6.50

D1797142

Beyond Post-Socialism

Beyond Post-Socialism

Dialogues with the Far-Left

Chamsy el-Ojeili
Victoria University of Wellington, New Zealand

First published 2015 by
PALGRAVE MACMILLAN

Palgrave Macmillan in the UK is an imprint of Macmillan Publishers Limited, registered in England, company number 785998, of Houndsmills, Basingstoke, Hampshire RG21 6XS.

Palgrave Macmillan in the US is a division of St Martin's Press LLC, 175 Fifth Avenue, New York, NY 10010.

Palgrave Macmillan is the global academic imprint of the above companies and has companies and representatives throughout the world.

Palgrave® and Macmillan® are registered trademarks in the United States, the United Kingdom, Europe and other countries.

ISBN 978–1–137–47452–0

This book is printed on paper suitable for recycling and made from fully managed and sustained forest sources. Logging, pulping and manufacturing processes are expected to conform to the environmental regulations of the country of origin.

A catalogue record for this book is available from the British Library.

Library of Congress Cataloging-in-Publication Data

El-Ojeili, Chamsy.
Beyond post-socialism : dialogues with the far-left / Chamsy el-Ojeili.
pages cm
Includes bibliographical references and index.
ISBN 978–1–137–47452–0 (alk. paper)
1. Communism.   2. Socialism.   I. Title.
HX45.E42 2015
335—dc23   2014049655

Typeset by MPS Limited, Chennai, India.

To my five great teachers – Sandy Davie, Charles Peter Fury,
Gregor McLennan, Brennon Wood, Peter Beilharz – to my
SOSC 401 students of 2014, and to my family

Contents

Acknowledgements

I would like to express my thanks to the following for kind permission to reproduce copyright material: John Wiley and Sons, Inc. for el-Ojeili, C. (2010). 'Post-Marxist Trajectories: Diagnosis, Criticism, Utopia', in *Sociological Inquiry*, 80 (2), pp. 261-282, which appears in modified form as Chapter 1; Sage Publications for el-Ojeili, C. (2008). '"No, We Have Not Finished Reflecting on Communism": Beyond Post-Socialism', in *Thesis Eleven*, 93 (May), pp. 110–129, which appears in modified form as Chapter 2; Sage Publications for el-Ojeili, C. (2007). 'Forget Debord?', in *Thesis Eleven*, 89 (May), pp. 115–127, which appears in modified form as Chapter 3; Sage Publications for el-Ojeili, C. (2004). '"Many Flowers, Little Fruit"?: The Dilemmas of Workerism', in *Thesis Eleven*, Number 79 (November), pp. 112–123, which appears in modified form as Chapter 4; Sage Publications for el-Ojeili (2014). '"Communism ... is the affirmation of a New Community": Notes on Jacques Camatte', in *Capital and Class*, 38 (2), pp. 342–361, which appears in modified form as Chapter 5; Sage Publications for el-Ojeili, C. (2014). 'Anarchism as the Spirit of Contemporary Anti-Capitalism? A Critical Survey of Recent Debates', in *Critical Sociology*, 40 (3), pp. 451-468, which appears in modified form as Chapter 6; Sage Publications for el-Ojeili, C. (2014). 'Reflections on Wallerstein: the Modern World-System, Four Decades On', in *Critical Sociology*, online first 9 May 2014, pp. 1–22, which appears in modified form as Chapter 7; and Sage Publications for el-Ojeili, C. (2011). 'Narrating Socialism: Three Voices', in *Thesis Eleven*, Number 105, May, pp. 102–117, which appears in modified form as Chapter 8.

A big thank you, as well, to Richard Bouwman and Dylan Taylor for their work on the manuscript. Finally, I would also like to acknowledge the following for their feedback, dialogue and intellectual camaraderie over the span of time during which this book was written: Esref Aksu, Peter Beilharz, Tim Corballis, Lincoln Dahlberg, Kevin Dew, Greg Gilbert, Patrick Hayden, Mike Lloyd, Gregor McLennan, Patricia Nickel, Sean Phelan, Alistair Shaw, Dylan Taylor and Warwick Tie.

Introduction

Some time back, over a decade ago now, two closely placed encounters had me reflecting on the contemporary situation of communism, both of them on the terrain of that horribly 'lost cause', Palestine–Israel. The first occurred during a meeting at which the Australasian representative of the Palestine Authority spoke. At the conclusion of his talk, a communist from a small Trotskyist group stood up and demanded that the Palestinian Authority immediately 'unleash the awesome power of the working class' on the Israeli settler state. The only thought that came to my mind in response to this demand was a *Simpsons* episode in which executives from a company manufacturing energy bars sloganize that their product 'unleashes the awesome power of apples'. Here, communism, socialism, Marxism would seem hopelessly out-of-time, exhausted and embarrassing, tediously and meaninglessly clichéd, a dead family of languages unable to speak to the present, let alone about the future.

The second encounter reverses or troubles this assessment, though. Around the same time, I was reading the chaotically humorous novel *The Secret Life of Saeed the Pessoptimist*, by the Palestinian communist Emile Habiby. Here, in spite of the four decades that have passed since its original publication, communism and Marxism remain powerful and present as analytical tools and as the imagination of other, better worlds, full, that is, of utopian significance, which Levitas (2013: 12) describes as 'a secular form of grace', encompassing loss, longing, redemption, fulfilment.[1] Communism, as represented by Habiby, can feel like *the* heroic, egalitarian, solidaristic and universalistic orientation, still, to the unyielding difficulties of our times. In one of the many lovely passages of the book, the anti-hero Saeed (whose stupidity and

1

cowardice see him recruited by Israeli intelligence) is trying to convince a woman he loves, Baqiyya, against involvement with the communists:

> Baqiyya opened her eyes wide and rained questions down on me.
> 'Who are the Communists?'
> 'Ungrateful people who deny the blessings.'
> 'What blessings?'
> 'The blessings of life which victors bestow upon the conquered.'
> 'But such blessings come from God.'
> 'Well, they deny God. They're heretics.'
> 'How are they heretics?'
> 'They claim, God preserve us from them, that they can change pre-determined fate'...
> 'Then we must seek help from the Communists.' (Habiby, 2003: 91)

Today, I think, many on the Left feel very much strung and pulled between these two poles, a sense of the urgency of the communist demand and a sense that, sadly, it might belong to a lost world. Above all, in this book, I want to lean in the more optimistic direction, exploring the question of what sort of help we are likely to get from the communists today. And, a decade on from the encounters I have just recalled, I think this question seems a much more reasonable one. A lot has happened since what we might variously name as the post-Marxist, end-of-history, triumphal liberal, happy globalist moments, between, let us say, 1977 and the middle of the 1990s,[2] where Marxism, socialism, communism were somewhat successfully consigned to the dustbin of history. For a start, I think we're now more likely to be attentive to just how much of the socialist past is still with us in the present – whether we are thinking about welfare states, widespread denunciation of sexism and racism, the continuing power and success of union mobilizations or the egalitarianism, irreverence and scepticism that inhabit popular culture and contest thinking animated only by questions of growth, profit and competition (Therborn, 2011). More than this, since the middle of the 1990s, with the emergence of the anti-globalization movement, and after a slow puncturing process of neo-liberal assumptions through that decade (Callinicos, 2003), there is perhaps a growing sense that we are in a moment of the re-opening or re-birth of history, as Alain Badiou (2012b) has titled his recent book – looking to the reawakening of interest in and creative debate around Marx, the still rolling, ominous financial crisis from 2008, the Occupy movement and the emergence of a harder parliamentary Left (for instance, in Greece), the Arab Spring and more. And we have some evidence, too, of this re-opening in the remarkable attention given to contemporary communist thinkers like Badiou himself, Slavoj Žižek, Hardt and Negri, in the proliferation of books and conferences effectively dedicated to thinking the possible shapes of twenty-first century socialism, and in Chibber's (2013: 294) compelling observation that 'For the first time since the 1980s, *everyone* is talking about capitalism'.

In this introduction, I want to provide a brief backdrop to the chapters that follow, beginning with a consideration of the broad shape of anti-communism today. Following this, and again in coarse strokes, I want to do something similar in mapping the ground and tone of contemporary socialist/communist discussion. Finally, I want to turn to reflect on a historical intellectual-political formation I have called Left communism. My interest in and continuing but critical fidelity to this Left communism informs the chapters ahead, where I seek to stage a series of conversations with contemporary socialist thinkers and traditions, with this Left communism and with what Santos (2006) has called an emerging Global Left, which appears to be moving beyond the older doctrinal and strategic disagreements and divides of an older Left. Convinced that we are, once more, at a point at which that Gramscian maxim 'the old is dying and the new cannot be born' (Gramsci, 1998: 276) holds, I want to approach the question of contemporary structures of knowledge, particularly around a constellation of communists who today offer us their assistance.

The communist society and its enemies

In mentioning Gramsci, I am suggesting, as do many, many others, that the concerns of the *Prison Notebooks* are really still pivotal for those on the Left – the organization of social groups, the links between knowledge, feelings and collectivities, leadership, the battleground for consent, popular culture as problem, ideology (Brennan, 2006; Morton, 2007; Santucci, 2010; Showstack-Sassoon, 2000; Thomas, 2011). It is particularly in thinking all at once about how capitalism is transforming, how groups are being organized and how those involved in the production and distribution of knowledge enter into these battles that Gramsci remains so alive today; as well, I think, in that he confronted an early, vigorous post-Marxism (Brennan, 2006), and he faced with supple intelligence the rise of fascism – just as, today, we witness the prominence of post-foundational thought in the human sciences, we see growing post-democratic tendencies, a hardening and thickening populist Right and a collection of closely connected, forceful religious reawakenings.[3] Gramsci's reflections on the organic function of intellectuals are central to my concerns in this section: what are the patterns of anti-communist intellectuality today? How are we to divide and explain the different strands that, at the least, come together over the non-contemporaneity of communism, who still posit communism as dominant dystopian figure? I want to approach this, in the spirit of Gramsci – though not according to the concrete philological letter – by way of ideal-typical idea clusters, which are, at once, diagnostic-explanatory, political-strategic and utopian-evaluative sets of references.

A first cluster we might name the 'cosmopolitical' – the world becoming one, often despite acknowledged disjunctures and threats. This position, connected to globalization discourse, announces our post-communist present as promising growing wealth, mutual understanding, expanding freedoms, and governing mechanisms (often technical and problem-solving rather than strictly democratic) more and more responsive to the choices and preferences of a global citizenry. The basic political variety of this set of commitments is liberal – the rule of law, the protection of life, liberty and property, tolerance and non-violence. Coming in various shades across a continuum that stretches from vague social democracy to sanguine neo-liberalism, and with various qualifications about, say, the continuing appeal of nationalism or the threat of global terror, this mode of intellectuality corresponds roughly to a real or imagined freedom from place, an elite subject at home everywhere (Friedman, 1995). In the narrative variations of this position, the really existing collapse of communism is, simultaneously, the moment of arrival for realistic hopes for world peace, the reign of global human rights, universal democracy, multi-cultural interchange, and the flattening of intra- and inter-societal wealth, power and status disparities.

A second cluster of thought elements presents us with an apparently opposing pole of diagnosis, strategic meditation and 'utopian reference' (Alexander, 1995; 2001). Here, the global is an illusion, or it mostly presents a multitude of threats, and a more realistic scale of social organization is instead sought. At its most ambitious, the proposed rescaling is civilizational; at its most modest, it is indigenous-ethnic or local; and it also comes in re-assertive cultural nationalist and traditionalizing-religious versions, which suggest the possibility of a re-enchanted life-world. What we have, here, are a series of appeals to a future – rooted and social – way of being, a response to atomization, dislocation and uncertain futures, organized around a variety of foes, often trading on significations that were once the property of social democracy, communism and national liberation movements, and visible among uneasy elites who elevate the particular (ethnic, national, local, confessional, civilizational) over the general. Communism, here, is read and rejected as rootless and abstractly universal, a project carried by intellectuals mobilized only by an Idea lacking in place, subjects and magic.

A final portrait of communists and socialism is often painted by, or implicit in, a third predominating thought cluster found among contemporary intellectuals – which we could, again after Friedman (1995), describe as a narcissistic-individualizing pole. Sometimes resonant with cosmopolitan or collectivist-traditionalizing impulses, this modality pivots around notions of the art of the good life, and individual self-construction and reconstruction. Found in libertarian and counter- and sub-cultural modalities (say, cyber-libertarianism or deep-Green activism), its black beast is, very often, statism, collectivism, or egalitarianism, with communism attached to any or all of these and implicated, therefore, in the crushing of difference, coercive uniformity and normalization, understood as a rageful and inevitably totalitarian project of levelling – in short, a moral disaster for the modern individual.

This is obviously highly schematic and far from exhaustive, but these structures of knowledge, these intellectual patternings, I think, co-exist and compete with the communist passions I am exploring in the chapters ahead, providing another set of appeals – once again, explanatory, political and utopian – on a terrain marked by all sorts of morbid symptoms, which provoke urgent efforts at answers: for instance – a more unstable, multi-polar situation in terms of geo-political power; financial crisis, economic concentration, severe austerity threats and growing inequalities; turbulent popular protests, including those from a Right-wing populist and religious direction, and in the face of post-democratic tendencies in the formal political sphere, including certain elements of a new authoritarianism; a popular cultural field marked by irony, consumption and irreverence.

Left reflections on the twenty-first century

I will elaborate on some of these issues in the chapters to come but, here, I want to turn my attention to the broad ideal-typical intellectual patterns that are visible on the Left of the political spectrum, which attempt to size up the contemporary terrain and to reflect upon Left results and prospects in the twenty-first century. Here, we could follow the compelling typology of critical intellectuals put forward recently by Razmig Keucheyan. This materialist analysis foregrounds changes in the intellectual field, especially in the academic field, the 'fate of the organizations to which they [the critical theorists surveyed] belonged' (Keucheyan, 2013: 51), the connections between early doctrinal orientation and later trajectory, and delineates six ideal-typical positions. The first ideal-type contains the 'converts' – for example, Irving Kristol, Andre Glucksmann, Lucio Colletti, Julia Kristeva – Keucheyan insisting on distinguishing the serious, thoughtful liberal conversion of Lefort from the 'fast motion' (2013: 54) case of the *Tel Quel* collective. The 'pessimists', combining radicality with resignation about substantial emancipatory change, meanwhile, typically end up in a 'form of "dandyism" or "decadentism"' (2013: 57) – for instance, Guy Debord after the death of the Situationist International. The third group, the 'resisters', often belonged to currents relatively 'unaffected by the collapse of real socialism' (2013: 61) – some anarchists (Chomsky or Daniel Colson) and Trotskyists, say. The 'innovators', engaging in hybridization of theory and turning to new theoretical objects (ecology, law, media, for instance), include thinkers such as Slavoj Žižek, Ernesto Laclau, Judith Butler, Hardt and Negri. Next, we have the 'experts' who often hail from 'disciplines of a highly empirical cast' to 'contradict the dominant discourse' (2013: 66) – Vandana Shiva, members of ATTAC's scientific committee, for example. And, finally, the 'leaders' are those rare thinkers who combine theorizing with active politics – Daniel Bensaid, Alex Callinicos, Alvaro Garcia Linera and Edward Said are examples here.

Keucheyan's analysis is excellent but, again, I will suggest a broader typology, avoiding the complicated and multiple positions of individual thinkers, some of whom I will engage with in the chapters to come, thinking about three major constellations of intellectuality across Left reflections today: first, a cool communism of the watchtower, an overwhelmingly pessimistic diagnostic modality; second, a thoughtful, rather Catholic and often more up-beat consideration of the conjuncture; and, third, an obdurate, sometimes, ecstatic militancy of Left renewal and socialistic possibility.

The first of these modalities I have described as a cool socialism of the watchtower, a sense that the co-ordinates within which an older Left had been formed and located are now significantly dissipated, that the contemporary field of possible socialist endeavour is unrecognizable, against that of yesterday. Defeat is the reality the Left must today face, confronting with sobriety and stoicism the necessarily long hard task of intellectual and political re-tooling, and re-imagining a twenty-first century socialism amidst the detritus and disorganization left by the decades'-long victory of capital. A second broad variation of Left response will typically register the scale of transformation and necessary Left re-thinking, but remains more light-hearted, discovering an array of promising ambiguities and encouraging signs on the street, as well as registering continuing Left resolve. Often welcoming of current pluralism, this interlocutory approach acknowledges the historic Left's limits and is attentive to opportunities for re-building, often considering some severe renunciations of time-honoured facets of the Marxian and wider socialist traditions. A third broad cluster of Left response contains militant variations of imaginative renewal and defiance. Assertive, combative and unrepentant, this strand often creatively re-occupies older Marxian outposts or seeks to inhabit new ones, detecting the current moment as both threatening and ripe – a forced and forbidding opportunity – for socialist re-emergence.

Returning to Left communism

Despite the differences in tone, each of these modalities of Left reflection have undoubtedly been buoyed by a general sense that something like a new Global Left has been in emergence since the close of the 1990s. Embarrassingly, when I was working first on a doctoral dissertation, then on a book on Left communism, between 1996 and 2002, I utterly missed the significance of what was taking place in Seattle and afterwards and, especially, of the affinities between what I was imagining was urgently alive in that Left communist tradition and what was happening on the ground of alternative globalization. My hope was that more attention be paid to this vigorous, neglected, defeated and variegated current of communism, after the collapse of 'really existing socialism' and the capitulation to neo-liberalism of Western social democracy (el-Ojeili, 2003).

This Left communist current contains a wealth of sometimes contradictory emphases – a group of thinkers whose ranks include anarcho-communists and anarcho-syndicalists, council communists and Bordigists, situationists and impossibilists.[4] To indicate the variety and complexity, here, I would refer the reader to Chris Wright's (2005) worthy but inescapably rather tortured and partial[5] effort to represent the Marxist side of this family tree. In his 'Libertarian Marxist Tendency Map', Wright begins with Marx and Engels, followed by major branches to council communism, Rosa Luxemburg, and Lenin and post-Leninist Leninism, which are then followed by a tangle of subsequent branches and their multiple interconnections – for instance, the Frankfurt School, the Johnson-Forest Tendency, Bordigist groups, Operaismo, the Situationist International, Open Marxism and so on. Adding in the numerous anarchist sub-currents[6] – such as anarchist communism, anarcho-syndicalism, individualist anarchism, eco-anarchism, communalist anarchism, post-anarchism, anarcho-feminism – their internal variations, and some representative groups and thinkers, we would make such a map infinitely more illegible.

In some ways, it is perhaps fair to say that if Left communism is an intellectual-political formation, it is so, first and foremost, negatively – as opposed to other socialist traditions. I have labelled this negative pole 'socialist orthodoxy', composed of both Leninists and social democrats. Of course, this is a grand simplification, and I would now be much more hesitant about any hard and fast separations, but this distinction still serves some purpose as a starting point for a consideration of the commonalities across Left communism, the unity amidst great difference. What I suggested was that these Left communist thinkers differentiated their own understandings of communism from a strand of socialism that came to follow a largely electoral road in the West, pursuing a kind of social capitalism, and a path to socialism that predominated in the peripheral and semi-peripheral countries, which sought revolutionary conquest of power and led to something like state capitalism. Generally, the Left communist thinkers were to find these paths locked within the horizons of capitalism (the law of value, money, private property, class, the state), and they were to characterize these solutions as statist, substitutionist and authoritarian. I will now seek to get closer by exploring some significant themes in this Left communist work – party and organization, knowledge and science, state, economy, democracy and state capitalism.

A first crucial theme is the debate around party and organization. Here, Left communists frequently distinguished themselves from Lenin's substitutionist strictures in *What Is To Be Done?*, often following Rosa Luxemburg's early insistence on the leading role of working-class self-organization, and her fears about where Lenin's contentions might lead. Therefore, it is frequently to forms of working-class or popular self-organization that Left communists look in answer to the questions of the struggle for socialism, revolution and post-capitalist social organization. Nevertheless, Left communists have often continued to organize themselves into party-like structures that undertake agitation, propaganda, education and other forms of political intervention. This is a vexed issue across Left communism and has resulted in a number of significant variations – from the absolute rejection of separate parties in favour of mere study or affinity groups, to the critique of the naivety of pure spontaneism and an insistence on the necessary, though often modest, role of disciplined, self-critical and popularly connected communist organizations.

We find similar dissensus around the problem of the origin and importance of socialist consciousness. Does it derive, above all, from material conditions, which might imply nothing more than 'revolutionary waiting' from the communist intellectual, or is it to be created through education and/or the formation of a communist counterculture within the shell of the old society? Some of these debates have a more contemporary ring to them, in a time when we often hear that we are now in a period of politics without parties or that vanguardism has been eclipsed after the end of 'really existing socialism', that new forms of rhizomatic, networked or horizontal organization are supplanting the older arborescent, pyramidal and vertical structures. And a reinvigorated and sophisticated return to Lenin today, which insists that minorities do count, that fidelity and discipline are not the equivalent of totalitarianism, and that organization is the permanent basis of any genuine politics, has made such questions even more difficult.

Tightly bound up with such questions around organization and the role of communist intellectuals is the problem of knowledge, power and communism, one significant part of which entails reflecting on the role and character of theory in social contestation and change. Here, again, Left communists sought to take a number of paths away from a socialist orthodoxy that often emphasized the completeness of Marxism, Necessity, science and prioritized communist intellectuals over the mass of people. For some, this orthodoxy was just not orthodox enough (Lenin and Kautsky as apostates), and a super-Marxian intransigence in theoretical matters was the order of the day. Another route has been an anarchistic hostility to Marxism as, in essence, a theory of the power of a new class, sometimes set against a wholly other set of emphases – will, morality, instinct; sometimes issuing in an Enlightenment, rationalist educationism, devoid of the more elaborate theoretical preferences of the Marxists.

Of course, in the Western Marxist current, the return to Hegel provided a further escape route from the discredit into which 'real communism' was falling – for Karl Korsch, for instance – while council communist Anton Pannekoek looked to Joseph Dietzgen, and others responded by breaking from an erstwhile theoretical paradigm

(Cornelius Castoriadis's break from Marxism, for example); and various Left communists turned their attention to a whole plethora of issues of culture, widely understood – everyday life, art, sexuality, ideology, media, consumption – as a guide to the maintenance of social order, the failure of revolutionary aspirations and as a well-spring from which truly emancipatory contestation and transformation might emerge.

A final set of problems concerns the state, democracy and the projected organization of post-capitalist life. Again the negative contrast with Marxist orthodoxy is decisive. Both the social democrats and the Leninists are often charged with positing a statist conception of socialism, equating nationalization with socialization of the means of production, and dependent on a socialism understood as the equivalence of party and state. As mentioned, the Russian Revolution is frequently associated with capitalism/state capitalism rather than communism – a social order still marked by class division, exploitation and domination, private property, and the law of value. Meanwhile, social democracy is viewed, very often, as establishing merely a social capitalism – the mixed economy, the welfare state and class compromise in the interests of national integrity and progress.

The alternative to such orthodox conceptions of socialism, as noted, has very often been centred on appeals to working-class or popular forms of self-organization, as the means to struggle against capitalism and as the foundation of post-capitalist organization – workers' councils, revolutionary unions, federated communes of locality – seen, frequently, as embodying direct democracy and a critique in action of alienated notions of representation.

Looking ahead

Because of my sense of the continuing relevance and richness of this tradition, because this is the tradition I have been formed in, intellectually and politically, the dialogues ahead are, for the most part, informed by and centred on Left communism. As I have said, I am now much more sceptical about the idea that we can think this formation as absolutely distinct from 'socialist orthodoxy'. I see that orthodoxy as vastly richer, more complicated and fertile than I once did, and I would tend, instead, to see communism or socialism as a large, variegated field of thought and action, from which we can draw somewhat pragmatically from the strengths of a whole range of very different thinkers, organizations and sub-traditions. At the same time, it is clear to me that the emerging Global Left is perhaps marked, above all, by crucial affinities with the currents and emphases of Left communism, and that this formation demands an acknowledged, explicit presence in any discussion of the Left, Marxism, communism and socialism today.

Above all, this Left communism provides us with still powerful ways of responding to the broken promises of neo-liberal capitalism today, as a robust critique and a compelling set of utopian proposals. First, the notion of neo-liberalism's broken promises, which is the suggestion that 'reality problems' (Alexander, 1995) have significantly eroded the 'narrative strength' (Dawson, 2013: 7) of neo-liberalism as an explanatory and utopian thought complex. Here, we might say that neo-liberalism proffers that the freeing of markets, the reduction of state interventions to a minimal level, and the ethos of competitive, self-reliant individualism will result in liberty, meritocracy, harmonious interchange, and knowledge, transparency and rationality.

I think it is increasingly clear that these promises have failed to be fulfilled. In the place of freedom, is it not plausible to argue that we see the disembedding of economic concerns from more widely social concerns, growing liberty for the already wealthy and powerful, along with the profound unfreedoms ('dis-emancipation' [Tosel, 2008]) generated by market anarchy, flexibilization, the erosion of welfare and other rights, and the unleashing of a culture of atomized consumerism that is quite at odds with freedom understood in the more robust sense of autonomy? Instead of meritocracy, might we not characterize the present as a time of growing inequality that, moreover, undermines liberty in manifold ways, and one of more and more precarious working and living conditions for the vast majority? Rather than harmonious interchange, we appear to have escalating violence, cultural polarization and a new state authoritarianism (including new forms of imperialism), with states serving ever more narrowly economic agendas connected to profitability, growth and competition. And in place of the promised arrival of a knowledge age, is it instead not more accurate to underscore the pervasiveness of a conformist culture industry centred on consumption and excess, the return behind Enlightenment to various forms of compensatory obscurantisms, and the disfiguration of science by its deepening attachments to money and power.[7]

More positively, moving from the resources of critique to the utopian dimension, Left communism, I believe, offers us a compelling alternative portrait of the good socialist life, of human flourishing and its pivotal principles and institutional conditions.[8] Moreover, these utopian elements are not merely disembodied ideas but they can be viewed as already operative within social movements, organizations, popular culture and everyday life. As a start, Left communists challenge common-sense views around the economy, that economic questions begin and end with emphases on growth, profit and competition. In a related vein, notions of value, worth and usefulness are detached from narrowly monetary conceptualizations and instead are deeply embedded in a vantage point that considers social life as a whole. In a similar manner, the separation of work and life is questioned, and alternatives suggested that are underpinned by notions of dignity, self-realization, and freedom from domination and exploitation. Here, a freedom that is not restrictively negative (as in neo-liberal conceptions) but is, as well, positive – connected, that is, to views about human flourishing – is important, a profoundly embedded understanding of freedom, which ties freedom to its social, communal conditions and, importantly, refuses to separate questions of freedom from those of equality (Dawson, 2013; Schecter, 2007).

Moving to the closely connected political realm, Left communism asks searching questions about the democratic nature of liberal democracy, often in light of an orientation that understands true democracy as autonomy or popular domination extended to all facets of our lives together, rather than to a restricted, narrow, separate 'political' stage. Sometimes, Left communists are less than enthusiastic about democracy, contending that democracy's fetishism of the majority and individualist premises should be replaced by arrangements expressive of something like our 'communal being'. They imagine, here, a range of possibilities for life beyond the state – councils, communes, plural popular associations – and a vision of another way of doing politics.

As I say, these values and institutional suggestions should be seen as extant, as operative in a range of ways and places, wherever critique (explicit or implicit) of neo-liberal values and practices and suggested or existing alternatives appear. Briefly, we can, for instance, detect such values within the field of alternative globalization: in the opposition to growth as the goal of social organization, in the name of sustainability and social justice; in critiques of privatization and commodification ('the world is not for sale'); in the insistence that limitations be placed upon markets (financial regulation, for example); in contestations of state authoritarianism, surveillance and militarism; within protests directed at monopolistic corporations unresponsive to wider social or ecological values; and in indignation at the excessive wealth and power of 'the one per cent' – to name just a few instantiations.

This Left communist tradition, as mentioned, is present, as analytical object or interlocutor, across the following chapters, where I critically discuss an array of Left thinkers, traditions and debates around socialism. Of course, given the expansiveness and diversity of this tradition, I cannot be exhaustive here, surveying certain traditions and thinkers rather than others, traditions and thinkers I take to be most illuminating, provocative, or illustrative of certain socialist strengths or dilemmas. I begin with a critical overview of 'post-Marxism' as an intellectual formation characterized by a series of challenges to Marxism and socialism, or a rubbing together of broadly Marxian concerns and post-foundational thinking. My scepticism about the theoretical, political and utopian gains of post-Marxism– a chronically residual socialism, submission to the post-modernist fixation on limits, despite the important attempt at a non-theological attachment to Marxism – runs through other chapters. In Chapter 2 for instance, I turn to the arguments of Claude Lefort, Cornelius Castoriadis and what we might call recent 'psychoanalytical Leninism'. Castoriadis, to my mind, is the most important contemporary representative of the direct democracy contentions of council communism, rethinking socialism by way of the notion of autonomy, which, importantly, encompasses both an individual and a collective dimension. Nevertheless, Castoriadis's and Lefort's post-Marxism often appears to limit both sociological analysis and the utopian dimension of their work, just as psychoanalytic Leninism remains imprisoned within some of the more damaging confines of a barely reconstructed Leninism.

A one-time member of Castoriadis's Socialism or Barbarism group, Guy Debord and his organization, the Situationist International (SI), are the subject matter of Chapter 3. While elements of Debord and the SI – diversion, the notion of spectacle, the attention to contemporary urbanism, as well as another passionate, more contemporary version of council communism – have travelled well into the present, the current attraction to this thinker and to the SI has tended to conceal a number of reasons that should, I think, provoke us to try to forget Debord. Especially troublesome, in this regard, is that the slavish admiration of the SI's cultural politics has tended to obscure Debord's intolerable dogmatism and vituperative and ultimately arid sectarianism. Italian workerism is the focus of Chapter 4, a current contemporaneous with the SI and, like them, best placed within the Left communist tradition. This chapter explores some of the great strengths (the creative optimism of the intellect, particularly around approaching changing patterns of subaltern resistance as the driving engine of the social world) and antinomies (an enthusiasm for

overstatement that undermines sober strategic reflection) of this tradition, a tradition that finds contemporary expression in the tremendously
influential work of Michael Hardt and Antonio Negri.

Chapters 5 and 6 turn to anarchism – the first exploring the work
of primitivist communist Jacques Camatte and his unique trajectory,
emerging from the much neglected Left communism of Italian Bordigism,
then breaking from Marxism to push a communal-being-centred
critique of modernity, of what he calls 'the wandering of humanity'.
This primitivism, while often somewhat eccentric, has the merit of
tracing a singular path of ecologically informed Left communism, and
combining this with an existentialist reflection on 'living otherwise'
and a 'community communism' that seem due a present-day comeback
of some kind. Chapter 6 focuses on the return of anarchism that many
have detected within anti-globalization currents, critically exploring the
claims of a growing literature that – on the streets, within contemporary
contestatory movements and in the world of ideas – anarchism is making
a return, as something like the 'spirit of contemporary anti-capitalism'.
Anarchism's clear strengths seem to lie in its appeal to individual freedom, its anti-statism and its open and experimental qualities, while, at
worst, this can issue in a politically obscure paean to liberty at the
expense of equality, an individualism that is socially threadbare, and a
hostility to analysis that is intellectually and strategically disarming.

Chapter 7 is an extended insistence on the continued relevance of
the tireless work of Immanuel Wallerstein and world-systems thinking.
Wallerstein's politics again belong somewhere within the field of Left
communism and his world-systems analysis joins to this the earliest
and still most ambitious attempt to map, at a global level, the fields of
economy, politics and culture, utterly out of step with post-modern and
globalization thought but still, in my estimation, defensible and, in fact,
indispensable for thinking our times. Finally, in Chapter 8, I examine
four recent narrations of socialism's life and times – important works by
Alain Badiou, Peter Beilharz, Lucio Magri and Goran Therborn. These
eminent, articulate voices issue from positions outside of that Left communist tradition, from Leninism and social democracy, but provide us
with a wealth of forceful and timely questions and theses with respect
to the past, present and future prospects of socialism, especially when
brought into conversation with Left communist contentions. My inclusion of these voices is partly a move against a Left communist sectarianism, which would consign Leninism and social democracy ineradicably
to the past, a Left sectarianism that would then be bereft of the vast
riches of ideas still offered by those thinking out of these traditions.

It is clear to me that Badiou (2010b) is right at least in designating ours a time of experimentation, and creative and critical exploration towards a new Left, and this necessary encompassing and open exploration accounts for the shape these dialogues have taken. Above all, Castoriadis's (1997a: 417) contention – 'It is not just what is, but what could be and should be, that has need of us' – still seems to me the point, and this point is still unthinkable without the wealth (intellectual, political, utopian) bequeathed to us by socialism. And, within this socialism, we can't, of course, tell which of the seeds of time will grow, but my hunch is that significant strands of what will be important in social movements, cultural contestation, and intellectual debate from the Left, in the next decade or two, will intersect with the debates and discussants addressed here, and that the Left communists I deal with, or draw from in addressing others, will and should engage us as still live and worthy interlocutors into the future.

1
Post-Marxist Trajectories: Diagnosis, Criticism, Utopia

Introduction

For over a century, Marxism and socialism have been intimately joined. Therefore, the idea of 'post-Marxism' is a vital one for any contemporary re-thinking of emancipation. But post-Marxism is a troublesome notion. Might it not be a pretentious codeword for ex- or non-Marxism (Geras, 1987; 1988), merely another moment in 'the weak thought' of 'the end of Modernity' (Said, 1994: 399), 'a dull and meaningless term ... [that] makes sense only in an autobiographical context' (Heller and Feher, 1991: 4)? Such scepticism and irritation were to the fore in an earlier phase of 'furious' post-modernism and anti-post-modernism (Beilharz, 1994), where Marxist critics were likely to read post-Marxism as a signal of the 'advanced stage of an intellectual malady' (Geras, 1987: 43), of a European Left moving rightwards or becoming ever more spectatorial, culturalist and theoreticist.[1]

Even after a more appreciative, or at least cautious, next wave of commentary,[2] it can't be said that the term is entirely clear, that it is attached to an instantly recognizable canon of works, an obvious set of theoretical and political co-ordinates, or uncontroversially identifiable adepts. One solution, here, would be to limit the label to self-identified post-Marxists (Howarth, 1998) – most prominently Laclau and Mouffe and their followers. Yet, this seems insufficient, given an obvious confluence of concerns and emphases that bring Laclau and Mouffe's work close to a number of other thinkers. In this respect, the collection of intellectuals surveyed in three more recent works – Stuart Sim's (1998; 2000) *Post-Marxism: A Reader* and *Post-Marxism: An Intellectual History*, and Simon Tormey and Jules Townshend's (2006) *Key Thinkers from Critical Theory to Post-Marxism* – looks about right: Laclau and Mouffe, Lyotard,

Deleuze and Guattari, Derrida, Bauman, Habermas, Castoriadis, Heller and Hartmann, for instance. However, when we consider the diversity here, when such lists are expanded to include the full range of plausibly post-Marxist figures – such as Jameson, Harvey, Žižek, Badiou, Rancière, Baudrillard, Offe, Castells, Balibar, Honneth and Gorz – the difficulties involved in thinking of post-Marxism as anything like a coherent intellectual formation are clear.

In his earlier work, Stuart Sim (1998: 2) summarized post-Marxism as 'a series of hostile and/or revisionary responses to classical Marxism from the post-structuralist/post-modernist/feminist direction, by figures who at one time in their lives would have considered themselves as Marxists, or whose thought processes had been significantly shaped by the classical Marxist tradition'. Here, Sim's (1998: 7–8) solution to the problem of post-Marxism's variety was to distinguish *post*-Marxism from post-*Marxism*, arguing, though, that both shared an 'element of nostalgia' and that, for both, 'the post- side ... drives the theoretical enterprise'. More interested in post-*Marxism*, Sim's introductory remarks are, on the whole, deflationary[3] – post-Marxism, most importantly, as an emotional rather than substantive matter: 'What remains in post-Marxism is not so much Marxism, I would contend, as a series of somewhat empty gestures whose content is emotional rather than theoretical' (Sim, 1998: 7). This emotion is, first and foremost, a nostalgia that marks an implicit or explicit recognition of defeat – the spectre of the totalitarianism, the deadness of socialist language today – alongside a reluctance to properly let go; and, in the end, Sim insists on the impossibility of any *real* conversation between an inherently monistic paradigm (Marxism) and an inherently pluralizing one (post-modernism).

Perhaps Sim is on to something, here, but there is more to post-Marxism, I think, than defeat and impasse, and there must be a coherence that runs beyond simple nostalgia. In this chapter, I want to think about this 'something more', to try and plot the 'co-ordinates of unity' (Anderson, 1976) of post-Marxism as a 'series of gestures' (Said, 2001: 160) that respond to 'reality problems' (Alexander, 1995) faced by Marxism and socialism, to the so-called 'crisis of the Marxist imaginary'. There is certainly, within post-Marxism, no 'elegant coherence' (Spivak, 1990: 15), we have, here, a field that is 'highly varied and contradictory in nature' (Beilharz, 2007), but I think there is an important unity to this moment, found in the engagement between, on the one hand, what Therborn (2008) describes as the Marxist triangle of historical social science, a philosophy of contradictions and socialist politics and, on the other, more recent, post-foundationalist currents in social theory. The best attempt to understand this unity, in my opinion, is provided by Simon Tormey and Jules Townshend (2006). In particular, the six problems these authors view post-Marxists as posing to Marx and Marxism allow us to track a certain coherence among otherwise very diverse thinkers: the problem of history, the problem of revolutionary subjectivities, the problem of ethics, the problem of positivism, the problem of vanguardism and the problem of democracy. In the second part of this chapter, I will follow Tormey and Townshend in very selectively surveying post-Marxist analyses of, and responses to, these problems.

It seems to me that we can read the post-Marxist moment, after Jameson (1996: 1), as emerging at a time 'in which capitalism itself undergoes a structural metamorphosis', a Marxian engagement, to be crude, that responds to, and wrestles with, the arrival of what world-systems thinkers refer to as an 'age of transition' (Wallerstein, 2000b) or 'systemic chaos' (Arrighi, 2010). In this vein, in the first part of this chapter, I will suggest that a cluster of systemic transformations post-1968 provide the crucial backdrop to the development of post-Marxism and that, together, these changes are implicated in the so-called 'crisis of the Marxist imaginary' to which post-Marxism responds. And I will contend that the uncertainty issuing from these transformations can be read along two intimately related axes, axes crucial to social theory as a whole – diagnosis and utopia: that is, first, questions of mapping and understanding the social; and, second, questions of 'utopian reference' (Alexander, 2001), the expressions of the desire for a better way of being (Levitas, 1990; 2013).

Overall, I think it is hard today not to feel somewhat torn about post-Marxism. Perhaps Beilharz (2007) is right in maintaining that, 'In the long run, postmarxism will surely be known as Marxism'. In that case, post-Marxism's pluralism might be viewed as a welcome, truly Marxian effort to be as radical as our times, renewing a complex and still important tradition, in contrast to a Marxist orthodoxy that appears unsustainably necessitarian and hopelessly out of touch with the institutional and imaginative peculiarities of our modernity. Given these peculiarities, given the decidedly pluralist moment we are in, obdurate, closed Marxism clearly doesn't do the trick in answering fundamental problems posed to Marxism, and there is plenty of interest contained in the moments of post-Marxist inventiveness – variously, philosophical, political, theoretical. Nevertheless – against many of the stronger post-Marxist gestures – I think it is hard to escape a sense that, having passed through and beyond phases of 'post-modern conjuncturalism' (McLennan, 2006) and 'happy globalization' (Stephen Holmes in

Outhwaite and Ray 2005: 19), we are as easily reminded of our proximity to Marx and Marxism as of our distance from them, that, at worst, post-Marxism simply lets go of the powerful socialist resources of critique (class, totality, production as social, the questioning of the prioritization of economic emphases, of value, of profit, and of self-interest, say) and institutional alternatives, and comes to occupy an analytical space behind and short of Marxism.

Reading post-Marxism: the crisis of the Marxist imaginary

A good place to start, I think, is Jameson's (1996: 1) contention that '"Postmarxisms" regularly emerge at those moments in which capitalism itself undergoes a structural metamorphosis'. Historically, we might think of Bernstein's 'revisionism' or the emergence of Western Marxism as examples. For Jameson, the shape that this metamorphosis takes today is conditioned by the transformation captured by the phrase 'multinational capitalism'.

This idea is worth exploring. And, objectionable as some might find reading post-Marxism through a basically Marxist interpretative framework, I think that the world-systems analysis contention about our entry into an 'age of transition' from the late 1960s to the early 1970s is the most convincing way to understand the important factors in the emergence of post-Marxism: that is, post-Marxism as a set of responses to transformations in economic organization, political formations, structures of knowledge, social movements and cultural repertoires. These changes appear immediately relevant, in that the majority of those thinkers that could reasonably be designated 'post-Marxist' were born between the early 1920s and the early 1940s,[4] making such transformations plausibly central in their political and intellectual formation or re-orientation. Laclau (1990: 97), for instance, strenuously places his own post-Marxism within the context of the following kinds of social reconfigurations:

> ... structural transformations of capitalism have led to the decline of the classical working class in the post-industrial countries; the increasingly profound penetration of capitalist relations of production in areas of social life, whose dislocating effects – concurrent with those deriving from the forms of bureaucratisation which have characterised the welfare state – have generated new forms of social protest; the emergence of mass mobilisations in Third World countries which do not follow the classical pattern of class struggle; the crisis and

discrediting of the model of society put into effect in the countries of so-called 'actually existing socialism', including the exposure of new forms of domination established in the name of the dictatorship of the proletariat.

There is, of course, something of a consensus around the reality of multidimensional social change post-'68, and a variety of attempts at characterization of such shifts – post-modernism, post-Fordism, informationalization, risk society, detraditionalization, reflexive modernity, globalization, for instance. What I would like to do is fairly loosely draw from the world-systems' framing of these transformations insofar as they might be seen as fundamentally reconfiguring the terrain on which Left intellectuals operate, both in terms of the horizon of the descriptive and explanatory tasks of social theory and in terms of utopian horizons. Interestingly, in these terms – theory, utopia – within commentary on post-1960s social transformation, we find two related narratives of decline: a decline of utopia narrative, and a demise of critical social theory and their intellectual carriers narrative, which can be translated into the world-systems language about a post-1970s 'crisis of the movements' and a simultaneous 'crisis of the ideologies/structures of knowledge' (Wallerstein, 1991b).

To begin chronologically, I will start with what Arrighi, Hopkins and Wallerstein (1989) have called 'the world revolution of 1968'. This revolution is crucial in the transformations we have seen subsequently. The argument runs that the 1848 rebellions across Central and Western Europe, and elsewhere, announce the arrival of the 'antisystemic movements', a family of movements with three principal variants – social democracy, communism and national liberation. Over time, these antisystemic movements became institutionalized features of the political landscape, and all three variants were, on one level, extraordinarily successful in coming to power and dominating the landscape of progressive thought and social change in the period 1945–1968.

These movements, Wallerstein (2002a) argues, shared some essential features – most prominently, increasingly wedded to a two-step strategy of social change, involving the capture of state power, followed by progressive social transformation. Despite their success, more and more these movements had a number of fundamental sets of complaints levelled at them, complaints that crystallize in the world revolution of 1968: that certain people had been left out, that they hadn't changed the world as promised, that they had been co-opted, and that they were repressive and exploitative and did not rule on behalf of the people

(Wallerstein, 1991b). For Wallerstein (1991b; 2002a), the crucial upshots of this revolution are a loss of faith both in these movements and in the state.

We might isolate four pressing sets of consequences of the revolution of '68 – three connected to the movements themselves, one a more general political consideration. First, the so-called 'social democratic consensus' and the related consensus around the notion of 'development', central in the period 1945–1970, are replaced by a period of neo-liberal commonsense and the so-called 'Washington Consensus' (Wallerstein, 2005b). Here, we witness the electoral and membership misfortunes of social democratic parties, and the capitulation of a good number of these parties to the neo-liberal agenda.

A second consequence is the end of the Bandung period of Southern unity and assertiveness, and of 'third worldism'. We have, here, the devastating impact on much of the periphery and semi-periphery of worldwide economic downturn, the debt crisis, and structural adjustment. In the face of this, the remnants of the national liberation movements still in power in the semi-periphery look ever more unlikely to regain any momentum and widespread support (Wallerstein, 1991b).

The third (arguably partial) consequence is the collapse of 'really existing socialism'. The events of 1989–1991 were, of course, immensely disorienting for many Left intellectuals, even those long critical of the Soviet alternative. In the world of theory, as Alexander (1995) points out, we witnessed a post-communist return to modernization and convergence themes; we see, likewise, 'capitalism' replaced by 'modernity' as starting point for social theory (Jameson, 2002); we see Left intellectuals wrestling with Fukuyama's end of history thesis and the equation 'end of socialism equals end of utopia equals end of history' (Kumar, 1993); and we see a burgeoning 'ethical turn' in social theory, one part of which obsessively concerns itself with the threat of 'totalitarianism', frequently located in the modern imaginary, and deployed as a moral brake on the utopian enterprise.

The fourth, more general, consequence is a widely commented upon generalized loss of faith in the state, and an accompanying transformation of politics. It is frequently said, of course, that, over the past three decades or so, we have seen growing scepticism towards the state, party machines and representative democracy. In the optimistic readings of such changes, we have, here, an expansion of the political, a bottom-up, reflexive, cosmopolitan politics, which stretches beyond the older hierarchies, channels and limitations of formal political involvement (Beck, 1997; 1999; Giddens, 1991). In the pessimistic readings, we have a series of crises – of the state, of democracy, of legitimacy, of the public sphere – and a post-democratic or post-political condition: where politics becomes increasingly empty and mediatized, more and more eaten up by economics; where political options converge around minor variants on the neo-liberal theme; where citizens withdraw from parties and electoral contests, and parties withdraw from citizens; where state sovereignty and a potentially expanded conception of citizenship are increasingly under strain (Bauman, 1999; Castells, 2000; Crouch, 2004; Mair, 2006; Martin and Schumann, 1998; Zolo, 2001).

Second, we have economic crisis and transformation. The revolution of '68, the US loss in Vietnam, a B phase of economic stagnation, the shrinking productivity gap between America and other economic powers – together these bring us, world-systems thinkers insist, into a period of hegemonic transition, the effects of which we are still living with. This analysis has important resonances with many of the interpretations of the emergence of a new capitalism post-1970: a post-industrial age (Bell, 1999); post-Fordism/disorganized capitalism (Offe, 1985; Lash and Urry, 1987); the knowledge or information society (Webster, 2002); multinational capitalism (Jameson, 1984a; 1996; Harvey, 1989); fast capitalism (Agger, 2004); flexible capitalism (Sennett, 1998; 2006); the aesthetic economy (Bohme, 2003); a new third spirit of capitalism (Boltanski and Chiapello, 2005); informationalism (Castells, 1997; 1998). Such characterizations have attempted to capture new or emerging axiomatic features of ultra-contemporary capitalist organization: for instance – information as a new, directly productive force; a new emphasis on flexibility in production and in labour; changes in patterns of production and consumption; neo-liberal restructuring; changes in class composition and a weakening of organized labour against capital; a reconfiguration of the international division of labour and a new, intensive, and highly competitive phase of global networking; changes to corporate structures; financialization.

Clearly, these sorts of shifts have had important implications for the ways intellectuals have mapped the world and for the societal and institutional alternatives connected to such theorizing. For instance, by 1970 the size and power of the industrial working class in the West had reached its peak (Therborn, 2001), and the neo-liberal assault (made possible, in part, by the crisis of the antisystemic movements already referred to), deindustrialization and growing internationalization arguably combined to transform labour, undermining the solidarity and power of that working class. One obvious consequence of this was to cast further doubt on the notion of this class as the primary agent of social transformation, as well as on the traditionally conceived-of direction of such transformation. More generally, neo-liberalism, for some, has shifted 'the parameters of commonsense' (Hall, 1988: 188), from equality, solidarity and justice towards liberty, competition and individualism, deflating utopian aspirations before the hidden hand (Fuller, 2005) and necessitarian rhetoric ('there is no alternative').

And, in a related vein, restructuring pressures within the university, and accompanying professionalization and commodification of knowledge, have been viewed as posing severe challenges to the historic tradition of critical intellectual life.

Such challenges are often seen as intimately linked, too, to cultural transformations. One of the consequences of the world revolution of '68 was the rise of the 'new social movements'. These movements are an important condition of the so-called 'cultural turn' in both social life and in social and political theory – for instance, in shifting what Nancy Fraser (2003) describes as the grammar of political claims-making towards emphases on identity, difference, cultural domination and recognition. We can link these movements (as well as the process of 'de-ruralization'), too, with what Therborn (2001) calls 'the erosion of traditional deference' (or what others have called 'detraditionalization'), which, in turn, is connected to a growing 'pluralization of lifeworlds' (Boggs, 1993) and individualization across social orders. For some, the changes entailed here have gone so far as to issue in a 'new personality' (Castells, 2000; Gauchet, 2000), which appears completely out of step with the collectivist, egalitarian, solidaristic anthropological premises of a former utopian imaginary.

We see such transformations signalled in social and political theory, as questions of selfhood and identity increasingly became central thematics, with constant underscoring of fragmentation, permanent construction and reconstruction, strategy over solidity, movement over rootedness. This is bound up with shifts in what Wallerstein (1991b; 1991c; 1997a; 1999a; 1999c; 2006b) calls the 'structures of knowledge', most importantly, a shift away from 'scientific universalism' – universal laws, progress, determinism, the canons, formal rationality, Eurocentrism and objectivity. The direction these shifts have taken, under pressure from challenges such as feminism, the critique of Eurocentrism and the questioning of science, is the post-modernization of intellectual life. This post-modernization, in part, appears to return to a liberal sense of limits around what we can know and do (Beilharz, 1994): the critique of universalist, redemptive, totalizing metanarratives, of closure, of capitalized Truth, Rationality, and Science (which are read as ineradicably particular rather than universal), and of the erasure of difference. Thus, for Therborn (2000b), at the beginning of the twenty-first century, social scientific answers to the traditional questions of social cosmology, directionality of the world and appropriate mode of cognition are answered, respectively, as follows: strategies, contingency, and understanding and discourse.

These changes, once again, appear to unsettle older ways of mapping our social worlds and established imaginings of progressive social change (diagnosis and critique, alternatives and transformatory strategy (Wright, 2006)). We see, here, Foucault's (1980) argument about an actual and morally positive movement from universal to specific intellectuals, and Bauman's (1987) congruent suggestion of a post-modern shift in intellectual function from legislation to interpretation. We see, too, in challenges to commitments to progress, aspirations to totalizing knowledge, and assumptions of unity, caution towards, or forthright criticism of, utopian blueprints and the idea of revolution, in the name of difference, for fear of totalitarianism, in an elevation of the ethical over the political.

Putting aside a raft of obvious objections, I think the case can be made that these transformations intertwine by the late 1980s and into the 1990s – the period of 'happy globalization' – into an overriding sense that 'the utopian mentality is withering away' (Kolakowski, 1990: 143), that 'the utopian itself has been in general suspension since the mid-seventies', bringing a 'remorseless closure of space' (Anderson, 2004: 71). And, related, these changes fed into a sense that the historic tradition of oppositional intellectual social theorizing and criticism was outmoded in the face of newly hegemonic emphases in theorizing – difference, reflexivity, post-positivism, ethical and cultural turns, anti-totalization, pluralism (McLennan, 2006), scepticism about the 'hermeneutics of suspicion' (Baudrillard, 1983), distance from those 'four sins of modernist theorizing' (universalism, reductionism, functionalism, essentialism) (McLennan, 1996) and so on. Thus Peter Wagner (2001a: 1) notes that doubts have 'arisen during the closing decades of the twentieth century as to whether the social sciences' way of observing, interpreting and explaining the world really brought superior insights into the social life of human beings'.

Post-Marxism, it seems to me, is clearly an expression of these sorts of transformations and a set of responses to the challenges posed by such changes to socialist intellectuals. I will return to these transformations in a concluding note, because I think that by the end of the 1990s we see another set of shifts that, in turn, troubled the assumption that post-Marxist trajectories had adequately answered questions tied to the 'crisis of the Marxist imaginary'.

The thematic unity of post-Marxism

I now want to turn back to those introductory remarks about the difficulties entailed in thinking the unity of the post-Marxist moment. Tormey and Townshend's (2006) identification of six problems addressed by post-Marxism to Marx and Marxism seems the best way in here, and I will work through these as a way of exploring some of the commonalities that can be detected in apparently very different post-Marxist trajectories. This approach also serves as a way of moving towards consideration of the dilemmas entailed by these trajectories and addressing the question, whither post-Marxism?

First problem – history. The problem of history is what Tormey and Townshend (2006: 212) describe as the 'common suspicion of the teleological narrative that is seen to underpin Marx's work'. Across post-Marxism, we find a critique of teleology, of functionalism, determinism, of 'external guarantees' (Badiou 2003a: 130); and we find a corresponding emphasis instead on 'the political' or 'politics'. Thus, Heller (1991; Heller and Feher, 1988) rejects the redemptive politics of 'radical universalism', which is underpinned by the notion of goals in History. Such universalism imagines the existence of rationally predictable institutions, and envisages single emancipatory gestures that would bring history to an end. We can see these emphases, too, in Castoriadis's early arguments against a Marxism that read history as rational and closed, which, for him, effectively eliminated struggle from history. More generally, Castoriadis (1987) came to reject traditional ontology's equation of being with 'being determined', underscoring instead the Abyss or groundlessness of being, insisting on the fundamental creativity entailed in the production of meaning and society, and the radical historicity and particularity of the forms and figures of social formations (Howard and Pacom, 1998: 87; Castoriadis 1987: 181; 1997a: 274).

What we are left with, as I have said, is something like the priority of politics or the political. That is, we are urged to face up to a world of constant struggle, of endless, undetermined political construction and reconstruction. In this vein, Gramsci has frequently been identified as an important ancestor to, and influence on, post-Marxist thinkers. As Bauman (2002: 334) puts it, 'Gramsci immunized me once and for all against brain-paralyzing bacilli of systems, structures, function, billiard-ball models of the agent and mirror models of the subject's mind, determined past and preordained future'.[5] This Gramscian turn is, of course, most pronounced in Laclau and Mouffe, where the political is deemed prior to the social, and systemness, cohesivity and patterning in social life are not to be thought of as grounds but as horizons, always threatened, always 'a hegemonic attempt at articulation' (Laclau, 1990: 214; 1996: 103). How to analyse this structuration in social life, or the degrees of institutionalization that are found within the social, then, has become the focus of Laclau's (1990: 61, 224; 2014) subsequent work of conceptual elaboration (demands, articulation, logics of equivalence and difference, horizons, frontiers, nodal points, empty signifiers, sedimentation and reactivation, and so on), as a replacement for historical materialism.

Second problem – revolutionary subjectivity. This problem centres on the critique of the notion of the working class as the primary force in progressive social change, and has variously involved the re-imagining by post-Marxist thinkers of transformatory agency, social struggles and political identity. Castoriadis and Lefort were, for instance, early observers of the increasingly differentiated struggles within contemporary capitalist social orders (Curtis, 1988); and Castoriadis (1988b; 2010a) initially recasts, and thereby expands and pluralizes, the fundamental division within modern societies as that between directors and executants, with self-management an aspiration underpinning and uniting the variety of forms of social contestation. Similarly, the Italian workerist notion of 'the social factory' is later reworked by Hardt and Negri (2000; 2004) in ideas of 'immaterial labour' and 'the multitude', underscoring plurality and singularity, against the automatic subaltern unity imagined by orthodox Marxism. The 'new social movements', of course, have been a constant point of reference for Laclau and Mouffe and others in the shift from class to demands, from Emancipation to emancipations, from identity as recognition to identity as construction, and from assumed unity and homogeneity to difference and articulation. No longer, for post-Marxists, is it sufficient to separate the material and 'objective interests' from the 'merely cultural' and chosen or constructed identities (Butler, 1998).

Third problem – ethics. As Lawrence Wilde (2001) notes, orthodox Marxism has a history of radical denial about ethical questions, a 'moral constipation', in Steven Lukes's colourful phrase. In response to the 'ethical deficit' of Marxist orthodoxy, and paired with anti-foundationalist, anti-teleological and pluralist emphases, a number of post-Marxists – Heller, Bauman, Derrida, Lyotard, for instance – have been important contributors to the so-called 'ethical turn'. On the other hand, the ethical turn is viewed sceptically by those post-Marxists insisting on the priority of the political (Castoriadis or Laclau [1990: 84], for instance).[6] At the extreme edge of such scepticism we find Žižek's (2001a) and Badiou's (2001; 2003a; 2005b) scathing rejections of Arendt, Levinas and ethical musings centred on the danger of totalitarianism,[7] our infinite responsibility to the Other, the prioritization of respect for difference and enthusiasm around the expansion of a global discourse of human rights. Nevertheless, even here we see something of an ethical impulse that provides a contrast to Marxist orthodoxy: for those who prioritize the political, in the responsibility and autonomy implied by the recognition of contingency and openness (Castoriadis's (1997b) 'ethics or mortality', for instance); for Badiou and Žižek, in some variety of a Lacanian ethics of the Real, a fidelity to Truths.

Fourth problem – positivism. Here, we find a distancing from the alignment between Marxism and the natural sciences found in the orthodox Marxist trajectory from Engels to the Second and Third Internationals, and a critique of the connections this alignment has with the exercise of domination (Tormey and Townshend, 2006). We see, too, a rejection of a 'theological' (Castoriadis, 1997a) approach to social criticism, and a corresponding pluralism and pragmatism in theoretical terms (Mouzelis, 1990). Often important, in this respect, is the post-modern questioning of Enlightenment emphases on truth, science, rationality and of the associated Modern desire to know, control and order (Bauman, 1987; Feher and Heller, 1987: 205), to pursue what Castoriadis (1987)[8] called the 'unlimited expansion of rational mastery'.

Fifth problem – vanguardism. This is the problem of the prioritization of the party within Marxist orthodoxy. As Lovell (1986: 30) notes, Marx was unclear about the relationship between his project and the working-class movement, about the links between leaders, intellectuals, parties and the mass of people. And, of course, there is an oscillation within Marx's work, and within Marxism more widely, between a materialist insistence that the liberation of the working class is necessarily the work of the working class itself and, on the other hand, the promotion of science and its carriers to a crucial role in progressive social transformation (Boggs, 1984; Femia, 1993; Gupta, 2000). It is arguably this latter tendency which dominates orthodox Marxism, where the question of the agents of socialist transformation is effectively answered by emphases on intellectuals, party, theory and programme (Tormey, 2004) while, at the same time, emphases on necessity, History and proletariat have obscured what is at stake here (Gupta, 2000).

Post-Marxists, by contrast, have been far more careful on issues of power and knowledge when addressing questions of theory, intellectuals and organization, and they have tended to distance themselves from the elitism, vanguardism and substitutionism of Marxist orthodoxy. For a start, 'really existing socialism' has, of course, been a crucial 'reality problem' for the Marxian tradition, and a number of post-Marxists have engaged in seminal analyses and critiques of these regimes – in doing so, attempting to separate them from socialism as it could be: for instance, Feher et al. (1986) on communism as a 'dictatorship over needs'; Bauman on communism as modernity at its most determined; and Negri and Castoriadis on communism as a form of state capitalism. In Castoriadis, Bauman, Heller, Hardt and Negri, for instance, we find clear echoes of the Left communist critique of both Leninism and social democracy, with emancipation instead equalling self-emancipation, with Science and its carriers dethroned. At the same time, ultra-Left spontaneism is seldom seen as an adequate answer, given the strong critique of teleological understandings of history and, for most post-Marxists, there still seems to be some sort of role for organization and intellectuals.[9]

Sixth problem – democracy. In light of the undemocratic history of Marxist orthodoxy, how do we approach the question of democracy today? What can socialism mean after Stalinism and the events of 1989–91, and within the context of what Boggs (1993) calls the 'crisis of Modernity', with the entailed 'turn to the local', 'dispersal of social movement activity', 'pluralization of social life-worlds and opposition', 'resurgence of civil society', and impacts of new technology and mediatization? There is, within post-Marxism, a real tussle with questions about the relationship between socialism, democracy and liberalism. For some post-Marxists, democracy (albeit a radicalized democracy) overtakes socialism as the goal of emancipatory action, with the old opposition between liberalism and socialism erased. The tone here is more cautious, plural, diffuse (Bauman, 2002; Heller and Feher, 1988: 32; Heller, 1987; Lefort, 1986; 1988). Here, liberalism and democratic institutions can no longer be casually dismissed (Laclau and Mouffe, 1985; Lefort, 1988). Gone, too, very often, is the Marxist demand for the end of private property, the withering of the state, the dictatorship of the proletariat and the dismissal of rights as so much bourgeois verbiage, with socialism now a sub-set of demands internal to a wider Democratic Revolution.

On the other hand, the ultra-Leftist critique of capitalism and the state remains the order of the day for post-Marxists such as Castoriadis,

Hardt and Negri, and Badiou. In a sense, though, even here, I think we could run with Boltanski's (2002) contention that we have witnessed a pervasive 'moderation' in utopian terms and a withdrawal from totalizing transformative schemes. Boltanski argues that we have seen, in recent times, a shift from the formerly dominant Left vision of, and commitment to, 'total revolution'. Today, says Boltanski, the Left speaks the language of democracy, rights, and citizenship. Thus, even in the ultra-Leftist imaginings of Hardt and Negri (2000) the programmatic moment consists of rights demands – global citizenship, a social wage and reappropriation (Žižek, 2004).

Evaluating post-Marxism

Each of these problems, and the variety of post-Marxist answers to them, seem pressing when reflecting on the issue of Marxism's 'broken triangle' of social science, philosophy and politics (Therborn, 2008) and on the question of the extent to which socialism still constitutes a significant counter-culture of our modernity (Bauman, 1976; Beilharz, 1999). Yet, as Tormey and Townshend (and others) point out, these post-Marxist responses are themselves open to a number of critical questions. This appears to me to be especially the case in light of another set of shifts, shifts that have made those parallel narratives of decline – of utopian reference and of the classical values and aspirations of social theory – look less convincing. In particular, I think that by the second half of the 1990s both of these narratives had unravelled somewhat – they and, with them, that moment of 'happy globalization' were simply facing too many 'reality problems'.

Particularly important, I think, were a number of key events, mobilizations and processes through and beyond the 1990s that, together, 'punctured' (Callinicos, 2003) both of these stories. I am thinking here of the following variety of factors: major mobilizations against neo-liberal restructuring (for instance, France 1995) – it hardly seems credible to say today, as Anderson (2000: 7) did at the beginning of the twenty-first century, that neo-liberalism stands as 'the most successful ideology in world history'; the East Asian Crisis of 1997 and subsequent 'contagion' followed, a decade later, by another profoundly dislocating financial crisis, of which we are still in the midst; the growth of right-wing populism, in Europe and elsewhere; the gathering momentum of the anti-globalization movement – from the Zapatista rebellion to the 'coming out party' at the WTO's third ministerial in Seattle, 1999 – and, more recently, the 'Arab Spring' and the Occupy movement; significant dissent in the semi-periphery against the Washington Consensus; the rise of political Islam; and a 'new pessimism' (Murden, 2002) about globalization bringing a 'clash of civilizations', a 'rise of tribes', 'Balkanization' and so on.

In a theoretical register, I think we have some corollaries. Gregor McLennan (2000; 2003) has spoken of an emerging 'new positivity' in the social sciences. Part of this involves a reaction against what McLennan (2003) calls the 'negativity' and 'excessive self-scrutiny' of post-modern theory. According to McLennan (2000: 18; 2002), this new positivity entails a somewhat deflationary attitude towards theory and a 'more substantive and affirmative' direction in theoretical work. We are seeing, here, a return to concern with the 'logic of the social' (McLennan, 2000: 18), to the 'state of things' (McLennan, 2002: 323), to the ambition 'to actually say something about the structure and direction of the world we inhabit, and about the values which will guide a better human future' (McLennan, 1999: 566). Here, the challenges mounted to social theory through the post-modernizing period – challenges to reductionism, functionalism, determinism, universalism, and the problematization of objectivism, realism, enlightenment, rationality and explanation (McLennan 1996; 2002) – are thought vital, progressive, inescapable; but this new positivity involves a recognition that the social sciences cannot do without some version of these emphases and values.[10]

The result of all this, I think, is that we are seeing something of a comeback both of utopian reference and of more affirmative social theorizing and self-assured criticism: we are seeing real productivity in terms of utopian reference since the late 1990s, with numerous thinkers calling for a return to utopian 'thinking beyond' and developing utopian alternatives that insist 'another world is possible';[11] and, at the same time, we are seeing projects of social and political theorizing that represent something of a return to the classical modality in terms of the combination of conceptualization, explanation and ambitious substantive work (McLennan, 2003).[12]

If these suggestions are plausible, then I feel that the post-Marxist identification of problems within Marx and Marxism, and its responses to such problems, might seem less weighty today. On this score, despite their sympathy with the broad thrust of the post-Marxist engagement with Marxism, Tormey and Townshend are critical before every one of those unifying problems and, again, it is worth running through some of what they have to say, before a concluding note that draws some of these hesitations together. With respect to the question of history, post-Marxists often caricature Marx and Marxism, and frequently simply offer a replacement meta-narrative. On the question of revolutionary subjectivities, have we not seen, since the emergence of the anti-globalization movement, precisely a return of 'materialist' political contestation spoken to by the Marxist tradition? In the case of the problem of ethics, the often accompanying retreat from radical politics by post-Marxists could be seen as again out of step with the radicality of transformative politics emerging today. On the issue of positivism, Tormey and Townshend are concerned that 'positivism' becomes an obfuscatory charge, especially given that many post-modern-influenced thinkers continue to work in a parallel way – totalization, grand-narratives, explanatory schemas and so on. With respect to the problem of vanguardism, Tormey and Townshend are sceptical about whether post-Marxists are able to completely escape from the charges they level at Marxists.[13] And, finally, with regard to the problem of democracy, Tormey and Townshend contend that many post-Marxists, while extolling the virtues of democracy, do not analyse with sufficient rigour the conditions for such democracy.

These all seem to me to be rather important, effective points and, in conjunction with my speculative comments about a late 1990s return of utopian reference and expansive social theorizing, they take some of the wind out of the sails of the idea of post-Marxism as a successor discourse to Marxism. Related issues are raised by turning back to initial definitional difficulties – that is, the character of the post-Marxist confrontation with Marx and Marxism. Centrally, there is a dialogue established within post-Marxism between Marx and Marxism, on the one hand, and post-foundational thought, on the other. It is clear that this is an uneven dialogue across post-Marxism. For instance, in Laclau, the Marx and Marxism side seems at the most residual and contingent. Wanting to hold on to certain (rather minimal) Marxian insights, such as 'human beings have no other nature than the one they give themselves in the social production of their own existence', Laclau (1990: 242) insists that Marxism was only *one* possible starting point in the development of the theoretical and political ideas outlined in *Hegemony and Socialist Strategy* (Laclau and Mouffe, 1985). Apparently, Marx and Marxism can almost be forgotten. Here, as in Castoriadis (1988b), we might have to put some or all of the Marxist body to death in order to save the spirit, a spirit equated with something like radical critique, autonomy.

For others, it is clear that the 'name "Marx" is – in a certain sense – entirely uncircumventable' (Derrida in Magnus and Cullenberg, 1995: x), providing, in Spivak's (1995: 113) words, 'dynamic materials'. For others still, the question of Marxism as a label is avoided, and perhaps for good reasons, since Marx himself, as we know, declared that he was not a Marxist. We might, in this vein, nominate Edward Said as a post-Marxist thinker and look at his approach to such an issue. Constantly drawing from Marx and Marxism – Gramsci, Williams, Adorno, C. L. R. James, and others – Said (2001: 441), in an exemplary post-Marxist move, insists that 'I am not concerned with schools of thought if the issue is membership ... we must eclectically choose specific elements and reformulate them in a new approach through our new discourses'. Proclaiming oneself to be a Marxist of this or that stripe makes no sense to Said if you are unattached to a political constituency, if Marxism is a 'compensation for the loss of the divine' (Said, 2001: 158) or a mere academic sub-speciality (Said, 2001: 42, 57, 77, 158, 222, 438).

And, finally, for yet others, Marxism still designates a political-intellectual endeavour that remains important in placing their thought – Jameson, Žižek, Badiou. A post-*Marxism* of this stripe, I think, could quite legitimately ask some probing questions of the more distanced iterations of post-Marxism that, at times, seem to assert that we are simply *beyond* Marx and Marxism. Marx and Marxism are surely plural; we have, here, a 'rich combination of cultures' (Beilharz, 2002: 5) and do not many of those post-Marxist critiques – Marxism simply as a mirror of production, as eliminating struggle from history, as a grand narrative we can do without, as irretrievably and illegitimately determinist and universalist – look a little harder to maintain today? Do they not seem a tad totalizing, inattentive to difference and caught in their own metanarrative about the passage from modernity to post-modernity? Those who have imagined we might pin Marxism down to a simple set of now irrelevant axioms are doing great violence to a tradition that can contain Gramsci and Adorno and Pannekoek and Luxemburg and Kautsky and Debord and Korsch.[14] And, on this note, in getting closer to this thing, 'post-Marxism', it is worth noting the apparent proximity of post-Marxism to Western Marxism – post-Marxism perhaps simply as 'Western Marxism, only up-to-date'. That is to say, both are rather culturalist in orientation, more pragmatic than Marxist orthodoxy and searching beyond the Marxian canon for resources, marked by defeat, contained largely in the academy (Anderson, 1976) and critical, even if this is sometimes muted, of Leninism as well as of social democracy (Aronowitz, 1981).

In a related vein, it is hard, I think, not to be tempted by Perry Anderson's (1983) argument that there is nothing that matches Marxism in terms of scope and moral force. Today, in particular, as

Tormey and Townshend argue, in the face of globalization and its pressing discontents, are we not drawn back to Marx and the Marxian tradition? Is there anything that compares when endeavouring to map our globalizing present? Does *post*-Marxism, for instance, ever offer us anything that comes near to the power of a world-systems analysis? Is there any analytical or political gain in dedicating ourselves wholeheartedly to post-Marxism? That is to say, across post-Marxism, we have a range of interventions at very different levels – ontological reconsiderations (Castoriadis, Badiou), conceptual reconstruction (Laclau), grand, totalizing theoretical work that seeks to map the world (Hardt and Negri). And the most interesting work, for me, is that expansive theoretical effort, attached to a more ambitious, emphatic *socialist* politics, in line with McLennan's argument about the 'new positivity' of our theoretical moment, and away from the sometimes paralyzing obsessions with reflexivity, difference and the cautious mulitdimensionality of the period of post-modernism's theoretical hegemony. For instance, I certainly believe that Laclau's development of a new conceptual apparatus provides a useful set of considerations as an analytical strategy (Andersen, 2003). Yet, doubts have to remain. In the substantive analyses stemming from the so-called Essex School, do we really find anything that a sophisticated Marxist thinker might not already be attentive to? Do we find anything that is a significant advance on the scope and subtlety of a Perry Anderson, a Fredric Jameson, an Eric Hobsbawm? I think the answer has to be a clear no. Instead, these analyses often seem rather *blank and formal*. This, to me, seems very clear in many Laclau-inspired analyses of political identities and discourses, which simply get pulled into their constituent pieces to reveal that there are no foundations, identity is precarious, relationally constructed, that identity coheres around some contingent nodal point that is, in truth, empty of substantive content, while viewed (incorrectly) by participants as 'points of supreme plenitude of meaning' (Stavrakakis, 1997: 274), etc., etc. But what is the real analytical and political purchase of such formulaic moves?

At the same time, stubborn Marxist orthodoxy hardly seems an option at our undoubtedly pluralist moment, and what Docherty (1996: 243) suggests that post-Marxism gives us – an interrogation of Marx 'in the interests of a proper historicity', a pluralizing move against aspirations to doctrinal purity and the illusion of orthodox Marxism as self-sufficient diagnostic template and remedy for everything – is inescapable for any socialist-minded reinvention of a theoretical lan-guage and compelling set of utopian references today.[15] Post-Marxism is, though, a 'series of gestures' some of which might, after all, come to be seen precisely as moments *within* Marxism (Beilharz, 2007), within the wealth of efforts made to establish a dialogue between Marx and contemporary social settings. Surely, this engagement, as Castoriadis (1987: 9) once said, remains 'immediate and inevitable' for anyone interested in society. In that case, then, Marx and Marxism are still there as indispensable, though not lone, figures on our (post)modern socialist horizons.

2

'No, We Have Not Finished Reflecting on Communism':[1] Castoriadis, Lefort and Psychoanalytic Leninism

Introductory comments

As noted in the previous chapter, Goran Therborn (2007: 67) has approached what has been called 'the crisis of the Marxist imaginary' by way of the elegant notion of 'Marxism's broken triangle'. This triangle – constituted by, first, 'a historical social science ... focussed on the operation of capitalism and, more generally ... the dynamics of the forces and relations of production', second, a 'philosophy of contradictions or dialectics', and, third, a socialist, working-class politics – has, Therborn charges, come apart under the weight of intellectual challenges and extensive social changes.

'Post-Marxism', despite being a fairly troublesome notion, represents a significant Left effort to take seriously, and wrestle with, these changes and challenges. Again, as previously mentioned, in the best book-length treatment to date, Tormey and Townshend (2006) suggest that post-Marxism's co-ordinates of unity centre on six crucial problems posed to Marx and Marxism – the problems of history, of revolutionary subjectivity, of ethics, of positivism, of vanguardism and of democracy. Each of the thinkers and works I am dealing with in this chapter – Lefort, Castoriadis and the 'psychoanalytic Leninists' – wrestle with these problems, rub up against, or would be considered instances of, post-Marxism, and engage with the question of socialism's continued significance within our modernity (Bauman, 1976; Beilharz, 2003). They allow us to get a better, closer feel for this thing, post-Marxism. In their very different ways, they illustrate that, as Therborn (2008: 179) remarks, 'left-wing creativity has not ceased'. At the same time, each of the trajectories represented here is beset by dilemmas: a premature erasure of the still-fertile resources of historical materialism, in

Castoriadis and Lefort; a rather all-embracing and one-sided pessimism, in Castoriadis, combined, though, with an attractively updated council communism; a confining liberalism, in Lefort, which sits uncomfortably beside Left communist insights; and a worryingly unreconstructed and uncritical Bolshevism, in psychoanalytic Leninism, alongside some stirring, novel cultural criticism and a refreshingly confident appeal to socialism. These dilemmas leave us, for better or for worse, without any fully satisfying replacement for that broken triangle. To explore this, I will work through a number of central theoretical and political issues, bringing these figures into conversation with each other and, towards the end of the chapter, with another protagonist – what might be called 'post-Marxism phase II', which, to my mind, suggests another path in addressing a predicament Santos (2005) has described as a combination of modern promises (the unfulfilled promises of modernity), alongside the disarray into which modern solutions have fallen.

Autonomy, politics, creation

A first way into these issues are the questions raised by Claude Lefort's (1924–2010) reading of the Democratic Revolution, which plays a crucial role in the best known instance of self-avowed post-Marxism, Laclau and Mouffe's (1985) *Hegemony and Socialist Strategy*. Serving as a condensation of the key emphases of his 'post-Marxist' turn (Bourg, 2007: 5), *Complications: Communism and the Dilemmas of Democracy* sees Lefort returning to his contention about the advent of liberal democracy as a 'mutation in the symbolic order' (Lefort, 1986; 1988) against monarchical domination – the discovery

> that power does not belong to anyone, that those who exercise it do not incarnate it, that they are only temporary trustees of public authority, that the law of God or nature is not vested in them, that they do not hold the final knowledge of the world and social orders, and that they are not capable of deciding what everyone has the right to do, think, say, and understand. (Lefort, 2007: 14)

Or, deploying the language of psychoanalysis – a common feature of all the thinkers treated here – democracy as a new 'imperative ... that the distinction between the symbolic and the real ... [is] tacitly acknowledged' (2007: 143).

Lefort's reading of this democratic mutation, which is equated with the advent of 'the political', comes close to the 'autonomy' of his one-time comrade in the legendary Socialism or Barbarism organization, Cornelius Castoriadis, the motor driving four posthumously published volumes by the latter, *The Rising Tide of Insignificancy, Figures of the Thinkable, A Society Adrift*, and *Postscript on Insignificancy.* (But, of course, Lefort's encounter with Machiavelli and his disillusionment with the notion of revolution, as well as the influence of Merleau-Ponty's focus on the 'flesh' of history, against scientism, Marxian and other varieties of social thought, make for a significant divergence of paths from Castoriadis.) The concerns covered in these works will be familiar to anyone acquainted with the three volumes of Castoriadis's *Political and Social Writings* or the two 1997 collections, *The Castoriadis Reader* and *World in Fragments*, but there's plenty of interest here, especially in the interviews and some of the provocative occasional reflections (the Gulf War, third worldism, the psychic roots of hate, chaos, C. L. R. James, the crisis of Marxism, for instance); and the web-publication of these four volumes, under unusual, controversial circumstances,[2] promises a well-deserved, long overdue expansion of Castoriadis's audience.

Born in Constantinople in 1922, Castoriadis was philosophically literate and politically active by his teenage years. Hunted in Greece in the early 1940s by both Stalinists and fascists, he left to take up a never-completed doctoral thesis in France, where he worked as an economist for the OECD, then as a psychoanalyst and finally as an academic in the school for advanced studies in the social sciences, passing away in France in 1997 (Curtis in Castoriadis, 1997a). Perhaps Castoriadis is best known for his tutelage of the group Socialism or Barbarism, which split from the Trotskyist Fourth International in 1949 (and dissolved in 1967) and whose ranks included not only Lefort, but also Jean-Francois Lyotard, Guy Debord and psychoanalyst Jean Laplanche. Socialism or Barbarism belongs within that rather neglected current of socialism I have chosen to label Left communism, which contested the orthodoxies of both social democracy and Leninism, interpreted the regimes of 'really existing socialism' as forms of capitalism ('total bureaucratic capitalism', for Castoriadis [1988a; 1997a]) and posited the possibility of a different type of socialism, often a directly democratic socialism of workers' councils, council communism.

As I have noted, Castoriadis (1988b) became more and more critical of Marxism, making a decisive break in 1959 in a lengthy text he circulated within Socialism or Barbarism, 'Modern Capitalism and Revolution'. Here, and from this point onwards, Castoriadis objected fundamentally to a range of Marxian notions: the economic determinism and teleological view of history, which eliminated struggle from human history;

the assumptions of growing working-class immiseration, uncontrollable crisis tendencies, the falling profit rate; the prioritization of the industrial working class as agent of socialism; the 'theological' character of Marxian social science; and Marxism's implication in the modern fantasy of 'unlimited rational mastery' (Castoriadis, 1988b; 1993; 1997a and b; 2010a and b). In place of such Marxian emphases, Castoriadis, again and again, underscored creativity and the imagination (indeterminacy as a crucial factor), against the relentlessly deterministic cast of modern thought, to focus on 'social imaginary significations' and 'webs of meaning' in terms of social analysis, and to reconceptualize the opposition capitalism-socialism, more in the order of the pairing heteronomy-autonomy, continuing to his death to hold to a notion of self-emancipatory and directly democratic socialism (Castoriadis, 1987; 1997a and b).

In Castoriadis (2003: 15), a heteronomous social order entails that 'people strongly believe ... that the law, the institutions of their society have been given to them, once and for all, by somebody else – the spirits, the ancestors, the gods, or whatever – and are not ... their own work'. On the other hand, 'autonomy' designates 'a society that knows that its institutions, its laws, are its own work and product'. Such autonomy, for Castoriadis, is to be found in two historical 'ruptures'. The first occurs within Greek Antiquity, from the eighth to fifth centuries BC (2005: 174). On this score, these volumes again demonstrate Castoriadis's attachment to this period. For instance, in a fascinating piece discussing *Prometheus Bound* and *Antigone*, Castoriadis (2005: 38) contends that, within the quarter of a century separating the two works, we witness an extraordinary shift from 'the idea of a divine anthropogony [humankind prior to Prometheus's gifts] to the idea of man's self-creation', 'the self-limitation of the individual and of the political community' (2005: 27). The second rupture commences from the eleventh to twelfth century in Western Europe, reaching a pinnacle in the years 1750–1950 (2005: 133). Here, we find Castoriadis praising the extraordinary creation in all domains during the height of autonomy's recommencement – the institution of a new anthropological type, the 'European citizen' (2003: 53), the workers' movement, the re-flowering of philosophy and art – as well as forthrightly defending the 'specificity of Western civilization' (2003: 142), against the growing popularity of anti-Eurocentrism and the related 'denigration of truth, autonomy, and responsibility' in post-modernism's equalization of all narratives (2003: 134, 103). (On this last score, despite certain resonances with his own work, post-modernism is designated by Castoriadis [2010b: 136] as 'trite and spineless'.)

These breaks, this autonomy, for Castoriadis (2003: 274), clearly reveal the Abyss, the absence of any 'extrasocial source and grounding of the law', over which meaning is built, and also the centrality of the creation that surges forth from such chaos – being and history, in Castoriadis (2005: 177, 334), as creation. This, once again, is in contrast to the traditional philosophical equation of 'being' with 'being determined'. Such fundamental creativity can be found, Castoriadis (2005: 127) insists, at the level of the psyche, which is 'radical imagination', the 'flux or incessant flow of representations, desires, and affects'; and at the social level – the social imaginary, the magma of imaginary significations and the institutions embodying these significations, which hold society together. These social imaginary significations have, for Castoriadis (2003: 209), three vital functions – structuring representations of the world, designating ends of action, and establishing types of affect characteristic of a society.

In both Castoriadis and Lefort, then, we find that common post-Marxist opposition to teleological History, foundationalism and determinism. Thus Castoriadis (2003: 150, 274; 2011) objects to the heteronomy implied by the Marxist notion of 'laws of History', charging that, in this, and in his submission to the capitalist imaginary of production, progress and the expansion of rational mastery, Marx failed to remain faithful to the project of autonomy. In both Lefort and Castoriadis we find, too, that post-Marxist exit from these problems – non-determinacy and politics/the political. Both, though, are rightly unhappy with the formulation 'contingency' as an answer to Marxist teleology, determinism and Necessity. In his interpretation of communism, for instance, Lefort (2007: 26) rejects both analyses that accent necessity and those that emphasize contingency: instead he posits communism bearing traces of the past but hardly ordained by this history; and Bolshevism as the product 'of an extraordinary condensation of heterogeneous processes that coexisted in the same space and at the same time' (2007: 136). In like manner, Castoriadis (2003: 186) insists that creation doesn't mean indetermination, but instead 'the positing of new determinations'; and radical creation, while not predetermined, is nonetheless 'conditioned' (2005: 355) by what 'precedes and surrounds' it (2005: 418). Here, Castoriadis (1987), borrowing from Freud, was to deploy the notion of 'leaning on' as an answer to the problem contingency/determination (Klooger, 2009).

The turn to contingency, of course, was a major concern in Marxian evaluations of the post-modern and post-Marxist enterprises – clear, for instance, in Anderson's (1983) critique of the post-structuralist 'randomization of history'. In one of the more searching, intelligent responses to Laclau and Mouffe, Nicos Mouzelis (1988; 1990) charged that the authors of *Hegemony and Socialist Strategy* had constructed an entirely unnecessary either/or out of the confrontation with Marxism – either absolute necessity or absolute contingency. The result for Mouzelis (1988: 110) was the demolition of the Marxian conceptual apparatus, without any 'Generalities II'-type replacements, leaving us with an 'institutional vacuum' and abandoning the central terrain of social theory – accounting for the constitution, maintenance and transformation of social orders.

While Mouzelis accurately points to the way conventionally Marxist concepts often get smuggled into post-Marxist analysis, and is rightly concerned with the consequences of prohibitions against 'society', Laclau (1990) clarifies that he is not denying a 'structuration' of, or a 'systemness' to, the social; and Laclau's continued development of a discourse-centred analytical strategy does, to an extent, answer concerns about the absence of theoretical replacements for the 'historical social science' corner of the Marxian triangle. Yet, a still lingering concern might hold that, as Sim (1998) has put it, the 'post' side of 'post-Marxism' is driving the endeavour. A central worry here is that, as Gregor McLennan (1996; 1999; 2002; 2003) argues, the thrust of such post-modern thinking has been unrelentingly 'negative' and 'excessively self-scrutinizing', focused on detecting and rejecting those various 'sins' of Modernist theorizing – reductionism, essentialism, universalism, enlightenment, objectivism and so on. Is there any way we can abandon those 'traditionalist' commitments, McLennan (1996; 2006) asks, if we are to remain committed to thinking 'the logic of the social', to explanation and to politically relevant social theorizing. And I think the overall tenor of the discourse-centred post-Marxist alternative is indeed rather negative. As I noted in Chapter 1, it seems questionable that discourse analytical approaches present us with any theoretical or political advances beyond the always subtle, illuminating interpretive work we could expect from 'straighter' sophisticated Marxian thinkers.

And we could equally pose Mouzelis's questions to Castoriadis and Lefort. Is Marxism too much of a prohibitive presence in their thinking for the construction of social theory at that level of 'Generalities II'? It might be that this dimension is underdeveloped, or left implicit, though there are some indicators of possible answers. In Lefort, for instance, the insistence on the 'concrete' (signalling the continuing importance in his thought of Merleau-Ponty) against contingency and necessity, and his rejection of the tendency to read totalitarianism as an outcome of ideas is a start; and his analysis of communism, seeking to understand the interweaving of political, social, economic, juridical, moral and psychic facts (see Lefort 2007: 24–8), is suggestive of a line here.

Similarly, Castoriadis's 'imaginary significations' appear to suggest an alternative analytical strategy and, more recently, Peter Wagner and others have sought to develop this in a series of important pieces on 'world-making' (Karagiannis and Wagner, 2007; Wagner, 2001b). However, as Klooger (2009) points out, Castoriadis is deliberately turning from explanation to elucidation here, and I would suggest that while Lefort's and Castoriadis's emphases on complex determinations, creativity and meaning demonstrates sensitivity to that difficult pairing, determinancy/indeterminancy – these just do *not* make for a theoretical social scientific orientation, but instead remain at the level of a broad ontological orientation.

Psychoanalytic solutions, totalitarian problems

The search for theoretical help beyond the Marxist canon has, of course, been a persistent socialist response to Marxism's periodic crises, and joining a more recent turn to post-modern ideas has been the remarriage of Left thinking and psychoanalytic concepts, one significant result of which is the contemporary prominence of a 'psychoanalytic Leninism'. Much of this prominence can undoubtedly be attributed to the extraordinary Slavoj Žižek, to the point of the effective existence today of a Žižekian school of social theory, as well as a more popular counter-cultural influence for Žižek's ideas. I don't want to say too much here about Žižek, who has received extensive critical treatment elsewhere,[3] but his primary and most startling contributions lie in the realm of what Balibar (2013) describes as a Hegelian–Lacanian dialectic of the superstructures and, above all, ideology, which is grounded by a psychoanalytic re-articulation of historical materialism, with capitalism and exploitation as the Real. At his best, Žižek's turbulent, sometimes impetuous and contradictory genius is turned to often surprising and entertaining analyses of the operation of ideology today (fetishistic disavowal; the superego imperative to Enjoy; perverse enjoyment in political discourse; today's 'they know what they're doing, but are doing it anyway' – as against the older 'for they know not what they do'), with some lovely contributions on the ideological mechanisms of fascism and right-wing populism, Western Buddhism and contemporary belief, current multiculturalist tolerance, the monster alliances in political life today (for instance, Christian fundamentalist support of Israel), delusions of ethical anti-capitalism and human rights, and much, much more. Filip Kovacevic's (2007) *Liberating Oedipus?* is a systematic, partisan treatment that responds to this psychoanalytic Leninist development, carefully unfolding the argument that a Lacanian interpretation of Marx and Freud represents the best option for theoretical-political engagement with our current reality: psychoanalysis 'carries the banner of the advance of human freedom in the history of humanity' (2007: 229).

Kovacevic begins with an optimist's reading of Freud, emphasising the 'priority of the communal presence' (2007: 11), the repression of feelings of love over the repression of aggressive urges in the establishment of morality (aggressive urges as 'the children of Eros' [2007: 31]), even if the later Freud would retreat from such insights under the shadows of war and fascism.

Interestingly, Kovacevic returns to the early Freudo-Marxists – Reich, Marcuse, Brown and 'the Liberation Thesis' – and he insists on the affinity between these thinkers and Lacan. In the case of Lacan, Kovacevic identifies three strands of his thought central to rebuilding emancipatory social theory. First, Kovacevic champions the contribution made by Lacan in the realm of ethical theory: the 'invitation to the revelation of [one's] desire' outside of 'the service of goods' (Lacan in Kovacevic, 2007: 118), the possibility that the signifying chain structuring the subject's existence could be restructured in an encounter with the Real. Second, Lacan's analysis of the discourses of the master, the university, the analyst and the hysteric is useful, insofar as Lacan's psychoanalytical enterprise is centred on 'the hysterization' of the analysand's discourse. This hysterization breaks with congealed, inauthentic understandings of the self and the world and replaces them with uncertainty: 'hysterics are, in my opinion, the proletarians of a Lacanian revolution' (2007: 144). Here, Kovacevic argues that a 'formalization' of the famous appeal in *The German Ideology* to the varied, accomplished activities of the communist day 'would look like a life lived according to the discourse of the hysteric' (2007: 146). The third, related, strand is Lacan's work on the logic of sexuation, with the feminine pole – the logic of the not-all, of supplemental *jouissance* – as 'the logic of revolutions' (2007: 143).

After dispensing with Deleuze and Guattari's and Irigaray's critiques of psychoanalysis, Kovacevic (2007: 205) turns to Žižek and Badiou. These thinkers are central, he contends, in moving beyond the situation we find ourselves faced with – 'market populism', the false universality of multiculturalism, the problem of the '*jouissance* accumulated in social and political structures'. Badiou's notions of the Truth-Event, the encounter with the Real, and fidelity to that Event are endorsed. However, Kovacevic is critical of the possibly quietistic consequences of Badiou's emphasis on the unknowability of such Events (what others have named their 'miraculous' quality – and what Badiou (2010a: 6–7) himself describes as their 'non-factual' element, the event precisely not as a realization of possibilities in a situation), suggesting instead that they might be caused 'by the individual or group of individuals who are, in their words and deeds, incarnating the discourse of the hysteric' (Kovacevic, 2007: 216).

I will return to aspects of Kovacevic's work shortly (and to Badiou at length in Chapter 8), but it is worth noting again the turn to psychoanalysis across post-Marxism – Deleuze and Guattari, Habermas, Laclau, Lyotard. Lefort, too, deploys the terms imaginary, real and symbolic in his analysis of totalitarianism. But it is Castoriadis's reading of psychoanalysis that is perhaps of most interest, because it is built tightly into his social and political thought and is particularly well represented in the first two volumes under scrutiny, here; in addition, it is an interpretation quite at odds – more straightforwardly Freudian and 'pessimistic' – with the position put forward by Kovacevic, Žižek, Laclau and others drawing from Lacan, and with the use of, and hopes for, desire in Deleuze and Guattari and Lyotard.

For Castoriadis (2005: 343), psychoanalysis has a political significance, being part and parcel of the project of autonomy. Here, Castoriadis (2005: 347) refuses a Lacanian line centred on an ethics or politics of the Real: 'far from being an "ethic of privatized desire" the project of autonomy is brought into play as indissociably individual and social'. Castoriadis also takes Lacan to task for failing to recognize the radical imagination of the psyche, for reducing the psyche's creation of representations, affects and desires to repetition-reflection of the already there. Again, in this, we have Castoriadis's insistence on being and history as creation. Of course, though, his insistence on the remarkable creativity of the psyche – the 'defunctionalization' of representation and pleasure, the 'capacity to posit as real that which is not real' (2003: 20), the 'flux or incessant flow of representations, desires, and affects' which equals 'continual emergence' (2005: 127) – does not incline Castoriadis towards the position of the 'philosophers of desire' who would seek to unleash these unconscious forces. Castoriadis is much more sober on this score, reading the goal of analysis as enabling the analysand to become 'lucid concerning her desire and concerning reality, and responsible for her acts' (2005: 163), to establish a *different* relationship with the unconscious (2003: 16). This sobriety is in order because of the radical madness of the original psychical monad who must be torn – 'hominization' requiring 'radical violence' (2005: 164–5) – from its enclosed world to enter the social world. And such hominization necessarily leaves inhabiting in the psyche 'an ineradicable negativity' (2005: 351).

Castoriadis (2005: 295–6) explores this in 'The Psychical and Social Roots of Hate', where he notes the 'extraordinary quantity of hatred contained in the psychical reservoir', issuing from the 'near need' for a closure of meaning attached to the institution of society, and from the psyche's search for ultimate certainties. Given this, the fight against racism, war and so on is inevitably 'an uphill struggle' (2005: 297).

For Castoriadis, totalitarianism, too, can be understood partly in psychic terms, as a search for mastery, for omnipotence. Castoriadis and Lefort, were, as mentioned, part of a Left communist tradition that produced some of the best analytical work on 'really existing socialism' – their ideas influential in the revival of the anti-totalitarianism discourse from the 1970s (Howard, 2007). For his part, Žižek (2001a: 3) has dismissed 'totalitarianism' as a 'prohibition against thinking': 'Throughout its career, "totalitarianism" was an ideological notion that sustained the complex operation of "taming free radicals", of guaranteeing the liberal-democratic hegemony, dismissing the Leftist critique of liberal democracy as the obverse, the "twin", of the Rightist Fascist dictatorship.'[4] Despite some well-aimed shots, and the usual entertainment he provides, Žižek goes too far, and it is very important, I think, not to conflate Lefort and Castoriadis with the new philosophers and other 'conformist liberal scoundrels' (Budgen et al., 2007: 2).[5]

Complications makes the differences, here, very clear. The impetus for Lefort's book was provided by two prominent interpretations of 'really existing socialism' – Francois Furet's (2000) *The Passing of an Illusion* and Martin Malia's (1995) *The Soviet Tragedy*. More than this, though, Lefort (2007: 32), in his gentle, careful way, takes to task the position found in these works and much more widely that 'Communism has fallen apart, and passions have cooled. The time for judgement has arrived'. Here, Lefort, as a long-time analyst and critic of 'really existing socialism', rejects the implication that judgement was previously off the agenda. Moreover, Lefort seeks to complicate the understandings of communism presented in these two works, which are as familiar as they are trying in the totalitarianism literature: communism as ruled by Utopia, connected to the reign of the Marxist idea, installing an 'ideocracy' (Malia); communism as based on an idea, an illusion (Furet).

Lefort makes a number of notable points across *Complication*'s short, dense chapters. Importantly, we see the persistence of themes from his Socialism or Barbarism days, where, in a typically low-key, modest register, he notes that non-Leninist Leftists had for many years analysed and criticized Eastern bloc socialism and had, for their efforts, been major targets of a well-placed Communist Party establishment. In related fashion, he praises as still important Castoriadis's text of 1949,[6] in which the latter analyses the combination in the USSR of ostensibly collectively owned means of production together with the appropriation of surplus value by a minority (Lefort, 2007: 122). In this vein, Lefort (2007: 47) refuses the tiresome attempt to connect Marx's writing with totalitarianism, insisting on 'the falsification of Marx's work' and the 'manipulated' Marx deployed by Lenin and the Bolsheviks. Chapters 5 and 6, in particular, demonstrate continued attachments to his Left-councilist roots – and indicate the *radical* democratic potential, as opposed to the often remarked-on liberal quality (Ingram, 2006), of Lefort's ideas – where Lefort returns to a forceful critique of Lenin's 'socialism', and where he questions Malia's and Furet's neglect of the February Revolution in favour of October. February is vital for Lefort (2007: 53, 54) because of the spontaneous 'surge of revolutionary organs' creating therewith a 'space of untamed democracy'.

Addressing recurrent themes in the anti-totalitarianism literature, Lefort (2007) carefully explores the pairings totalitarianism–revolution, totalitarianism–democracy, and totalitarianism–egalitarianism: arguing that communism must be situated within a world 'transformed by the democratic revolution', within 'a universe that had ceased to be fascinated with aristocratic values' (2007: 69), but, at the same time, hardly a necessary development out of democracy; insisting on the plurality of meanings contained in 'revolution' and, again, recalling Left communism in his insistence that revolution means, first up, 'a popular uprising' (2007: 47); and separating radical egalitarianism from Bolshevism, arguing that, for Lenin, 'the construction of socialism was expressly subordinated to the introduction of the norms of industrial capitalism' (2007: 184).

In reflecting on the character of the Soviet social order, Lefort prioritizes the role of the party as an 'embryo of a new state' (2007: 123), possessed of a will to 'organize all the forces of society' (2007: 58). Against the Trotskyists, Stalinism was a mutation 'inside a new political space' (2007: 59) constituted by the unprecedented invention of the Bolshevik party (a feature that clearly distances the Russian from the French Revolution). In 'the interweaving of power, law, and knowledge in the party' (2007: 171) in its 'fabrication of the social', a new mode of domination and politics emerges: a domination 'in which many kinds of signs were effaced at one and the same time: the signs of a division between the dominating and the dominated; of distinctions among power, law and knowledge; and of a differentiation among the spheres of human activity' (2007: 25); and a politics 'entirely guided by the destruction of the autonomy of individuals, of every mode of sociability that escaped the mastery of the party, and of all opposition within the party itself' (2007: 68).[7] Arguing that 'the system of representations that governed the party likewise governed society' (2007: 138), Lefort explores the communist 'capture of the individual' (2007: 107), the invention of a new kind of person, possessed of 'communist traits': 'love of discipline of action and thought; their love of authority ... their love of order ... their love of conformity' (2007: 107). On the related question of communism's power of attraction in the West, and against the idealism of Malia and Furet, Lefort underscores the actions of the 'local' parties, with some fascinating anecdotal reflections on his encounters with the *Parti Communiste Français* (PCF). Equally interesting is Lefort's examination of 'soviet legality', the extraordinary 'combination of law and the arbitrary' (2007: 161), 'a perversion of the idea of law' (2007: 158), where, for the system to function, people were, in fact, forced to disobey the operative rules. In the book's final chapter, Lefort insists on the need to situate 'really existing socialism' on the terrain of globalization:

> ... it is rarely observed that the formation of a *single world-space* provided the resources to conceive, beyond different cultures, political systems, and inequalities in development, a *single social state*; a total mastery of human relations under the name of One; an abolition of divisions that, no matter their manifestations, had always implied an experience of the Other; and, lastly, a system in which the positions of dominating and dominated would be eliminated. (2007: 185–6)

Between the triumph of the capitalist imaginary and the Leninist re-opening of history

All of this could not be further from the style and substance of the Budgen et al. (2007) 'provocation', *Lenin Reloaded*, which urges us to 'repeat Lenin'. The Žižekian reading of Lefort would, as noted, draw the latter together with Laclau and Mouffe as submitting to the dictates of mere liberal democracy. Kovacevic (2007: 201), for instance, connects Laclau and Mouffe, Stavrakakis and Lefort, charging that the common positive emphasis on the Democratic Revolution's empty place of power equates to advocacy of changes only within a given economic and political realm, leaving 'unquestioned the fundamental rules of the liberal democratic game' – an essentially 'conformist' position that abandons the still pressing goal of universal emancipation. In a similar vein, in the introduction to *Lenin Reloaded*, the Žižek/Badiou rejection of the 'return to ethics', and the reading of human rights as a moralization of politics characteristic of our 'post-political consensus', stands in striking contrast to Lefort's readings. It is interesting here to note criticisms similar to this made by Castoriadis. Addressing the so-called 'ethical turn', Castoriadis (2003: 261) views it as a 'false conclusion' to be drawn from the experience of totalitarianism,[8] as a 'dodge, and a mockery of ethics', arguing instead that ethics only appears with autonomy, that it communicates 'necessarily and immediately' with politics. On rights, while rejecting (like Lefort) the Marxist emphasis on their merely formal and capitalist character, Castoriadis (2003: 350) sees them essentially as 'partial and defensive'. And while Castoriadis (2005: 207, 213) notes the affinities between his own thought and the notion of the empty place of power instituted by the modern democratic rupture, he vehemently denies that this can be taken as the case in our 'liberal oligarchies', which, in actuality, display a 'highly occupied "site of power"'.

In a sense, these sorts of criticisms are unfair to Lefort. On the question of rights, Lefort (1988), for good reasons, refused the hard Marxist critique of the welfare state, the maximalist reading of liberal democracy as the mere dictatorship of capital, and the understanding of rights as simply individualistic and property-founded veils of power. And this is again evident in *Complications*, where Lefort (2007: 72) remarks on the importance of the modern recognition of civil life and of rights: 'The rights to speak, to hear and understand, to read, and to write – these are indeed indissoluble. If the freedom of opinion is the freedom of expression, it is also the freedom of communication', this opening up a common space, and allowing expansion and deepening of such rights. In addition, clearly remaining committed to egalitarianism, and refusing the equation in the totalitarianism literature between communism and fascism (Lefort, 2000), Lefort reflects on contemporary globalization and the connection made between totalitarianism and utopia in the following way: 'And if one speaks of utopia, one must also recognize it in the pole opposite to socialism, namely, economic liberalism, the generator of practices that, if they had evolved freely, would have been devastating' (2000: 190).

Nevertheless, there are obviously points to be made about a broad post-Marxist retreat from forthright critique of capitalism and liberal democracy, the effects of what Jameson (1989) calls 'the [post-modern] war against totality', and the replacement of 'capitalism' by 'modernity' in explanatory-diagnostic terms (Alexander, 1995; Jameson, 2002; Wagner, 2001a; 2001b). Castoriadis is something of an exception that proves the rule here, continuing to display his Left communist credentials until the end,[9] and lamenting the 'incredible ideological regression' (2005: 81) that had seen the marginalization of criticism of representative democracy and capitalism. With respect to democracy, equated with politics and autonomy, Castoriadis (2005: 204) insists that this demands equal possibility for all to participate in power, and he finds the post-communist 'triumph of democracy' narrative risible. Today, the public sphere is private, the possession of the political oligarchy, with politics submerged beneath 'hobbies and lobbies' (2003: 217), with decisions of any substance completely disconnected from popular sovereignty, with a regime that simply guarantees 'the reproduction of the same' (2005: 208). The participatory democracy of the thin red line of workers' councils remains inspirational (2003: 216), against the mixture of 'the bureaucratic-hierarchical norm' and 'the money norm' of our 'fragmented bureaucratic capitalism' (2005: 213).

Articulating a contemporary version of council communism, a central element of democracy for Castoriadis should involve what takes place in the now highly separate realm of the economy. If modernity is the period of the re-birth of a potentially radicalized autonomy, it is also entwined with a second animating social imaginary signification, the 'demented capitalist project of unlimited expansion of pseudo-rational pseudo-mastery' (2003: 135). This attempt to extend rational mastery, taken to the furthest point in totalitarianism, is, for Castoriadis (2005: 94), the core imaginary signification of capitalism, involving 'the positing of the economy ... as the central site and supreme value of social life' (2005: 87), the contemporary 'autonomous movement of technoscience' (2005: 95) and an anthropological mutation wherein 'economic motivation tended to supplant all other motives' (2005: 96). In addressing the 'rationality of capitalism', Castoriadis returns to what he fears is a now-forgotten socialist critique: the fiction of the separability of the economic sphere; the preconditions of the creation of the market – violence, fraud, extortion; the absence of a 'perfect' let alone competitive market – state intervention, capitalist coalitions, withholding of information, manipulation of consumers, violence against working people; and the reduction of society and of rationality to the increase of production and the minimization of costs – 'neither the destruction of the environment, nor the flattening of human lives, nor the ugliness of cities, nor the universal triumph of irresponsibility and cynicism, nor the replacement of tragedy and popular festival by televised sitcoms is taken into account in this calculation' (2005: 116).[10] Castoriadis's alternative again recalls his councilist past – a directly democratized economy.

In these ways, Castoriadis looks decidedly singular, even eccentric, amidst the general direction of post-Marxism, but the Left defeats marking the post-Marxist moment equally mark these four volumes of his, which are almost unrelentingly pessimistic. Such pessimism makes Castoriadis's continuing radical political commitments appear rather impossibilist, intellectualist, lonely. For instance, in a 1990 piece on democracy, Castoriadis (2005: 246) says, 'so long as this collective hypnosis endures, there is, for those among us who have the weighty privilege of being able to speak, a provisional ethics and politics: unveil, criticize, and denounce the existing state of affairs. And for all: try to behave and to act in exemplary fashion wherever they find themselves'. Whereas a number of post-Marxist thinkers have shown a good measure of optimism about the 'crisis of Modernity', as expanding politics, as entailing a renewed and positive sense of limits (for instance, Laclau, 1990), for Castoriadis (2003: 76), the radical rupture of the project of autonomy, this unprecedented 'calling into question of the significations, institutions, and representations', is today in grave danger in the face of a threatened return to heteronomy. Today, says Castoriadis (2003: 44), we face a 'wearing out of [society's] ... imaginary significations': 'Society has discovered itself to be without any representation of its own future, and projectless as well' (2003: 37); we see a world-wide 'collapse of an emancipatory future' (2003: 69), signalled in the desperate clinging to a 'foundational past' – ethnicity, nation, religion; we have a 'dilapidation of the public space' (2003: 85); apathy and cynicism reign in political affairs; we see the 'total disappearance of prudence, of *phronesis*' (2003: 111); the artistic avant-garde is exhausted (2005: 138); a 'crisis of criticism' prevails (2003: 130) – 'there are no more philosophers' (2005: 138); we have witnessed the disappearance of social and political conflict; 'generalized corruption' (2003: 137), 'generalized conformism' (2003: 303) and privatization spread. All of this is clearly linked by Castoriadis (2010a: 250) to the 'fully-fledged domination of the capitalist imaginary'. This wearing out of imaginary significations promises, as well, serious anthropological consequences. Here, Castoriadis (2003: 30) suggests a shift in symptomology towards 'disorientation in life, instability, peculiarities of 'character' or a depressive disposition'. With the collapse of these imaginary significations, the 'dislocation of the family', education in crisis (2003: 31–2) and the dissolution of roles, we are faced with a 'destructuration ... [of the] personality' (2003: 30) – individuality reduced to 'a patchwork of collages' (2003: 223) and to the production of the 'greedy, the frustrated, the conformist' (2003: 302–3) individual – and a crisis of the identification process – contemporary identification centred on 'who earns the most and enjoys the most' (2003: 218).[11]

Perhaps we might read Castoriadis's endlessly pessimistic cultural criticism as a provocation, a call to arms but, over the four volumes – even moderated by his underlying optimism about history as driven by human collective and psychic creativity – it can't help but seem tiring, demobilizing and plainly one-dimensional. Here, Klooger (2009), for instance, makes an insightful critical point about Castoriadis's overly monolithic analysis of heteronomy, which is deemed in urgent need of revitalization and sophistication. Perhaps what we see with Castoriadis, after a brief brightening of mood in the 1960s, is a reflection of the terrain on which what might be called first-phase post-Marxism emerges and develops in the 1980s and 1990s – extensive social reorganization, the post-modernization of knowledge, the crisis of the ideologies and movements (Wallerstein, 1991b). This terrain, as Anderson (2000) mournfully remarked, had by the close of the twentieth century eclipsed the entire landscape on which the New Left was formed. And my suggestion is that the 'negative' and 'self-scrutinizing' theoretical register (McLennan, 2003) and the 'residualization' of utopianism found in 'phase one post-Marxism' are explicable in these terms.

However, I have suggested that, as 'globalization' increasingly replaces post-modernism as a 'social scientific master trend' (Arjomand, 2004: 341), as the discourse of 'happy globalization' (Holmes in Outhwaite and Ray, 2005: 19) comes unstuck – financial crisis, spiralling inequality, new anti-systemic movements, what Mann (2001) calls 'ostracizing imperialism' and 'zones of turmoil' – we have seen a shift. This shift can be seen in what McLennan (2000) argues has been a 'new positivity' in social theory from the second part of the 1990s and also, from about the same time, in what appears to be something of a rejuvenation of utopian themes.

Without a doubt, this more assertive, reconstructive mood is in evidence in the Budgen et al. volume, which is brimming with intelligence, decisiveness and energy, despite – from a Castoriadian-Left communist vantage point, at least – being wrong-headed in just about every imaginable way. In the introduction, Budgen, Kouvelakis, and Žižek (2007: 3) insist that the name 'Lenin' is urgent today, given the latter's determination to intervene in the situation, to adopt 'the unequivocal radical position' and thus to offer the possibility of changing the co-ordinates of our situation. The Lenin to be retrieved, they argue, 'is the Lenin-in-becoming, the Lenin whose fundamental experience was that of being thrown into a catastrophic new constellation in which old reference points proved useless, and who was compelled to reinvent Marxism' (2007: 3) – 'What Lenin did for 1914, we should do for our times' (2007: 4). On this score, war, globalization, 'the human face of market tyranny' (Bensaid, 2007: 148) are, throughout the collection, the connecting, mobilizing points – Labica (2007: 228–9), for instance, emphasizing this link in reading contemporary globalization as a higher, higher stage of capitalism, as imperialism with some new twists: 'the predominance of speculative finance capital, the technological revolutions ... and the collapse of the so-called socialist countries'. Lenin as philosopher, then, is read in the context of this earlier 'dramatic turning point of history', which pushed him towards Hegel (the *Philosophical Notebooks*) and towards strategic reformulations (the 'April Theses', *The State and Revolution*) (Michael-Matsas, 2007: 102). Similarly, Etienne Balibar (2007) argues that these circumstances moved Lenin away from laws of history, unfolding capitalist dynamics and so on towards the discovery of the 'field of the overdetermination intrinsic to class antagonisms', to the 'analysis of concrete situations' (2007: 211), to the 'non-predetermined constitution' (2007: 212) of theory and practice.

While my reservations about this sort of line are legion, there's obviously a great weight of intelligence in play here, some of the best stuff coming from the French thinkers – Badiou, Balibar, Lazarus, Lecercle. The boldness of assertion and declarative style is often bracing and provocative: Badiou (2007b: 9) on the 'short twentieth century' as 'a century of the act', whose 'subjective determination is Leninist'; Lazarus (2007: 255) on the twentieth century's 'new figure of politics', politics as 'party-like' and on the contemporary need for 'an intellectuality of politics without party or revolution' (2007: 265) – 'The end of the nation-state, which must be dated from 1968, is basically the end of the state as object of an "inherited" conflictuality' (2007: 266); Lecercle's (2007) reading of Lenin's qualities – firmness, hardness and subtlety – as forces towards a much needed new direction for the philosophy of language. It is also interesting to see Callinicos (2007a: 35) taking up the problem of what can be seen as Žižekian/Badiouian decisionism in favour of 'an ethics of political action' – improbably constructed by way of Trotsky. The problem of this decisionism is taken up nicely elsewhere by Balibar (2013: 27) who locates it in a major problem Žižek sets himself in constantly demonstrating capitalism's 'capacity to locate itself beyond the reach of ... class struggles', his attentiveness to the new types 'of control that modern capitalism performs on subjectivities'. Balibar (2013: 28–9) connects this aporia to notions of 'divine violence', the 'uncompromising wager', 'perilous excess' (read as 'returns of the death drive') and to the Leninist problematic in Žižek.[12]

And, here, a central issue, casting a shadow across the entire collection, is the question of the party – foregrounded, in a very different way, in Lefort's *Complications*. In noting the necessary encounter with the Real for any genuine change, Žižek (2001c) has previously pointed to the crucial facilitating role of three figures from the outside – God, Analyst, Party. In line with this emphasis, Kovacevic (2007) endows the discourse of the analyst with special significance, in 'making desire emerge, stimulat[ing] the creation of new frameworks for the life of the analysand' (2007: 205), arguing that, in the world of politics, this role is played by leaders, a 'responsible, emancipatory, analyst-type leadership' (2007: 207). In the Budgen et al. collection, Jameson (2007: 71) puts forward something similar – Lenin in the position of the discourse of the analyst, 'who listens for collective desire and crystallizes its presence in his political manifestos and "slogans"'.

Again, there are some good points made, here, on issues of organization, intellectuals, strategy: for instance, Eagleton (2007: 46) arguing that 'intellectual' 'designates a social or political location ... not a social rank or origin', distinguishing between elite and vanguard, and making some sound arguments against the easy, thoughtless rejection of authority *per se*. But, on the whole, for anyone influenced by the efforts of Castoriadis and Left communism more widely, the whole endeavour will smack of a magnificent regression.[13] For all its sparkle, we might want to read the volume as a sort of Sorelian myth around Lenin and Red October, bearing very little connection to the realities of Bolshevism or to any political realities and possibilities currently in play or ahead of us. For instance, Shandro (2007: 329–30) considers the relationship between the Bolsheviks and the workers' movement, arguing against the image of Lenin as Machiavellian opportunist formulating conflictual positions solely in the interests of power, contending instead that, in Lenin, 'vanguard and masses play different, potentially complementary but sometimes essentially contradictory parts in the class struggle'.

Lenin, then, is seen as steering an intelligent path beyond both naïve spontaneism and substitutionism, delicately, dialectically thinking the relation between different actors in social change. At times, there seems an implicit 'bid' at work here in relation to the present and future course of the alternative globalization movement – Bensaid (2007: 162), for instance, arguing that

> A politics without parties (whatever name – movement, organization, league, party – that they are given) ends up in most cases as a politics without politics: either an aimless tailism toward the spontaneity of social movements, or the worst form of elitist individualist vanguard-ism, or finally a repression of the political in favour of the aesthetic or the ethical.

This connection – globalization–socialist organization – is interestingly in play in the most uncomfortably out-of-place piece in this otherwise solidly united psychoanalytic Leninist collection, the contribution of Antonio Negri (2007), who makes some effort to begin with Lenin but is clearly nowadays of another tradition – 'Lenin beyond Lenin', 'Everything has changed' (2007: 300), 'the limitations ... of the Leninist point of view' (2007: 305). And I would suggest that, for all the problems with Hardt and Negri's *Empire* and *Multitude*, we have here an instance of second-phase post-Marxism,[14] alive with a bold return to 'logic of the social' theoretical synthesis, and reconstructive ultra-Left/ anarchistic utopianism. In this 'post-Marxism II', I think we can see movement past demobilizing, one-sided cultural criticism, really existing liberal democracy, post-modern deconstruction and Leninist retrievals – some decent attempts to offer replacements for Marxism's broken triangle and chart paths beyond the post-socialist condition.

3
Forget Debord?

Introductory comments

Guy Debord, as Derrida said of Althusser, traversed many lives – actor in the radical wing of the post-surrealist avant-garde, innovative film-maker, political militant and theorist, leading light of the Situationist International (SI), provocateur, classical stylist. By the time of his suicide in November 1994, Debord was a counter-cultural figure of some repute, equally able to command fierce devotion and to provoke hysterical denunciation.

Entering into the milieu of the avant-garde Lettrists as a young man, Debord very quickly took an independent path, breaking in 1952 to form a tiny splinter group, the Lettrist International (LI).[1] In 1957, the LI, together with the International Movement for an Imaginist Bauhaus, formed the now legendary Situationist International. Throughout this LI–SI period and beyond, Debord continued his work as filmmaker, authoring a total of seven films, which, in characteristically abrupt style, he made unavailable in protest at the assassination of his friend Gerard Lebovici in 1984.

Debord is, though, perhaps best known for his political and theoretical contributions – in particular his *The Society of the Spectacle*, written the year before May '68. The spectacle, manifesting itself in 'news or propaganda, advertising or the actual consumption of entertainment', was, for Debord (1995: 5–6), 'the heart of society's real unreality', a 'a weltanschauung that has been actualized'. Here, 'All that once was directly lived has become mere representation' (1995: 1), and 'mere images are transformed into real beings – tangible figments which are the efficient motor of trancelike behaviour' (1995: 18). This spectacle is explicitly connected by Debord to capitalism: 'The spectacle is capital accumulated to the point where it becomes image' (1995: 34); 'the spectacle corresponds to the historical moment at which the commodity completes its colonization of social life' (1995: 42). However, the fragmentation, alienation and illusion of the society of spectacle can be reversed, Debord pointing to the direct democracy of the workers' councils as the path towards 'establish[ing] truth in the world' (1995: 221). Two decades later, in *Comments on the Society of the Spectacle*, Debord's revolutionary optimism appears dissipated. Here, a new integrated spectacle had succeeded in absorbing all dissent and raising a generation according to its impoverished laws, erasing personality and the distinction between truth and fiction, and leaving 'nothing, in culture or in nature, which has not been transformed, and polluted, according to the means and interests of modern industry' (Debord, 1990: 10).

Arguably, Debord's most important work coincides with the life-span of the SI. Originally a collection of artists seeking the reconfiguration of life, it evolved more and more into a militant ultra-Leftist outfit. Nevertheless, the SI's origins remained significant in both the form and content of its publication, *Internationale Situationniste*. Within the pages of this journal, one finds a still sparkling and distinctive combination of concerns – from avant-garde proposals on urbanism, the 'drift', diversion, the construction of situations,[2] and the revolutionizing of daily life, to cultural criticism, to polemics against prominent figures and competitor organizations, to an array of decisive political readings of everything from the Algerian War, to the history of the workers' movement, to the character of 'really existing socialism'.

In these pages, the affinities between the situationist undertaking and the events that rocked France in 1968 are clear, and the situationists were authors of, or the inspiration behind, much of the most remembered graffiti that appeared during those events: 'I come all over the paving stones', 'Humanity will only be happy the day the last bureaucrat is hanged with the guts of the last capitalist', 'I take my desires for reality because I believe in the reality of my desires', 'Beneath the paving stones, the beach', 'Move quickly, comrade, the old world is right behind you'.

As Homer (1998: 74) notes, though, 1968 was a paradoxical moment of 'euphoria *and* disillusionment, liberation *and* dissipation', and the SI was unable to maintain momentum, falling into inactivity (the last issue of *Internationale Situationniste* appeared in 1969) and finally disbanding in 1972. In Debord's (1990) upbeat reading, the collapse of the old world having begun, situationist theory having passed over to the masses, and the SI in jeopardy of becoming an object of passive contemplation, the organization as a separate group could be happily dissolved into the new revolutionary wave.

For anyone compelled by the political and moral constancy (despite unrelenting defeat) of the twentieth century's thin red line of non-Leninist communist currents, inspired by the bourgeois baiting of the now vanished avant-garde, and attuned to the growing aestheticization of economy, politics, even war today, the attractions of the situationists are immediate. There is still much of considerable interest and relevance in their work: the appeal to direct democracy, grounded in the historic experience of workers' councils; the bracing cultural politics and focus on the shape and transformation of everyday life; the analysis and critique of spectacle/image capitalism; some of the wonderfully utopian proposals. Inevitably, though, this appeal starts to wear thin, and a number of recent studies of situationism's chief architect, Guy Debord, show why, sometimes despite the intentions of their authors.

In this chapter, having touched on the appearance of psychoanalytic Leninism, I turn in detail to another contender for a compelling contemporary socialist cultural politics, exploring the current high regard in which Debord is held, as well as reasons for weariness – in particular, the fruitless sectarianism and elitism, as well as the intervening social transformations that separate us from Debord and the SI – using the recent, much-heralded account of Vincent Kaufmann, as a way in to some of the important issues here.

The most radical gestures?

Sustained work on Debord and the SI was, for the most part,[3] slow in appearing. Then, from the late 1980s/early 1990s, the output grew steeply – for instance, major books by Marcus (1989), Sussman et al. (1989), Plant (1992), Bracken (1997), Jappe (1999), Sadler (1999), McDonagh (ed., 2004), Merrifield (2005), Wark (2011; 2013). By 1988, Robertson was already suggesting that the spectre of situationism was haunting the Left. Combining an avant-garde sensibility and a radical politics that remained credible after the generalized loss of faith in 'really existing socialism', and seen as something of a hidden hand behind the events of May '68, punk and post-modernism (Plant, 1992; Robertson, 1988), the SI, over a decade and a half after its dissolution, could still apparently seize the imagination. Vincent Kaufmann's (2006) claim in his *Guy Debord: Revolution in the Service of Poetry* that today Debord is on everyone's lips – while doubtless a bit of diversion ('our ideas are in everyone's heads') rather than something the author seriously believes – does get at this remarkable appeal and at the continuing resonance of the most widely known of Debord's contributions, the notion of 'spectacle'.

Why this prolonged initial silence, though? The author of a 2003 Debord biography, Andrew Hussey (2001: xi), reports a letter from Debord's widow, Alice Debord, warning him – in true Debordian style – that she had 'friends who violently regretted calumnies'. This communiqué brings together the love of the clandestine, the hostility to academic scrutiny, the aura of dangerousness, and the grandiosity one finds across the situationist project. It also serves as a signal to the jealous guardianship that situphiles have attempted to exercise in relation to the situationist legacy: one thinks here of the pathological exchange of the 'pro-situ' accusation among the situationist-influenced milieu, indicating that the accused was opening the SI to recuperation, turning situationist thought into an ideology.[4]

On this score, it is refreshing to see Kaufmann unabashedly using the term 'situationism', which once was officially designated a 'meaningless term' (SI, 1989: 45), and read as a sign of apostasy. Happily, it seems that today the situphile battle against proper analysis of Debord and the SI has been decisively lost, with situationism now a wholly legitimate topic of academic attention. Nevertheless, in many respects, Kaufmann's biography – while offering some daring and convincing interpretative moments and adding more credible detail on a life that has hitherto proved somewhat inaccessible – often reads as a sophisticated exercise in justification and protection of Debord. We have, here, the apparently reasonable plea that we not forget Debord,[5] and, simultaneously, what, at times, seems like an elegant attempt to close down certain avenues of discussion and development. Kaufmann, it appears, is only too ready to take Debord at his own word: the volume is dedicated to Alice Debord; again and again, when Kaufmann seems to be on the brink of scepticism and critical commentary, he retreats; by the end of the volume there are signs – for instance, in a footnote on the Hussey biography – that the author has succumbed to the appeal of the master's voice and vituperative style.[6] The introductory disclaimers about his only recent arrival to Debord, his lack of far-Left credentials, and the absence of any 'ideological axe to grind' have not, then, produced the expected critical vantage point; and the work reads all too much as though Kaufmann is coming dangerously close to becoming another victim of situphilia. Here, I think, we need to more resolutely ask ourselves the question, 'what is living and what is dead in the legacy of Guy Debord?' – in short, 'forget Debord?'

Kaufmann insists on the singular, consistent, 'unclassifiable' character of Debord's life and, quite clearly, the latter did exhibit a rare constancy of purpose and intransigence in the face of a monolith that he viewed as threatening to leave nothing outside. This life, which Kaufmann insists cannot be viewed as separate from the body of work, appears heroic: against all compromise, identification, vanity and spectacular visibility; passionately dedicated to authenticity, communication and freedom. This much-admired life accounts for what Jappe (1999: 167) describes as 'a bizarre cult of Debord ... threatening to transform him into a pop idol, a sort of Che Guevara for the more refined taste'. But to paraphrase Gilles Dauve (1979), from his lucid critique of situationism,[7] 'is this a life that could be lived?; was this a life that was actually lived?' It seems doubtful. Debord boasts of having never having regretted anything: everything was done in 'exemplary' (Debord, 1991: 6) fashion; no one can dare raise any questions. Yet, it is a life, like every other life, littered with question marks, moral, political, aesthetic. At every one of these junctures, Kaufmann seems determined to appear as expert witness in Debord's defence, down-playing or simply not mentioning unfavourable evidence and, in the end, so heavily underscoring the 'singularity' and the life-work unity of Debord that these questions slide smoothly from view.

Debord was taken to spectacular breaks and exclusions, literary executions, in fact, all carried out, as Hussey (2001: 187) rightly notes, with a 'combination of megalomania, irony and intransigence'. Debord's own writing,[8] and a number of accounts by former comrades are consistent here: Jacqueline de Jong describes Debord as 'Jesuitical in his manner, very strict in his ideas, very arrogant and superior ... [a] Napoleon' (in Hussey, 2001: 149); and Alexander Trocchi, devastated by Debord's sudden refusal to have further contact, maintained that 'He was like Lenin; he was an absolutist, constantly kicking people out, until he was the only one left. Ultimately it leads to shooting people' (in Hussey, 2001: 188).

Kaufmann's response to the obvious charge of pathology here is to insist on Debord's great warmth across many letters and friendships, and to read such exclusions (in line with the SI's own claims [SI, 1989: 140]) as, most importantly, an insistence that the excluded individual continue autonomously on their own path – such exclusions, then, as the very opposite of Stalinist purges.[9] It is clearly important to be sceptical of that imprecise, reductive, obfuscatory charge 'Stalinism'. Yet, there is more than a whiff of the worst of the Leninist tradition – sectarianism, bureaucratic authoritarianism, an obsessive 'passion for the Real' – in Debord's behaviour within his 'party'. And, just as importantly, there is plenty of evidence of Debord's radical inconsistency in these matters. Why, for instance, when he broke with – and with great portent and vehemence relegated to a living death – comrades who had failed him in apparently minor or potentially correctable ways, did he never break with Asger Jorn (who continued to work as an artist after the SI's 1962 announcement of the end of art and the expulsion and derision of those persisting in a 'separate' artistic practice)? Why could a friendship with film producer and impresario Gerard Lebovici be countenanced, when Vaneigem, Khayati and Sanguinetti had been consigned to the dustbin of history? Kaufmann remains too quiet on these matters.[10]

In a similar vein, the SI proudly chose to index the names of persons insulted in their publications and, in his later years, Debord came to perfect the 'letter of insult' (Hussey, 2001: 317) in collaboration with Lebovici, who published these sorts of communiqués in Champ Libre's *Correspondances*. The SI insult is initially rather bracing and amusing – uncompromising, full of the bravado and an appealing certainty of judgement and, at times, hitting a deserving target in the right spot. Ultimately, though, the invective is repetitive, rasping, fairly empty and depressing stuff – all too much of the world the SI claimed to have rejected, including, yes, the Stalinist world too. It seems hard not to conclude, with Debord's first wife, Michelle Bernstein, that this trajectory 'was pathetic and stupid, a waste of his [Debord's] mind' (in Hussey, 2001: 324).

Further, this practice frequently appears to have functioned so as to relieve Debord (and the SI) of the demanding task of dealing in a rigorous and intelligent way with many of those designated as opponents. Across the span of Debord's and the SI's writings, there is a real dearth of sustained argumentation against the many thinkers who had so raised their ire. This in contrast to Castoriadis, say, who deals at length, and with great precision and passion, with the likes of Sartre (a bashing pet of Debord's). This lack of detailed engagement, I think, looks today like a failure of some magnitude on Debord's part, a failure of the circumscribed but still important tasks of the communist intellectual as formulated by Gramsci. Certainly, Debord was not an academic, and the term 'intellectual' has a consistently pejorative connotation for him; and the argument that we need to read the life and work as crucially unified as a project of existence is convincing to a point. However, too much insistence on this sort of thing can come close to resisting a proper interrogation of Debord and his legacy – the genesis and significance of the work in its period, the way it is situated and can be read against other intellectual-political currents of the time.

Of interrogations stalled

On this score, Kaufmann stops for some time on the questions of the debt owed by Debord to Lefebvre and to Socialism or Barbarism (SoB). The situationists, of course, came to write them off with familiar vehemence and lack of rigour.[11] Kaufmann, as well, seems only too ready to minimize what Debord received from these dialogues. Again, Kaufmann appears determined to see such matters through Debord's eyes: he (Debord) didn't owe anyone anything, an absolutely free and self-created individual who sought and managed to escape all forms of identification.

This just doesn't stand up to scrutiny. Debord's dialogue with SoB, for instance, was clearly vital to the subsequent politics of the SI and to Debord's *The Society of Spectacle* – for example, the discovery of the workers' councils, the attempted reconceptualization of the proletariat (as those who had no control over their own time-space) following on from Castoriadis's analysis of the division between *dirigeants* and *executants* (Hastings-King, 1999). And Debord's reasons for breaking off the dialogue with Castoriadis and company remain, in Kaufmann, Jappe and Hussey, rather nebulous. Kaufmann importantly points to crucial differences in emphasis between the two groups – for instance, SoB with its attention to the shopfloor, against Debord's slogan 'never work' and his culturalist bent. And Kaufmann correctly points to Debord's criticisms of the organizational dimension of SoB, though he doesn't interrogate further Castoriadis's far from simplistic approach to organizational questions, or the way in which precisely such criticisms could well be levelled against Debord and the SI. Kaufmann's treatment of this fascinating SoB–SI encounter, while not searching or detailed enough, is, though, far in advance of many accounts. For instance, Jappe merely resorts to misrepresentation and invective: in typically situphile mode, Jappe (1999: 93) imagines that the subsequent academic recognition of Castoriadis and Lefort is equivalent to an argument against their work, and he comes to the preposterous, thoughtless conclusion that Castoriadis came to 'completely' turn his back 'on any serious critical approach to society' (1999: 153).

Certainly, Debord's reported responses on this issue make things no clearer. When Castoriadis tried to persuade him to stay, Debord is said to have replied, 'Yes, but I don't feel up to the task', and 'It must be very tiring organising a revolutionary organization'.[12] What was going on here is, evidently, a matter of some speculation, but, thankfully, we do have the systematic and convincing account of Stephen Hastings-King

(1999), who plots the arc of the SoB-SI/Debord relationship. This account highlights Debord's debts, as well as the differences between the groups – the differences in the approach to culture and organizational questions,[13] for instance. But most interesting is Hastings-King's reading of Debord's venomous attitude towards Castoriadis and SoB after 1963, when Castoriadis pushes to its conclusions his notion of a crisis of the Marxist imaginary and the need to rethink revolutionary theory. For Hastings-King (1999: 50), this precipitates Debord's evolution into a 'defender of Marxist orthodoxy from heresy': Debord attempting to have the SI assume SoB's 'mantle of revolutionary vanguard' (1999: 48), and to place himself as 'the cultural arbiter of the Left' (1999: 49). This culminates, Hastings-King (1999: 49) argues, in a blurring of 'the organizational distinction between the inside and outside and the individual distinction between psyche and social world', with Debord ultimately positioning *himself* as 'the oppositional movement: he was what the bourgeois order feared. He was the spectre haunting Europe'.

We should ask ourselves, at this point, a more general question about Debord as social theorist. Situphiles have consistently attempted to separate Debord's contributions here (most notably, *The Society of the Spectacle* and *Comments on the Society of the Spectacle*) from the theoretical, and therefore the academic, realm – Debord's work as utterly distinct and thus immune from analysis on a theoretical terrain. Something like this is suggested by Wark (2011) in his estimation of the situationist project as useable low theory, as opposed to high theory, putting particular emphasis on the practice of diversion. And, in the end, Kaufmann appears content with an anti-intellectualist line of response to theoretical issues: Debord 'provides a "theoretical" form for a unique subjective position, for a life' (2006: 74); Debord as a poet rather than a theorist. This is not completely without weight; it is even perhaps an important consideration in approaching Debord. Certainly, the theoretical work demonstrates Debord's melancholic, poetic opposition to representation, his desire for an authentic life, and so on. But surely he is not, cannot be, immune from substantive analysis and criticism in theoretical terms. How, and under which influences, we need to ask, did he (and does he still) provide us with a descriptive, explanatory and evaluative mapping of the world? What, and with what possible consequences, do his conceptual torches help us illuminate dimensions of social life? Kaufmann evidently reads his own brief as elsewhere, and this precludes consideration of the many relevant commentaries on those two aforementioned books and their concepts. To mention just a few instances of attempts to take up such important questions,

Plant, Jappe, Hussey and Merrifield do good work in locating the web of theoretical elective affinities that can be read through the concept of the spectacle – Dada, Breton, Sartre, Lefebvre, Lukács, for instance; Levin (1991) notes a crucial slippage in this concept – sometimes referring to the realm of representation, sometimes to concrete existence; Wollen (1991) places Debord's and the SI's work as both a summation of the historic avant-garde and a summation of Western Marxism; Roberts (2003b) interrogates Debord's analytical division between the diffuse and integrated spectacle, developing a typology of the spectacle in modernity, while, elsewhere (2003a), considering the related notion of an 'aesthetic economy'; Craig (2004) provides a fascinating account of Debord's location of the origins of the spectacle in the late 1920s – the moment of the perfection of TV, *The Jazz Singer*, Benjamin's arcades project, fascist and Stalinist propaganda; and Plant (1992) claims that the work of the SI underwrites post-modernism and examines the continuities and breaks between these two fields of thought.

Overall, it is hard not to feel somewhat torn about the contemporary relevance of Debord's theoretical work. On the one hand, Debord (1995: 6) appears a still compelling commentator on the 'real unreality' of our society of the spectacle, where 'the real world becomes real images, mere images are transformed into real beings' (1995: 18), where people end up passively watching themselves, hopelessly alienated from authentic life. On the other hand, today the analysis seems to lose some of its shine: after the criticisms of the elitism and pessimism of Marxian *kuturkritik*; after the pairing of a negative with a positive hermeneutic in the interpretation of popular culture (in Jameson or Žižek, for instance); after cultural studies' insistence on the activity and creativity of audiences; after the critique of Western Marxism's capitalocentrism;[14] after the variety and richness of post-Marxist challenges over the past couple of decades. Not amended by borrowings from or interchange with more recent social and cultural theory, Debord's contributions might look like faded and tattered maps whose features no longer quite correspond to the contemporary terrain.

Perhaps it is reasonable to suggest that all of this is beyond the scope of Kaufmann's task, but it is a pity that he and most other commentators on Debord have nothing to say on such matters. What Kaufmann does best, perhaps, is explore (and, in fact, prioritize) the aesthetic moment in the work of Debord and the SI (which is, for him, in any case, merely Debord writ large[15]). And, here, Debord seems to fare better today. Despite all the out-of-time quality of the millenarian, self-inflating and often obnoxious aesthetic interventions Debord was involved in, he is, of course, the central figure in the development of the political-aesthetic technique of *diversion/detournement*. This contribution, at least, has travelled fairly well over time and can be seen at work today in some of the wonderfully sharp 'culture jamming' of the anarchistic wing of the anti-globalization movement. The desire to have done with the art–life separation for a total remaking of everyday life, too, while continuous with much of the historic avant-garde, was a remarkably generative impulse and, surely, must be repeated today by an emerging Global Left. Psychogeography, the drift, unitary urbanism – all of these contributions have been valuable for a certain strand of cultural geography, and they stand as lively utopian interventions that have not exhausted their value. On the other hand, today, one can't help but think how *inattentive* the SI were to the marvellous contained within the everyday, especially in light of the aforementioned theoretical developments in the Marxist-influenced study of culture.

This is relevant, too, in considering Debord's own artistic practice as a filmmaker. It is common to delineate an initial artistic phase that gives way to a political phase in the SI after the 1962 declaration of an end to art as a separate sphere ('It is a question not of the elaborating the spectacle of refusal, but rather of refusing the spectacle' [Situationist International, 1989: 88]). Kaufmann interestingly refuses to acknowledge such a break – Debord continues to respond as a poet in search of freedom and authenticity. There is an important point to be made here in light of the clear political emphases to be found even within the Lettrist International and, conversely, in light of the continuation of the Bohemian, aesthetic rebellion current within the SI post-1962. However, I would maintain that it is hard to sustain the idea of any smooth continuity: from the title, diverted from Marx's response to the collapse of the First International, and throughout the entire text of *The Veritable Split in the International*, we have clear signs of how won over Debord was by an easily recognizable far-Left politics – 'what are considered "situationist ideas" are nothing other than the first ideas in the period of reappearance of the modern revolutionary movement' (SI, 1990: 12); and Debord's and the SI's political trajectory is also clear in the increasingly irreconcilable tension within the SI between those impulses represented by the two key SI texts of 1967 – Debord's *Society of the Spectacle*, on the one hand, and Vaneigem's (1983) aesthetic-existential *Revolution of Everyday Life*, on the other. It is true that in the SI you do have a certain joining together of what Boltanski (2002; Boltanski and Chiapello, 2005) calls the artistic and social critiques,[16] and this looks, today, rather worthy and exciting – given that, subsequently, the social critique went into a downward spiral, while the artistic critique succeeded only too well, Boltanski (2002: 13; Boltanski and Chiapello, 2005: 101) suggesting that many of Vaneigem's[17] sentences would not be out of place in 1990s management books – but, from the early 1960s, this is an uneasy cohabitation.

And perhaps, post-1962, something is lost (whatever we might think of the resulting gains). Michelle Bernstein notes the changed physiognomy of the group: 'The new members after 1962 were extremely dry and dogmatic ... They had no sense of the wit or fun with which we had done things previously' (in Hussey, 2001: 182). This lack of fun is clear in Debord's films, as he abandons generating any new images and relies on found footage with a soundtrack diverting these images, 'revealing' the truth about our society of spectacle. Today, these films are close to unwatchable, demobilizing rather than politicizing and, again, close attention to even the trashiest of Hollywood productions – as I think Žižek often demonstrates with great verve – can be more politically and culturally revelatory and politicizing than Debord's filmic offerings.

Now, the SI?

Here, Kaufmann would, I am certain, come back to the centrality of Debord's signature, to style – a style of life. Intransigent, resolute, original Debord certainly was. And sometimes there is little to recommend Debord's books outside of style, though Kaufmann's (2006: 207) claim that 'Debord's writing will last eternally, well beyond the death of a French language ...' is overblown to the point of merging again with Debord's own self-evaluations. Because, ultimately, one detects a profound emptiness in many of those later writings: endless allusions to great learning and privileged insight that are never substantiated; paranoid clandestinity, tiresome military strategizing, delusions of grandeur – 'These *Comments* are sure to be welcomed by fifty or sixty people ... Having, then, to take account of readers who are both attentive and diversely influential, I obviously cannot speak with complete freedom. Above all, I must take care not to give too much information to just anybody' (Debord, 1990: 1); and a need, of almost Oprah-like dimensions, to speak about himself – here, Kaufmann (2006: xvi) shows some skill in reconciling the claim that Debord 'refused his own visibility' and sought to leave no trace of himself with works such as *Considérations sur l'assassinat de Gerard Lebovici, Panegyric, Cette mauvaise reputation,* and the volumes of *Correspondance.*

Melancholy, as Kaufmann rightly points out, is a dominating under-current of much of the work Debord has left us. But, against those who would insist that this is most marked in the later period, and joined by withdrawal, bitterness, paranoia (all moving Debord inexorably towards his spectacular exit as another 'Dada suicide'), Kaufmann insists on continuity and sees just more of the same – experimentation, game playing, alert and engaged strategizing. This cannot possibly ring wholly true. Debord insider Emmanuel Loi contends that, in the later years, 'the philosophy of combat was insidiously replaced by a pathol-ogy of despair' (in Hussey, 2001: 345). And it seems convincing, too – as Gerard Guegan maintains – to see the later Debord as a man out of step with the culture and struggles of his time (Hussey, 2001). Some sense of this is gained from the following anecdote. When a friend of Debord's, Lucy Forsyth, challenged him about the strict gendered household division of labour between him and his wife, Debord replied 'She does the washing up, I do the revolution' (in Hussey, 2001: 329). If Debord and the SI had indeed been able to provide the '68ers with 'a sense of style, a singular voice, a new voice' (Kaufmann, 2006: 183), it seems that, by the end, Debord – increasingly suffering at the hands of his alcoholism, politically distant and nostalgic for the period between his 'second birth' (1951 and the Lettrist encounter) and the heroic phase of situationism – could no longer read what Marshall Berman (1984) has called 'the signs on the street'.

And, here, very crucially, in thinking about Debord today, is not nos-talgia the dominating modality, the reason we are so reluctant to forget what is, and should be, forgettable in Debord? As noted, Stuart Sim (1998) has suggested that we might best read post-Marxism as an emo-tional matter rather than a substantive contribution. Whichever side of the hyphen is italicized, post-Marxism signals, above all else, nostalgia. This nostalgia marks at least an implicit recognition of defeat – the spectre of the totalitarianism, the deadness of socialist language today; at the same time, it marks a reluctance to let go, to simply acknowl-edge the impossibility of any real conversation between an inherently monistic paradigm (Marxism) and an inherently pluralizing one (post-modernism) to find a new language. Even if this is very contestable as far as post-Marxism goes, might we not say something similar about the appeal of Debord today?

And, on this question of nostalgia, we might be tempted to avoid the seductions of Debord's melancholia and ask about a more productive coincidence of affect and politics in our own times. Rather than retreat-ing to the comforts of an age now gone, and represented heroically by

Debord and the SI, there are plenty of places to look and think about these connections, both already extant and as possibilities on our political-cultural horizon. Here, I feel, when thinking about Debord today, we need to read him as a remarkable figure living through remarkable times, to be clear-headed on how uneasily that life and work has journeyed across the decades, and to be hesitant about whether it can or should be translated politically into the contemporary period – given all of the socialist and non-socialist material produced since, given the need for dialogue beyond the old divisions and debates for a new global Left. In this respect – if not, by any means, in all – I think we must courageously seek to *forget* Debord.

4

'Many Flowers, Little Fruit'?: The Dilemmas of Workerism

Introductory comments – *Empire, Multitude, Commonwealth*

By any count, Michael Hardt and Antonio Negri's (2000) *Empire* is a remarkable work. Here is an accessible, sweeping Left vision, apparently equipped – with a mix of rhetoric and scope reminiscent of the *Communist Manifesto*, a smattering of post-structuralism's intellectual highlights, the catchiest aspects of post-industrialism, network and globalization approaches to contemporary social change, as well as an extraordinary optimism and confidence ('the irrepressible lightness and joy of being communist' [Hardt and Negri, 2000: 413]) – to compete with Fukuyama's narrative of the end of history. The impact that *Empire* has had – immediately recognized by some as a *Manifesto* for our times, denounced by others as a silly book capable of inflaming only Leftists hopelessly out of touch with new realities, and viewed by some commentators as the closest theoretical and utopian expression of an emerging anti-globalization movement – demands an analysis and evaluation of its conditions of emergence, of its political-intellectual heritage. In good part, these conditions, this heritage, can be found in Italian *operaismo* or workerism, a Left communist strand contemporary with situationism. This is clear from the important tonal and conceptual similarities between *Empire* and a number of workerist texts: for instance, the demand for a social or political wage for all; the notion of the real subsumption of society to capital; the reconceptualization of the proletariat – most recently, as multitude; and the insistence that this multitude 'is the real productive force of our social world' (Hardt and Negri, 2000: 62). Here, Steve Wright's (2002) *Storming Heaven: Class Composition and Struggle in Autonomist Marxism* provides an exceptional way into thinking the lineage of Hardt and Negri's recent interventions, as one of the few books in any language, including Italian (Bologna, 2003), that soberly surveys Italian workerism in its quite daunting complexity,[1] indicating certain crucial dilemmas – especially the potentially rich focus on changes in class composition, combined with an enthusiasm that sometimes encourages a hyperbolic stress on social shifts rather than continuities – carried over from that tradition into Hardt and Negri's current work, and, more widely, laying open for analysis some of the central conundrums (for instance, around class and organization) within that rich and complicated tradition, Left communism. I begin here by briefly summarizing the major lines of argument of Hardt and Negri's trilogy – *Empire* (2000), *Multitude* (2004) and *Commonwealth* (2009) – before turning to Wright and workerism in some detail and, in the chapter's final section, I will critically connect Hardt and Negri's work to issues within the Italian workerist tradition and to Left communism in general.

Antonio Negri was born in 1933, studied at Padua University in Italy and received a professorship at an early age, specializing in state theory (Murphy, 2012). He gravitated from Italian socialism to become a participant in the far-Left movement in Italy and, as the temperature of contestation increased from the late 1960s, became a casualty of the 'years of lead', arrested in 1979 and connected to the activities of the Red Brigades. In 1983, he was elected to parliament as leader of the Radical Party and was released, but when his parliamentary immunity was subsequently revoked, Negri fled the country, making his way to France, where he taught for 14 years. In 1997, he decided to return to Italy and prison, in order to draw attention to the plight of those still imprisoned or in exile and, after a period under house arrest, he was given full parole in 2003. Michael Hardt was born in Maryland, USA, in 1960 and studied engineering and then literature, working in between degrees in the Christian sanctuary movement in Central America; he subsequently moved to Paris to write a thesis on the Italian Left under Negri. He is currently Professor of Literature and Italian Studies at Duke University, USA.

The pair had already collaborated in the 1994 work, *Labour of Dionysis*, which continued, in a more accessible vein, Negri's concerns with state theory but, as noted, it was *Empire* and their two follow-up volumes that attracted extraordinary academic and popular attention. In this work, Hardt and Negri (2000) suggest that the period between the first Gulf War and the war in Kosovo sees the emergence of what they call Empire – a new logic and structure of rule, of sovereignty. The power of the nation state, they contend, has gone into serious decline, along with the old Westphalian international order, and a 'series of national and supranational organisms' have been 'united under a single logic of rule' (200: xii). Empire, in contrast to the imperialism of old, is decentred and deterritorializing, and it progressively incorporates the entire global realm within its open and expanding frontiers. Today, they charge, no nation state is at the centre of rule. There is no Rome in this new Empire ('the coming Empire is not American and the US is not its centre' [Hardt and Negri, 2000: 384]), and there is no Winter Palace to storm (Beilharz, 2005b). Neither, any longer, is there purchase in thinking of the world in terms of cores and peripheries (given the 'smooth' space of today's Empire). In addition, now, the *object of rule* has changed: power seeks to rule social life as a whole; power works as bio-power, encompassing 'the production and reproduction of life itself' (24) – a claim indicative of the influence of French thought (particularly Foucault and Deleuze and Guattari) on Negri during his period of exile.

For Hardt and Negri, Empire offers new possibilities for liberation, and we should not be pessimistic about this new global order – it is a step forward in liberatory possibilities. That is, the machine of power seems to have no outside, power is everywhere but, at the same time, this means that resistance today is at the very centre of the social – Empire can be attacked from any point. Furthermore, Hardt and Negri contend, it was the very resistance of the dominated that called Empire into being. Regarding capitalism and class, Hardt and Negri claim that the old industry-centred capitalism has been transformed (horizontality, networking, decentralization) and that today what they call 'immaterial labour' – affective labour plus labour centred on service, cultural products, knowledge and communication – is in a position of dominance. This is intimately linked to Hardt and Negri's conceptions of contemporary social change, revolution and the new revolutionary subject – the multitude. For them, while we are witnessing the consolidation of this new Empire, we are simultaneously seeing the growth of the multitude, which sustains Empire, as the real productive force in our world, and this multitude is also capable of constructing a counter-Empire, an alternative political organization of global flows and exchanges – a new socialism, in short. The multitude is visible in a range of events and struggles – Tiananmen Square in 1989, the 1992 LA riots, the uprisings in Chiapas from 1994, the French industrial strikes of 1995, the Palestinian Intifada. What they say about multitude and resistance is this: 'First, each struggle, though firmly rooted in local conditions, leaps immediately to the global level and attacks the imperial constitution in its generality. Second, all the struggles destroy the traditional distinction between economic and political struggles. The struggles are at once economic, political and cultural – and hence they are bio-political struggles, struggles over the form of life' (Hardt and Negri, 2000: 56).

Refusing to offer blueprints for the future, Hardt and Negri do offer some thoughts on the construction of counter-Empire. Here, the Industrial Workers of the World (IWW) offer some suggestions of the modes of struggle that might lie ahead – decentralized and nomadic, universalist in orientation, insistent on the need to create the new in the here and now. In terms of the modality of resistance to Empire, we have moved, argue Hardt and Negri, from the older tropes around organized and resistant industrial labour to a new emphasis on desertion – defection and migration. The positive moment in this is the need/desire to create a new mode of life and a new community. In more concrete terms, they speak of the need to resist the encroachments of privatization and to create new commons, and they suggest three immediate rights demands – the right to global citizenship, the right to a social wage and the right to reappropriation.

In many ways, *Multitude* and *Commonwealth* really only unfold in greater detail emphases already found in *Empire*. *Multitude*, as the title indicates, focuses on this 'emerging class formation' (Hardt and Negri, 2004: xvii), which, 'working through Empire' and driven by a desire for democracy, is creating 'an alternative global society'. Again, here, 'resistance is primary with respect to power' (2004: 64), capital simultaneously dependent on the creativity of the multitude, but constantly thrown into crisis by its contestations. Multitude, Hardt and Negri (103) insist, 'is a class concept', clarifying their thoughts on immaterial labour as the 'hegemonic tendency' (2004: 106) today, producing communication, social relations and co-operation, blurring older distinctions between the economic, political, social and cultural. The heterogeneity of this multitude is again underscored – the multitude as a set of singularities (2004: 99), an inclusive concept (2004: xiv), working by way of swarm intelligence and exodus to collectively produce new subjectivites and forms of life, to produce the common, which capital limits and seeks to appropriate. In an interesting and somewhat lateral move, for Hardt and Negri, writing in the aftermath of 9/11 and the invasion of Iraq, the primary obstacle to the genius of the multitude and true democracy is the current global state of war (2004: xi), (post-modern) war becoming general, global and interminable, with the suspension of democracy as the norm (2004: 3, 17).

Finally, in *Commonwealth*, Hardt and Negri (2009; see also Hardt, 2010) take up and develop further the notion of the common and that of love as a political concept, with an emphasis on the expanding common produced by the multitude, despite the fettering efforts of capital to privatize/expropriate it. Bio-power (domination), here, is contrasted to bio-politics, the becoming power of life to resist and produce (2009: 56), with resistance again emphasized as prior to power (2009: 81) and, as always, autonomous and exceeding the bounds of capital (2009: 149). This common is quite other than the older public of socialism; 'really existing socialism' is read as a powerful machine of primitive accumulation and economic development (2009: 93), and liberation is equated to transformation beyond the older worker identity (2009: 311), with love understood as the production of the common, the escape from solitude (2009: xii), refusal, and the creation of a new society within the shell of the old (2009: 8, 180).

'Permanent critique' – early themes

As will become clear, many of the themes in Hardt and Negri's trilogy are recognizable within Italian workerism, as soberly treated by Wright, as well as bearing deep traces of Negri's engagement with French thought and of his prison-turn to the work of Spinoza – immanence, collective humanism, life, desire, creativity (Callinicos, 2007b; Murphy, 2012; Negri, 2004). And Wright's very important contribution, as I have noted, both treats with great care the 'multiple pathways', the 'stunning diversity' (Wright, 2008: 114; Brophy, 2004: 297) of workerism,[2] and opens crucial questions about Hardt and Negri and the wider tradition of Left communism. Wright (1980) had already confronted this broad tradition in 1980, in his review of Australian J. A. Dawson's odyssey across the 'outside left'. Dawson's commitments had spanned De Leonism, the closely related impossibilism of the Socialist Party of Great Britain, the IWW and, finally, council communism (Dawson corresponded with Paul Mattick and Anton Pannekoek, and he published the latter's *Workers' Councils*). While sympathetic, Wright maintained that Dawson's 1940s ultra-Leftism was, now, decidedly outmoded and, in his concluding comments, he suggested a more up-to-date, relevant Left path ahead lay with *operaismo*.

As Wright (2002; 2008) notes, Italian workerism travelled into the English-speaking world after the 1970s largely through the *wages for housework group*, influenced by the ideas of Mariarosa Dalla Costa, and through the efforts of the American journal *Zerowork*, taking up the workerist notion of the refusal of work as central in contemporary anti-capitalism.[3] Workerist ideas are, though, best known through the later writings, often dense and demanding, of Antonio Negri, which involve the following: an analysis of the modern state and 'juridico-economic mechanisms of capitalist control' (Hardt, n.d.); the examination of Keynesianism as a response to the struggles of the working class – a confirmation that 'The world is labour' (Negri and Hardt, 1994: 11); the turn from *Capital* to the *Grundrisse* in the name of proper attention to subjectivity,[4] and the idea of proletarian self-valorization as labour's struggle for alternative subjectivities and organization against the structures and imperatives of capital; and development of the notion of 'real subsumption', the subsumption of life by capital, inspired by the 1970s turn to Marx's unpublished sixth chapter of *Capital* (Hardt, n. d.; Murphy, 2012; Negri, 1996; 2010). Negri's pre-eminence here gives little sense of the heterogeneity of Italian workerism, and that tradition is made more illegible because of the articulation of Negri's later work with the ideas of Deleuze and Guattari[5] – new subjectivities, deterritorialization, nomadism, lines of flight. Yet more problems are added by the connection of workerism's *cattivi maestri* (bad teachers), Negri, Scalzone and Piperno, with Red Brigades' terrorism – Negri, as mentioned, under house arrest until 2003, held 'morally' and 'objectively' responsible for, as an 'intellectual author' of, the Left terrorism of the 1970s in Italy (Cuninghame, 1995; Hardt, 1996). Wright's book clears some of the cluttered terrain here by examining workerism in all its contradictory and messy reality.

Like a number of other creative far-Left currents that peaked in the late 1960s and early 1970s, Italian workerism has its beginnings in the 1950s, with the 'unforgettable year' of 1956,[6] and with (at least in Italy and France) a profound post-war social, economic and cultural reconfiguration – captured by Mario Tronti (2010) as 'neo-capitalism'. Central, too, was the new status and role of, and discontents around, those two major modes of working-class organizational capacity – the party and the union apparatus. The *Partito Comunista Italiano* (PCI), for instance, emerged from the war flush with resistance prestige, but disappointed many communist militants with its apparently overly cautious commitments – economic prudence, industrial growth, inter-group accommodation and a 'strong democracy'.

In these conditions, Left spaces opened up – significantly here within the Socialist Party (PSI) – and were occupied, first and foremost, by the figure of Raniero Panzieri (1921–1964). Panzieri was struggling with that ineradicable problem across the far-Left – the relationship between class and organization; he was suggesting that the study of capitalist development should be understood as involving the entirety of society, with crisis understood by early workerism as not mechanical-economistic but as more widely *social* (Bellofiore, 2006); and he was critical of the orthodox Leninist equation truth=party=class, insisting that Marxism should again become 'permanent critique' (in Wright, 2002: 16). Unsuccessfully attempting to win over a quiescent PSI hierarchy to a more radically Leftist set of emphases – the creativity and centrality of that which emerges from below, 'total democracy', the need for new economic institutions – Panzieri imagined a fruitful path ahead through an exploration of 'the reality of the proletariat and organizational movement of the popular classes' (Wright, 2002: 17, 33), a mode of inquiry at least partially separate from the analysis of capital (Bellofiore, 2006).

In terms of exploring this emerging surge of Left creativity, the place of Antonio Gramsci in Italian workerism provides an interesting parenthesis, and is unfortunately left largely unexplored by Wright. The Gramscian tradition in Italy has been largely split between Togliatti's social democratization of him and Bobbio's liberal reading (Hardt, n.d.). It is unsurprising, then, to find a prominent workerist figure such as Mario Tronti (1931–) consigning Gramsci to the past, as an idealist philosopher wrestling, above all, with the work of Croce, and offering little help in the most pressing task – the move from ideology to political economy (Wright, 2002: 28) – even though Tronti (2012) views *operaismo* as, in many ways, attempting something quite Gramscian, as a form of cultural revolution. This avoidance of or ambivalence towards Gramsci continues into the recent work of Hardt and Negri (2003: 372) who admit that 'Gramsci ... has never been among our favourites'. Nevertheless, at this early stage, Panzieri turned to the political Gramsci of the *L'Ordine Nuovo* period, an apparently obvious resource given Gramsci's sometimes syndicalist leanings and given *L'Ordine Nuovo's* enthusiastic reaction to the new struggles and organizational forms of the period 1917–21.[7] And Panzieri's position is congruent with a moment in Gramsci (1977; 1978), immediately after the collapse of the factory councils movement, in which he is championing both the factory councils as 'model of the proletarian state' and the party as 'furnace of faith'. Panzieri could thus insist on 'the principle of class action as the autonomy of the exploited and oppressed classes in the struggle for their liberation', while also viewing the party as 'the *instrument* of the class movement's political formation' (in Wright, 2002: 18–19).

Of much interest in Panzieri's and especially Romano Alquati's (1935–2010) early formulations is the imperative that socialists explore the proletarian world of work, 'workers' inquiries' – as Tronti (2012: 121) puts it, a 'new way of doing sociology'. This is, of course, precisely a strong and distinctive line of analysis within Socialism or Barbarism; and the young thinkers who gathered around Panzieri and the journal *Quaderni Rossi* were looking across to both Castoriadis's group and to the early work – *The American Worker* (1947) and *Punching Out* (1952), for instance – of the Johnston–Forest Tendency (C. L. R. James and Raya Dunayevskaya) in America. A more intricate analysis of the precise lines of development and influence here would be interesting,[8] as would more specific and rigorous determination of the links mentioned between workerism and the ideas of Adorno, Della Volpe, Hobsbawm, Kuczynski, American sociology and (later) Deleuze and Guattari. For instance, the Italian workerists were close to Castoriadis and company in their critique of Russian capitalist relations as the inspiration and model for private capitalism, but it is not clear if this was as well developed in the Italian context, particularly in light of the continuing widespread attachment to Lenin, which was soon abandoned by Socialism or Barbarism. Similarly, some workerists temporarily adopted Castoriadis's notion of a new social division between order givers and order takers. A more theoretical, as opposed to historical, interrogation of this would be useful, as there is little sense, in the English-language context, of the balance of forces involved in these adaptations and shifts.[9] Nevertheless, the major confluence of concerns are clear: dissident Trotskyism's turn to '*l'experience proletaire*' is a potentially enormously important departure point, in its assertion that – as Castoriadis (1988a: 20) was to frame it – 'Everything that has happened in the Western world for the past one hundred and fifty years is, in enormous part, the result of working-class struggles'. Thus, studies such as *The American Worker*, along with the workplace accounts of Socialism or Barbarism militants Daniel Mothe and Henri Simon, compelled Italian dissident Marxists to examine the self-expression of the workers through 'co-research' – a 'hot' rather than 'cool' analysis (Hardt, n.d.). The central gain or insight here, against a mainstream communist party perspective in which 'Whatever fell outside the party, fell outside history, and vice versa' (in Wright, 2002: 176), against an economistic and pacified Second and Third International view of workers (Bellofiore and Tomba, 2008), was that – in Danilo Montaldi's words – 'it is in production that the revolt against exploitation, the capacity to construct a superior type of society ... are formed' (in Wright, 2002: 23–4).

'Class composition' – between class and party

It is perhaps fruitful to reflect on the negative connotations often attached to the term 'workerism' in the French and English-speaking contexts. One of the concerns from critics is that this line of analysis proves too narrowly factory-focused, never getting beyond empiricist point-of-production description. There seems some basis for such a concern here, because Gramsci's culturalist lessons appear somewhat lost on much of Italian workerism,[10] as do those offered by the Johnston–Forest Tendency and by Socialism or Barbarism. C. L. R. James, for instance, was keenly attentive to the wider cultural aspects of the investigation of proletarian working life: '[F]rom the stories that we get everyday ... we can see a new form of struggle emerging ... its existence is continuous ... This is the struggle to establish here and now a new culture, a workers' culture ... We must watch with an eagle eye every change or indication of the things that these changes reflect' (James in McLemee and Le Blanc, 1994: 236). Thus, while Castoriadis and James were focused, early on, on a range of emerging struggles and perspectives, much of Italian workerism, even into the 'creeping May', and surrounded by a new and powerful student movement, was capable of such startling misapprehensions as *La Classe's* argument against those 'who instead of making a correct class analysis, identify the "left" of the people" in those most disconnected, ultimately organizing only poor devils, the sexually repressed, adolescents with Oedipal complexes, students in conflict with the family, lunatics, wretches, filmmakers in crisis, anguished noblewomen, sex maniacs, bourgeois anxious for expiation, the phobia-ridden etc.' (in Wright, 2002: 123–4). Although elements of the later Autonomia moment in the 1970s were to lean towards the counter-cultural, towards these 'stray dogs' (Cuninghame, 1995), Wright notes how little workerism really ever said about the content of subjectivity 'in its totality of behaviours, needs, beliefs, knowledges, cultures etc' (Borio et al., 2002 in Wright, 2007: 277). The obvious insufficiency of some workerists' perspectives around new social questions incited an important challenge from feminists (Brophy, 2004; Cuninghame, 1995) – for example, in Mariarosa Della Costa's analysis of domestic labour.[11]

A second concern around workerism emphasizes its tendency to manifest an increasingly distanced and uncritical spontaneism or *attentisme* ('revolutionary waiting'). Such a direction appears visible in some of the outgrowths of Socialism or Barbarism. Lefort and Simon's *Informations et Liaisons Ouvrières* (ILO) and its successor, *Informations Correspondance*

Ouvrières (ICO), broke from what they saw as the lingering Leninist substitutionism within Socialism or Barbarism and, here, liaison and information gathering and broadcasting took precedence over work, theoretical or otherwise political, that might be understood as a quest for separate leadership. On this score, one joke circulating at the time had it that ICO conducted debates as to whether stapling together workers' communiqués constituted an act of bureaucratic, vanguardist interference. While Italian workerism appears to be just as convinced as some of the French far-Left of the socialist direction of the historical process, *attentisme* seems not to have resulted. It is unclear, though, whether and to what extent this was the result of an explicit critique of the naïve notions of working-class spontaneity and independence, such as that articulated by Castoriadis,[12] which was paired, in the latter, with a critique of Leninism that – as workerism's long and tortuous struggle with Lenin's ghost shows – often seems absent or weak among the Italians.

At about the time of Panzieri's unsuccessful attempts to modify the PSI, Mario Tronti was developing a number of arguments that would be key for Italian workerism. For a start, Tronti claimed that the working class could force capital 'to modify its own internal composition' (in Wright, 2002: 37). Here, Tronti was to speak in terms reminiscent of Castoriadis of the two sides of Marxism – a science of capital side, and a revolutionary side (Bellofiore, 2006). By the first issue of his journal *Class Operaia*,[13] Tronti had reversed the primacy between labour and capital, in what Moulier calls a 'Copernican inversion': 'the beginning is the class struggle of the working class' (in Wright, 2002: 64); 'first the workers, then capital' (Tronti, 2012: 124–5); Tronti turned back to Marx to declare, '[T]he labour theory of value means *labour-power first, then capital* …. *Labour is the measure of value because the working class is the condition of capital*' (in Wright, 2002: 84). Tronti had also ditched Lenin's distinction between economic and political struggles, as the fundamental relations of force in society were now located in the sphere of production. For Tronti, the factory had come to extend its 'domination over the whole of society' (in Wright, 2002: 38). This *social factory or factory-society* – a concept developed more fully only later by Negri in the direction of viewing all labour as socially productive – necessitated a vital role for the state and planning, and it provoked continual working-class resistance (Bellofiore and Tomba, 2008; Bologna, 2003; Wright, 2002).

Some of the objective and subjective processes illuminated by this factory focus were explored earlier in *Quaderni Rossi* by Alquati and his associates, in studies of the FIAT and Olivetti firms. It is here that Wright locates the beginnings of workerism's discourse on class composition, 'understood as the various forms of behaviour which arise when particular forms of labour-power are inserted in specific processes of production' (Wright, 2002: 49), an analysis stressing the relations between material conditions and subjectivity. This theory appears to be a long way ahead of the simple-minded but persistent ultra-Left conclusion that questions of class consciousness, action and organization are solved by Marx's (1978: 134–5) contention that 'It is not a question of what this or that proletarian, or even the whole proletariat, at the moment regards as its aim. It is a question of what the proletariat is, and what, in accordance with this being, it will historically be compelled to do'.

Such enquiries into class composition inevitably raised questions about working-class organization. After failing to drag the PSI with him, Panzieri had turned to the CGIL (Italian General Confederation of Labour) in a period of renewed industrial struggle and growing concern over the possible revival of fascism. And later, though he was sceptical of the unions – and despite the influence of Castoriadis, James and company's critique of them as cogs in the capitalist machine – Alquati avoided a head-on confrontation for strategic reasons.

Things are similarly complex regarding the party form. As noted, Italian workerism, unlike other Left communist-leaning groups of the time, retained Lenin as a central point of reference. In the *Class Operaia* phase (1964–7), some workerists imagined an entryist strategy that would reclaim the PCI for the workers and for revolution – thus the Bordigist-sounding phrases of the time, such as 'the intervention of revolutionary will', the 'collective brain', and the following corruption of Lenin's famous claim in *What Is To Be Done?*: 'Give us the party in Italy and we will take Europe' (in Wright, 2002: 71). On this score, Tronti was to return to the PCI in the later part of the 1960s (Wright, 2008) and was to criticize workerism as unable in that decade of struggle to 'develop a force that could become a power' (in Brophy, 2004: 283). On the other hand, Alquati attacked the PCI as not organic enough to the working class and its daily struggles on the factory floor; while arguing that Lenin was correct in the idea of introducing socialist consciousness from without, he deemed the Bolshevik leader wrong in imagining that this outside was outside of production; and he contended that Lenin was also wrong to see the factory as providing the requisite discipline for the proletariat, as the organization of the proletariat (as in Castoriadis) is the very result of the irrationality of the capitalist division of labour.

Lenin's place is also complex in Negri's thought. In the period between 1969 and 1973, Negri deployed the paradoxical notion of the 'mass vanguard'. Here, Negri rejected Lenin's economics–politics distinction, and he also jettisoned Lenin's professionalized vanguard party based on the now passed primacy of the professional worker, seeing organization as situated *within* the class. But Negri also called for centralization (Hardt, n.d.); late in the piece he defended Lenin against the ultra-Left 'infantile disorder', and he viewed the party as 'the army which defends the frontiers of proletarian independence' (in Wright, 2002: 185, 213). According to Hardt (n.d.), Lenin remained important for Negri through a reading that accented the centrality of the philosophy of the will, of subjective affirmation in remaking the world, the emphasis on organization as specific to a certain mode of production, the aspiration for 'total critique', and an anti-statism congruent with *The State and Revolution*.[14] Arguably, this is a hardly recognizable Lenin, but Sergio Bologna's (1937–) later critique of Leninism made workerism more closely resemble the far-Left outside Italy: 'organization is obliged to measure itself day by day against the new composition of the class; and must find its political programme only in the behaviour of the class and not in some set of statutes' (in Wright, 2002: 207).[15]

'Projective Marxism' – end-game, concluding reflections

For Wright, the entryist idea signals a striking dearth of analysis of PCI reformism – though perhaps it is also a signal of the significant openness and debate peculiar to Italian communism.[16] Such theoretical and political under-elaboration is, for Wright, endemic to workerism, alongside much that he regards as potentially productive and insightful. If Tronti's assessment – 'Many flowers, little fruit' (in Wright, 2002: 225) – is judged a little harsh by Wright, the weight of the argument nevertheless rests on lost analytical opportunities and revolutionary delirium. This becomes clearer in workerism's next incarnation, as *Class Operaia* splits in two, as Italy's student movement gathers force and as the country enters the period of the 'Creeping May', with 303 million lost work hours in 1969, the year of the 'hot Autumn' (Meade, 1990: 31). On the one side, here the workerists were in a promising position to analyse the new forces and movements, by way of the notion of class composition; on the other hand, for many workerists, the student movement seemed merely personal, and a factoryist perspective was rigidly held to, or workerism's hasty theoretical innovation and revolutionary exuberance obscured the pressing strategic questions involved.

The key conceptual figure, at this point, was that of the mass worker (deskilled, rootless, unattached to established class organizations [Turchetto, 2008]): '[T]he working class is increasingly closed and compact internally, and searches within itself to articulate its ever greater unity in organization ... today the whole working class in struggle is the vanguard' (Negri in Wright, 2002: 77). This mass-worker thesis, though, did not stifle the workerist critique of the notion of self-management, in line with the ultra-Left challenge to that position – that self-management remained trapped within a capitalist imaginary, at the expense of a commitment to the complete transformation of labour and the world – with the end result of the idea of the *refusal of labour*. A go-slow at the Milan tyre firm Pirelli gave some signal to the workerists of these new forms of struggle – sabotage, for instance, and the 'heretical' idea of the struggle against work, 'self-valorization' (Murphy, 2012; Tronti, 2010). And the new organization *Potere Operaio* was to focus on the question of the wage, the refusal of the existing division of labour, and the appropriation of social wealth outside of the logic of commodity relations, with the rejection of work as a major theme.

By 1972, this emphasis on the rejection of work had elements within workerism questioning the necessary relationship between the labour process and class behaviour. Here, revolutionary subjectivity was to be created outside of and against capital, and Negri, as noted, championed the broad proletariat over factory workers. In this analysis, class conflict was equated to a proletarian assault on the social wealth accumulated by capital. After a period in which priority returned to factory-based struggle, with another acceleration of industrial conflict from the mid-1970s, attention turned again to the newer social struggles, flagged in Negri's development of the idea of the 'socialized worker' (*operaio sociale*), an idea that sought to recognize both questions of production and reproduction, and which took seriously individual needs and heterogeneity as part of the class struggle (Murphy, 2012; Wright, 2002): 'Nothing is richer or finer than being able to connect the immediate needs of individuals to the political needs of class' (in Wright, 2002: 157). For Negri, this socialized worker signalled a new period in class composition, where people at large attempted to fulfill their needs outside of capitalist relations of production. Nevertheless, while wider social questions appeared frequently on the workerist agenda, even Negri was still, at times, privileging the factory worker as 'absolutely hegemonic' (in Wright, 2002: 156);[17] and his socialized worker thesis was widely criticized within workerism. Negri's intervention was viewed by some as ignoring the reformist hegemony within the factories and the difficult organizational questions that lay ahead, as moving too quickly to discover a transformatory figure that was not yet a political subject, and as too casually piling together heterogeneous groupings without concern for the connection between material conditions and political action.

It is clear that such problems continue to plague Negri's recent work, as articulated by Dyer-Witheford (2001: 73) in his critique of Negri and Hardt's notion of 'immaterial labour': this concept too hastily pulls together 'multimedia designers, primary-school teachers, machine operators in a computerized car plant, and strippers'. Strategically, Dyer-Witheford counts this an enormous difficulty, for this concept and that of multitude (the newest figures in class recomposition) assume the automatic progressiveness of social struggles and they neglect the problems – in more Gramscian terms – of articulation and hegemony:

> With the very real disjunctions and frictions between different strata of labour occluded, *Empire* can celebrate the spontaneous solidarity of the multitude without descending to the awkward business of sorting out just how much commonality there really is between participants in say the Tiananmen Square revolt, the Intifada, and the French general strike or the Seattle showdown, or how they might actually be tied together. In reality, there are potentially deep differences and complex contradictions both between and within these revolts. (Dyer-Witheford, 2001: 95)

I will return to this question soon.

When Negri defended his analyses of this new period of class composition, arguing that his reluctant comrades' memories were imprisoning them, Bologna responded: 'If we toss everything away, we live in a condition of permanent schizophrenia' (in Wright, 2002: 175). Again, this sort of criticism might appear to carry some weight in light of Negri's subsequent theoretical development, where he appears forever to be discovering fundamental shifts, new revolutionary subjects and strategic breakthroughs – for instance, the suspension of the laws of economics (Negri, 1988), peace as the alpha and omega of the revolutionary programme (Guattari and Negri, 1990) or the irreversibility of the welfare state (Negri and Hardt, 1994). This innovation is, in part at least, an important, daring series of attempts by Negri to respond to new and emerging social coordinates, to a wider loss of faith in the working class, and to the strategic question of the forces now potentially inclined towards socialist change. Here, we have the 'antici-patory' (Brophy, 2004: 281) power of workerism/autonomy, what Tronti emphasized as the 'dangerous leaps', the emphasis on *discontinuities* (in Wright, 2008: 115). Thus in his *The Politics of Subversion*, Negri (1989) follows Castoriadis's and Debord's attempts to redefine the working class according to the appropriation of time; but, as in Debord's efforts to equate the new movements with a general challenge to alienated labour, Negri's thesis could easily be read as more hopeful – a 'consolatory ideology', in Turchetto's (2008: 298) brutal assessment – than analytically convincing or empirically substantiated.

Wright adds to workerism's internal criticisms of Negri another related to the latter's disablingly schematic portrait of the relationship between the PCI and the workers as one of pure repression, in a period that saw an increasingly *complex and differentiated* political reality. Similarly Negri's triumphalism – '[T]he working class, its sabotage, are the stronger power ... We are here; we are uncrushable; and we are in the majority' (in Wright, 2002: 173) – is deemed by Wright unsuitable to what was a profoundly contradictory reality. On this note, Wright connects the praise of violence among workerists like Negri with workerism's fast and virtually complete eradication by the state. That is, moving after '68 to a view of the PCI as, in Piperno's words, 'the working class articulation of capitalist social organization' (in Wright, 2002: 117), elements of workerism tended to a view of a new phase where an 'acting minority' (Bologna in Wright, 2002: 100) might detonate class struggle – a modern version of the insurrectionist German far-Left of the period of the disastrous March Action of 1921. As the pace and ferocity of struggle grew towards the 'years of lead' of the 1970s, many workerists, never having developed a proper critique of Leninism and faced with state repression and fascist violence, turned towards the notion of building a party of insurrection. Here, in Wright's view, political impatience and a growing loss of touch with political realities saw militarization touted as the way ahead; Bologna (2003) contends that isolation from factory struggles accentuated a political impatience, in the 'voluntarist and late-Leninist character' of elements of the struggle; and Bellofiore (2006) notes the irrationalism characteristic of workerism in this period, visible in Negri's implication that development, crisis and revolution were all the same thing. Hereafter, *Autonomia Operaia*, a heterogeneous, fluid, and marginal set of groups, which arose after the collapse of *Potere Operaio* in 1973, split into libertarian and civil war wings, the Moro affair dislocated the whole movement with subsequent arrests and exiles affecting 5,000 militants, with over 1,000 convicted to more than 10 years in prison (Bologna, 2003), and an employer offensive saw the dispiritingly fast demise of workerism into 'the years of cynicism, opportunism, and fear' – the 1980s (Balestrini and Moroni in Wright, 2002: 198).

Undoubtedly, a number of the workerists themselves would contest Wright's reading. In a 1983 tract, 'Do You Remember Revolution?', Negri and ten other intellectuals imprisoned in Rebibbia Prison in Rome maintained that they had *absolutely nothing* to do with terrorism, that they never fetishized violence and that there was an unbridgeable gap between the Red Brigades (whose actions merely mirrored state violence) and the revolutionary groups of Workers' Autonomy (Virno et al., 1996). Here, the massive struggle of the mid-1970s and the decline of the movement are read in terms of the passing of a whole phase of struggle and the emergence of a new phase – post-Fordist class composition. In particular, from 1973–74 onwards, we see the historic compromise – one part of labour drawing nearer the government, a decline in the central role of large factories and workers in those factories and a subjective change across the movement. The Red Brigades are, in this reading, viewed as expressing the reaction of an older class composition to this restructuring and to state repression, and against the new composition of the movement of 1977 – though, interestingly, the authors of the tract admit that militarization meant many resemblances and, in some instances, a real joining of forces.

For Wright, the most potentially fruitful concept and substantive analyses of workerism – the closer examination of class composition – were never, in the end, properly realized. Wright's charges of simplicity and one-dimensional analysis are fairly convincing. The penchant for overambitious theoretical categories such as the social factory yielded little, anticipating results out of what looks like impatience, extrapolating nascent trends, and being far too sanguine, for instance, in ignoring the tendencies to class *decomposition* simultaneously taking place (Wright, 2002: 224; Brophy, 2004).[18] The workerist reply, though, would equally cogently accent – as Harry Cleaver (n.d.; 1993) does – the gain involved in workerism's rejection of the variety of Marxist analysis that views capitalism as a self-perpetuating system within which the working class are hopelessly integrated. Instead, another story, a 'positive hermeneutic' (in Jameson's words), is discovered: as Hardt (n.d) puts it, if critical Marxism manages to get at the construction of the subject in its receptivity and plasticity, workerism gets at its spontaneity. On this reading, in the case of Italian workerism, Perry Anderson's (1976: 93) harsh judgement of Western Marxism – 'method as impotence, art as consolation, pessimism as quiescence' – is completely out of order, a judgement perhaps facilitated by the surprising absence of workerism from his *Considerations on Western Marxism*.

Here, it is worth making just two final comments – one critical, one appreciative – that link workerism to Negri and Hardt's influential trilogy. First, Wright draws attention to an important contradiction within workerism, one that is evident, too, in Hardt and Negri's *Empire* and, more generally, across Left communism. This is the tension between the notion of labour-power's permanent antagonism against, and power within, capitalism, and the various opposed theses that appear to suggest that capital has now achieved total domination. Thus Negri (1989) speaks of capital insinuating itself everywhere, and – in a letter to Felix Guattari – he talks of the consolidation and victory of capitalism. As Bologna notes, workerism was both an exaltation of the power of the working class *and* of the power of capital in subsuming that class, the latter emphasis providing an explanation of the strong line of specialization in state theory among workerists (Wright, 2008). In *Empire*, this sort of antinomy is glaring. For instance, a sanguine commentary about the massive creative and resistant power of the multitude and the fragility of Empire (which is, after all, called into existence by that very multitude) sits with difficulty alongside a discourse in which 'struggles have become all but incommunicable' (Hardt and Negri, 2000: 54; see also Negri, 2010) and an uneasy use of Guy Debord's *Comments on the Society of the Spectacle*. Debord's conclusions are hardly congruent with the 'lightness and joy of being communist' and far more harmonious with his own miserable decline into alcoholism, pathetic intrigue in the role of 'the prince of division' and bad-tempered withdrawal to the socialist watchtower (Hussey, 2002). In what way could the integrated spectacle described by Debord be a step forward?

Second and related, if it is easy to feel concerned about the politically adventurist and theoretically sanguine results of workerism, a progressivist utopianism of the present, including the paean to subjectivity oblivious to its real ambivalence; about a certain science-fiction quality to Hardt and Negri's analyses of the present – on, say, bio-political production and immaterial labour as hegemonic, as against counter-tendencies at work (a deconstruction of the working class?); about a globalism that appears, despite assurances, to gloss over the continuing unevenness of power in the world, the way in which place still matters; about a lack of analysis concerning precisely how this multitude might be practically and politically linked – in what ways is this in fact a class concept? Is there not a dearth of strategic and hegemonic thinking here?; about the dangers of a 'post-secular' temptation in their work and the implications of the Spinozean–Deleuzian ontology of life running beneath the analyses (Bellofiore, 2006; Brophy, 2004; Callinicos, 2007b; McLennan, 2010)[19] – it is hard, even in the face of all this, not to feel at least somewhat positively disposed to later worker-ism's 'optimism of the intellect'. For a start, whatever its failures, it can hardly be less attractive than curmudgeonly, one-sided *kulturkritik* or an obdurate Marxism that sees nothing new anywhere and refuses to read the 'signs on the street'. In addition, this 'projective Marxism' (Hardt, n.d.), which looks to the Marx of 1848 and the Marx of 1871 (Hardt, n.d.), which has seemed able to 'mutate along with the times' (Brophy in Wright, 2008: 112), seems an important flipside to Anderson's (2000) grim insistence that we take stock of the massive tasks ahead and really feel the defeat amidst an all-powerful neo-liberalism and total American foreign policy hegemony. Workerism's joyful side provides some relief, and is a good match for a capitalism that works through pleasure, as a 'desiring machine'. Here, as Hardt argues, such exuberance is vital, and with globalization and the Left's present condition of 'theorizing without movements', *Italy is brought close to us*. Hardt is right that Left asceticism, defeatism and masochism must be abandoned, but Wright's book shows clearly why we must still remain sober.

5

'Communism ... Is the Affirmation of a New Community': Notes on Jacques Camatte

Introduction

It is unlikely that the thought of French communist Jacques Camatte is widely known to those working in the field of social and political thought. Nevertheless, it contains plenty of interest – beyond what might be delivered by a distanced history-of-ideas treatment of intellectual novelties or oddities. For a start, Camatte's distinctive later work was built from a platform provided by a fascinating but relatively neglected (even in Italy) wing of Italian communism – the Bordigist line – distinct again from the Left communist workerism examined in the previous chapter. Second, the development of Camatte's thinking in the direction of what has commonly been referred to as primitivism is both unusual (because of his Bordigist roots) and is one of a number of important resources for English-speaking primitivist intellectuals and collective projects. Furthermore, while this peculiar Left communist current appears to have peaked and subsequently declined in influence from the middle of the 1990s, it contains plenty to chew on, and its emphases and impulses continue to have an at least subterranean life within the broad field of anarchist thought, which has, moreover, been reinvigorated since the close of the 1990s in alternative-globalization currents, and to which I will turn in the next chapter.

In this chapter, I will seek to touch on these issues, drawing on the work by Camatte currently available in English. I will begin by providing a background to his thought by exploring the ideas of Amadeo Bordiga at some length – such is the continuity of themes between Camatte's early work within the International Communist Party and his later primitivist phase. I will then examine the movement of Camatte's thought, from the early Bordigist writings to the primitivist positions taken after 1968, which provide a novel, ecologically directed Left communist optic. Here, Camatte re-orients his thinking around community, organization and the character of contemporary capitalism, breaking from Marxism, and presenting an impassioned plea that humanity end its 'wandering' – rejecting domestication, technological development and domination in the name of the re-establishment of 'Gemeinwesen' (communal being). In a concluding note, I draw Camatte's later work together with more contemporary Anglo-American primitivist currents, considering in broad strokes what might be alive and dead in such work. While much of this formation of thought appears today to be naively romantic, worryingly irrationalist, and inadequately political, there are, I suggest, certain aspects that still have significance – in particular, the questioning of growth and the human consequences of new technological developments, the existentialist note struck in response to capital's 'running away', and the impassioned utopian demand for another way of being and being together.

The Bordigist inheritance

In a review of a Cristina Corradi's recent *Storia dei marxismi in Italia*, Peter Thomas (2009: 129) notes the significant absence of Amadeo Bordiga: 'the mention of his name, revealingly, still has the capacity to prompt a Wittgensteinian silence in some areas of the Italian left.' Thus, nearly 60 years prior to Corradi's story, the editors of the first edition of Gramsci's letters from prison had felt it necessary to erase references to the continuing and warm connection between Gramsci and Bordiga and, very often, Bordiga is only mentioned as a dogmatic and one-dimensional vulgar Marxist foil to Gramsci's subtle and rich explorations in the philosophy of praxis.[1] Yet, within the history of Marxism and Left communism, Bordiga is a fascinating figure in his own right, whose thought is indispensable in approaching the work of Jacques Camatte.[2]

Amadeo Bordiga was born in 1889, and became politically active as a young man, within the dynamic milieu of the Italian Socialist Party's (PSI) youth section, opposing the colonial war in Tripoli in 1911 and founding 'the Karl Marx circle' in Naples in 1912 (Camatte, 1972; Craver, 1996). Already, at this point, Bordiga's very clear stance on knowledge, culture and revolution was evident, a position that was to provide a striking contrast to that which a young Antonio Gramsci would soon take up. In a widely influential clash from 1912 with Angelo Tasca and the Turin 'culturalists' (Craver, 1996; Fiori, 1970), Bordiga declared: 'The need for study should be proclaimed in a congress of school teachers, not socialists. You don't become a socialist through instruction but through experiencing the real needs of the class to which you belong' (in Davidson, 1977: 88).

Bordiga's impressive early radicalism was also clear during the First World War, where he and the youthful 'intransigents' around him rejected the PSI line of 'neither adherence nor sabotage', taking a decided anti-militarist position, together with a more Leninist view on the imperative of transforming war into civil war (Camatte, 1972; Craver, 1996). At around this time, too, Bordiga had been expressing deep-seated scepticism about the democratic (read as the negation of socialism) and electoral orientation of Italian socialism, a posture that was to become a distinguishing and unrelenting focus of his later activity (Camatte, 1972; Craver, 1996; ICC, 1992).[3]

It was in this moment, in 1917 at a conference in Florence, that Gramsci and Bordiga encountered each other for the first time (Davidson, 1977). Here, it is interesting to note the immediate contrasts between the two, noted at the time by an observer, Giovanni Germanetto, who described Bordiga as 'tall and imposing', 'a powerful and impetuous speaker', and Gramsci as 'thin, small, and sickly', 'a thinker' (in Cammett, 1967: 58). Both men, in their own ways, were increasingly struggling with the compromises of the PSI, in the turbulent context of major social change and proletarian militancy in Italy, war and revolution in Russia. From December 1918, Bordiga's *Il Soviet*[4] was pushing an abstentionist line (Cammett, 1967), captured in the slogan, 'Not one socialist at the polls!' (Fiori, 1970: 131). On the other hand, for Gramsci, the immediate point of re-thinking and re-evaluation was the growing Italian suffering towards the end of the war, expressing itself in the engineering city of Turin in growing working-class unrest and, ultimately, the factory councils experience of 1919–20. The differences between the two men here are significant, with Gramsci moving in a more syndicalist and councilist direction under the influence of the events in Turin, seeing these new forms of proletarian organization as the leading edge of revolutionary action, and Bordiga, meanwhile, insisting that control over production was a question to follow after the capture of political power, the immediate task being the formation of a strong and unified party that might conquer state power (Bordiga, 1977; Camatte, 1972; Cammett, 1967; Davidson, 1977). Bordiga's position was that, at this point in Italy (in contrast to Russia), the political dimension was primary, that the party must take precedence over the councils, that, in any case, the factory councils were more limited than soviets (which would certainly be important after the conquest of power), and that to underscore councils/soviets too heavily was mistakenly to 'emphasize a form over a force' (Bordiga, 1977: 219): 'Those who can represent the proletariat *today*, before it takes power *tomorrow*, are workers who are conscious of this historical eventuality; in other words, the workers who are *members of the Communist Party*' (Bordiga, 1977: 205); 'there are no organs which are revolutionary by virtue of their form; there are only social forces that are revolutionary on account of their orientation' (Bordiga, 1977: 220). On the other hand, Gramsci was to find the abstentionists too restrictive in their view of the party, ignoring, he felt, the urgent need for 'wide contact with the masses' (in Fiori, 1970: 131), and he refused the idea of a party that tended towards 'a collection of dogmatists or little Machiavellis ... which makes use of the masses for its own heroic attempts to imitate the French Jacobins' (in Adamson, 1980: 58).

Nevertheless, after the defeat of the Turin movement, and influenced by the failure of the Hungarian Revolution, we see Gramsci drawing closer to Bordiga's positions, and a new attention to the question of the party in his work (Davidson, 1977; ICC, 1992; Piccone, 1983: 136). As Davidson (1977: 158) glosses this, after 1920 Gramsci is forced to confront the question, 'why can men not make their own destinies?', rather than the question of how they can. This convergence builds towards a split from the PSI.[5] And it was at the January 1921 PSI Congress at Livorno that the communist group left and reconvened, coming to constitute the Italian Communist Party (PCd'I), a party dominated in its initial phase by Bordiga (Fiori, 1970).

However, rather soon afterwards, as the prospects for revolution began to dim, and as fascism strengthened its hold in Italy, Bordiga's contentions were increasingly assailed, and he progressively lost control of the party from 1923 (Fiori, 1970). Foreshadowing some of the issues that were to arise, Lenin (1966: 113) himself famously entered into the debates around some of the further Left positions with his *'Left-Wing' Communism – An Infantile Disorder* of 1920, commending Bordiga's criticism of 'Turati and company', but rejecting the conclusion that 'parliament is harmful in principle'. Lenin's argument was that communists needed to be involved in every sphere of proletarian life, rather than fencing themselves off from difficult but inevitable problems. Bordiga's (1977) unrelenting stand, on the other hand, was that participation in parliament necessarily entailed a contradiction with the imperative of constituting a strong communist party capable of seizing power.

This stance is tightly threaded together with Bordiga's resolutely anti-democratic politics. For Bordiga (1922: 56), there was absolutely no intrinsic value to the principle of democracy, being based on the 'simple and crude arithmetical presumption that the majority is right and the minority is wrong'. Centrally, democracy relied upon an individualism alien to the conceptions of historical materialism: democracy 'considers each individual to be a perfect "unit" within a system made up of many potentially equivalent units, and instead of appraising the value of the individual's opinion in the light of his manifold condition of existence, that is, his relations with others, it postulates this value *a priori* with the hypothesis of the "sovereignty of the individual"' (1922: 50). In contrast, the properly Marxian position was: 'The collectivity is born from relations and groupings in which the status and activity of each individual do not derive from an individual function but from a collective one determined by the multiple influences of the social milieu' (1922: 52).

This is a central emphasis for Bordiga, and one that was to be constantly rearticulated. In a 1946 piece, for instance, Bordiga insists that the dialectic focuses upon 'collective phenomena', against the 'myth of the individual' and its associated language of personality, dignity, duties and liberties. We must always start with a properly materialist focus on needs, which are, above all, social. So opposed was he to bourgeois personalization, so convinced that all work was collectively and historically produced, and so intent on avoiding a party of passive followers of leaders (in contrast to a party centred on a rigorous and consistent political programme), Bordiga refused to allow the individualized identification of his own theoretical contributions, insisting on revolutionary anonymity (ICC, 1992) – something that has made precise identification of his contributions somewhat difficult in certain cases. From early on, then, we have a strong sense of communism for Bordiga as the 'affirmation of social man' (Bordiga, 1950), 'the joyous harmony of social man' (Bordiga, 1965), a focus that is rather more troublingly linked to the vision of the communist party as future 'social brain' (Buick, 1987: 128).

In my discussion of Camatte, I will return to a number of these points – anti-individualism, the community-centred vision of communism, the anti-democratic stance. Resuming a more chronological account, growing tensions between Bordiga's positions on elections and the response to fascism and those taken by the Comintern rose to an initial peak around 1923 (the year of Bordiga's first arrest) (Davidson, 1977). As Davidson (1977) notes, already by 1921 there were divergences between Gramsci and Bordiga over the interpretation of fascism, with Gramsci taking a more culturalist position, and coming to a more lucid recognition of the cross-class support it had succeeded in marshalling. Here, Bordiga's 'immovability' and long-remarked-upon determinism were seen as problems by a part of the movement, Bordiga tending to lump the fascists and social democrats together (Fiori, 1970) in a formula that equated both democracy and dictatorship as simple, ultimately indistinguishable forms of the rule of capital. As Bordiga was to put this in 1946–8, 'Democracy is class collaboration through lots of talk, fascism is plain class collaboration'. At the time, this equation, fascism=social democracy, was out of favour in the International, and behind the scenes, attempts to were being made to displace Bordiga.[6]

The opposition between Bordiga and Gramsci on such issues only grew over time, the two engaging in an extraordinary 14-hour debate in 1924 at a Congress in Naples (Davidson, 1977). A series of events and encounters in 1926 proved decisive in effecting a scission. At the PCd'I Congress of Lyons in January 1926, Gramsci's theses rejected historical determinism and put forward a novel analysis of the Italian situation, of fascism and of the tasks ahead (Cammett, 1967). Here, very notably, Gramsci – articulating a more dialectical understanding of class and party – argued as follows:

> Bordiga has said that he is favourable to the winning over of the masses in the period immediately preceding the revolution. But how do we know when we are in this period? It depends precisely on the work which we know how to develop among the masses whether this period begins or not. Only if we work and achieve some success in the winning over of the masses will we arrive at a pre-revolutionary period. (in Showstack-Sassoon, 1980: 102)

In response, Bordiga reiterated his position on the necessary purity of the party, on liberalism and fascism as but two methods of essentially identical class rule, and he criticized Gramsci's 'ordinovist' positions as 'derived from philosophical conceptions of a bourgeois and idealist nature partly inherited from Benedetto Croce', which led in the direction of reformism (Bordiga, 1926a). Particularly at issue were the questions of the united front and the process of bolshevization (Bordiga, 1926a).

On 23 February in that same year, at the Sixth Enlarged Executive Meeting of the Communist International, Bordiga strongly voiced some of the same objections, here notably distinguishing himself as the last

Western communist to confront Stalin in person, as the gravedigger of the revolution (Goldner, 1991; Piccone, 1983).[7] In his speech, Bordiga (1926b) emphasized the specificity of the Russian path to communism, and criticized the emerging 'regime of terror', stating that 'the spectacle of this session of the plenum has filled me with dark forebodings'.[8] Bordiga's provocative suggestion was that, given that communism was a truly internationalist movement, all the communist parties of the world should jointly rule the Russian communist state (Goldner, 1991).

Contacted in that same year by Karl Korsch about the possibility of breaking away and forming a counter-international, Bordiga (1926c) thought it too early, rejecting Korsch's suggestion that the revolution was bourgeois, but also raising concerns about the future degeneration of Russia in the absence of other revolutions.[9] From almost the beginning, Bordiga had maintained few illusions about Russia's backwardness and the implications of such underdevelopment: 'The historical conditions within which the Russian revolution has developed do not resemble the conditions within which the proletarian revolution will develop in the democratic countries of Western Europe and America ... The tactical experience of the Russian revolution cannot be integrally transposed to other countries' (in Piccone, 1983: 157). It was, though, only after the war that Bordiga was to develop his distinctive reading of the character of the regime in the USSR (Camatte, 1974) – a reading that has certain connections with those developed by the non-Leninist Left (Pannekoek, Mattick, Rühle, for instance), although he came to designate the USSR (as an early type of) 'capitalism' rather than 'state capitalism' (Fernandez, 1997; van der Linden, 2007). While 1917 did see a proletarian political revolution, for Bordiga, the important real content was its bourgeois, anti-feudal side (Goldner, 1991; ICC, 1992; van der Linden, 2007). According to Bordiga, capitalism is *the agrarian revolution* (Goldner, 1991). The Russian socialists' capitalization of agriculture and the development of the forces of production were capitalist, not communist, tasks: 'One does not *build* communism' (in Goldner, 1991); one only destroys obstacles to its development (Camatte, 1974). The absence of a capitalist class was beside the point for Bordiga (1953) as the Russian economy 'is founded upon wage-labour and internal and external market exchange': 'where there is money, there is neither socialism nor communism, as there isn't, and by a long way, in Russia' (in Buick, 1987: 139):

> to define communism by 'state property' is a nonsense because the idea of 'social property' is itself one: when society as a whole becomes

the master of its conditions of existence because it has ceased to be torn by internal antagonisms, it is not at all 'social property' that comes into being but the abolition of property as a fact and so as an idea. For how is property to be defined if not by the exclusion of the other from the use and enjoyment of the object of property? When there is no longer anyone to be excluded there is no longer any property nor any possible property-owners, 'society' less than any other. (in Buick, 1987: 134)

1926 is also the year in which Bordiga and Gramsci were arrested.[10] Bordiga was to remain in prison until 1930 – the year he was expelled from the PCd'I for supporting the Trotskyist opposition – after which time he withdrew from politics until 1943, and was accompanied constantly by two police agents (Bourrinet, n.d.; Bourrinet, 1998; ICC, 1991).[11] The Bordigist Internationalist Communist Party was formed in 1943, growing fairly rapidly, and producing the journal *Prometeo* from November that year (Buick, 1987; ICC, 1992). While politically active from 1943, Bordiga only joined the party in 1949,[12] after which time a split in 1952 saw Bordiga and his followers leaving to form the International Communist Party (Buick, 1987; ICC, 1992). In this postwar period, Bordiga continued to reaffirm his fundamental arguments: the 'invariance' of the communist doctrine formulated by Marx in 1848; the priority of the party in the establishment of communism,[13] and the need for the party, in unfavourable circumstances, to 'survive and hand down the flame, along the historical "thread of time"'; anti-democracy and anti-individualism, with communism's content given by its community-centred premises; criticism of anti-fascism, and the equation of social democracy and fascism; analysis and critique of the USSR; and a radically materialist reading of the link between material conditions and consciousness[14] (Bordiga 1946; Bordiga 1946–8; Bordiga, 1950; Bordiga 1965; Buick, 1987). Interestingly, from the 1950s Bordiga also wrote a number of rather early pieces on the connection between capitalism and environmental degradation (Bordiga, 1951a and b; 1952; 1953; 1963).[15]

From Bordiga to Camatte

This rather lengthy treatment of the main lines of Bordiga's political thought is, I think, an indispensable prefatory note to a consideration of the work of Jacques Camatte. Camatte was born near Marseille in 1935, and first corresponded with Bordiga in 1954, meeting the latter for the first time the following year in Naples.[16] Bordiga's influence, as we will see, is direct in Camatte's early work, Camatte consulting with Bordiga (who lived until 1970) on a number of those texts.[17] Furthermore, even when Camatte breaks from the International Communist Party and Marxism, his distinctive new communist trajectory is written both against and in continuity with these Bordigist roots, with his emphases on communal being, the despotism of capital and the environmental consequences of capitalism indicative of strong continuing affinities.[18]

Camatte's work during the majority of the 1960s is, then, firmly placed within the Bordigist current. His 'Origin and Function of the Party Form' (co-written with Roger Dangeville in 1961), for instance, involves detailed Marxian exegesis on the question of organization, reading very much as an internal International Communist Party text – with, for instance, prominent reference to the Rome Theses of 1922 and the Lyon Theses of 1926 as central documents.[19] Already notable, here, is the great emphasis placed upon Marx's usage of the term 'Gemeinwesen',[20] which proves to be a consistent preoccupation across the entirety of Camatte's work and is altogether consistent with Bordiga's central emphasis on the anti-individualist and social, collectivist premises of Marxism. 'Gemeinwesen' carries connotations of 'common essence', 'commonwealth', 'common system', 'common being', 'communal being', and is thus not translatable simply as community understood in a restrictively spatial sense (Nicolaus, 1993; O'Malley, 1970). Further, its use cannot be read as a straightforwardly communitarian moment in Marx's work – the term indicating a transformation of the human being, an ethical revolution, beyond a bourgeois commonsense that opposes individual and society/community (Brenkert, 1983; Marx, 1993; Ollman, 1976). As O'Malley (1970: xliv) explains this,

> Man is essentially social, and society is precisely the actualization of his social nature. The being of society is not to be distinguished from the being of its members; nor is the essence of man in its actuality to be distinguished from the ensemble of social relationships of which he is the focus and subject, and which, taken as a whole constitute the matrix of his life as an individual. In his individual existence he embodies society [...] the individual and society are one in essence and being.

This notion is tightly connected to Marx's critiques of state and private property, of illusory community and illusions about sovereign individuality, of the dualism individual–society and, furthermore, for Marx, at this point, one could see, in the proletariat, a glimpse of this potential future Gemeinwesen (O'Malley, 1970; Thomas, 1983).

Alongside, and connected to this, we find the expected emphases of Bordigist thinking on organization: capitalism can only be surpassed if a party of the proletariat is organized; this party is a representative of the proletariat and is, in its invariant programme and existence, 'the prefiguration of communist society' (Camatte, 1961: 4), 'an organ of foresight' (1961: 7); the party, rejecting democracy (in favour of 'organic centralism'[21]), is to seize power, setting itself up as a ruling class as the social brain, the social state; the communist revolution must ultimately be international – it knows neither nations nor individuals (the revolution will be anonymous [1961: 5]). Similarly, 'The Democratic Mystification', begun in 1962 (also with the support of Bordiga) and published in Camatte's journal *Invariance* in 1969, is largely a work of Bordigist orthodoxy. Democracy is, here, defined as 'the organization of those who have lost their original organic unity with the community'. Implying division, individualism and a reconciliation between classes, democracy is merely a mechanism used by the ruling class to attain domination over society,[22] Camatte equating social democracy with fascism.

Despite this apparent orthodoxy, there are already emphases here that foreshadow the break Camatte makes towards the end of the 1960s from the Bordigist current. In particular, the exegetical references to Marx's *Grundrisse* (which includes reference to the fall of ancient Gemeinwesen and money establishing itself as 'real community' [Marx, 1993: 223–6]) and mention of 'formal domination' are indications of shifts in emphasis that become more apparent in Camatte's major work *Capital and Community* (1964–72). This, again, heavily exegetical work is a long intervention on the significance of a number of then non-canonical works by Marx, the most important being the so-called unpublished sixth chapter of *Capital*, 'Results of the Direct Production Process'. In this text, Marx (1994) analyses the capitalist production process and, importantly for Camatte, distinguishes between the formal subsumption of labour under capital (linked to absolute surplus value) and real subsumption (linked to relative surplus value). In the moment of real subsumption, says Marx (1994: 429), the mystification in the capital-relation 'is now much more developed', the social character of labour appearing as something entirely autonomous, 'as a *mode of capital's existence*' (1994: 457). Here, the products of labour 'stand on their hind legs vis-à-vis the worker and confront him as "capital" – but also the social forms of labour appear as *forms of the development of capital,* and therefore the productive powers of social labour, thus developed, appear as *productive powers of capital'* (1994: 457–8). What we have, here, in essence, is a critique of the growing penetration of capital into human existence, a reformulation of the notion of ideology, away from those versions found in *The German Ideology,* and reflections on aliena-tion and human essence underscoring the loss of communal being.

Occurring at a moment of a number of returns to Marx, in search of renewal,[23] Camatte's (1964–72: 22) interpretation is that this chapter 'articulates' the whole corpus of Marx's work. More closely, Camatte (1964–72: 10) suggests that the draft brings together the four different ways in which Marx had confronted the critique of political economy: 1) in terms of alienation in the *Economic and Philosophical Manuscripts;* 2) in beginning with the commodity, in *Capital;* 3) in Marx's considera-tion of the autonomy of value in the original version of the *Contribution to the Critique of Political Economy;* and 4) in his assessment of the obstacles to capitalist development in the *Grundrisse.* This articulation is glossed by Camatte as the study of the domestication of human beings by capital, the autonomization of the non-living, the progressive 'capitalization of everything' (1964–72: 40–2). In this process, capital becomes social, 'an animated monster', seizing 'all the materiality of man' (1964–72: 106). In short, capital 'has become the material com-munity of man' (1964–72: 107). As this is summarized in a text included from 1971, 'Apropos Capital', 'Men are reduced to pure spirits who now receive their substance from capital, which, as the material community, has also become nature' (1964–72: 177).

Sometimes repetitive, dense and difficult, the value of *Capital and Community* is partly in its collection of a number of texts written over such a long stretch. The main body of the work was begun in 1964 and published in 1968. In 1966, Camatte broke from the International Communist Party over questions of organization and over diver-gences caused by the particular direction taken by Camatte's otherwise Bordigist emphasis on communism as equal to communal being. On the one hand, then, there are a number of rather straightforward Bordigist characteristics within the text: social democracy as 'the fitting resolu-tion of fascism' (1964–72: 69); communism as defeated in 1926–8, with the 'socialism in one country' line of the Russian Party and the Third International, and the subsequent triumph of capital in Stalinist Russia; democracy as 'founded on the illusory sovereignty of man as an isolated individual' (1964–72: 108); the party as social brain, and instrument of socialism.[24] On the other hand, within the main text, and in appended texts written after 1968, we find some fundamental departures – for example, in terms of the issue of communist organization, and class analysis (most notably, an apparent widening and de-proletarianization of communism's agent); or in terms of questions of community, history and emancipation ('all human history is that of the loss of its community' [1964–72: 182]). I want to turn now to this post-1968 break.

One of the texts additional to the main body of *Capital and Community* is 'On Organization', a letter of 1969, which, Camatte (1995: 19) notes, 'led to the dissolution of the group that had begun to form on the basis of the positions set forth in *Invariance*'.[25] Here, we see a major shift from a Left communism of the party to one more in line with spontaneist and anti-substitutionist stances found among councilist and anarchist currents that gained greater prominence around 1968. Camatte's (1995: 25) contention is that, just as the state is a 'gang' that mediates between particular capitals and between total and particular capitals, so, too, all parties, including the International Communist Party, have evolved into gangs. In fact, all forms of working-class political organization have disappeared and have been replaced by various 'rackets', competing with each other for theoretical and organizational prestige. Constituting an 'illusory community' (1995: 31), the gang merely 'replaces all natural or human presuppositions with presuppositions determined by capital' (1995: 26–7). This process is linked by Camatte (1995: 26) to capital's achievement of real domination. Rejecting all political representation as a 'screen' and an 'obstacle to a fusion of forces' (1995: 20) and insistent that emancipation must be self-emancipation based on materialist premises (consciousness follows action), Camatte (1995: 32–3) looks to Marx's reflections on the Communist League, insisting that, at this moment, one can only recognize the party in the *historic* (as opposed to formal) sense: 'The revolutionary must not identify himself with a group but recognize himself in a theory that does not depend on a group or on a review, because it is the expression of an existing class struggle ... the desire for theoretical development must realize itself in an autonomous and personal fashion and not by way of a group that sets itself up as a kind of diaphragm between the individual and the theory'.

Camatte (1995: 19) rejects that this is any sort of retreat to a 'Stirnerian individualism', and the text is still replete with references to Marx and attached to the notion of the proletarian movement. However, very soon, we see some further important shifts that entail a decisive move away from Marxism. These shifts are clear in two pieces from 1973 – 'The Wandering of Humanity' and 'Against Domestication' – and one from the following year – 'This World We Must Leave'. Pivotal to these texts, again, is the notion that capital has now achieved real domination over society and established itself as the material community. The perhaps logical endpoint of this assessment, though, comes more clearly into view, here. For Camatte (1995: 40), that is, in our period of the 'despotism of capital', we see 'the integration of human beings in the process of capital and the integration of capital in the minds of human beings' – or, to reformulate, the autonomization of capital and the 'domestication' of the human being.

As noted, in these texts, we see some major departures from orthodox Marxian presuppositions.[26] Camatte (1995: 39–40, 54) charges that, in 'running away', capitalism has now overcome the law of value, has been able to absorb crises, and, in a Debordian formulation, he contends that capital is, today, representation.[27] Here, against the thesis of contemporary capitalism's 'decadence', Camatte argues that the productive forces have not at all stopped growing and that, in truth, it is human beings who are decaying. Centrally, capital has finally negated classes through the 'universalization of wage labour', creating a 'collection of slaves of capital' (1995: 41). It is, then, 'humanity that is exploited' (1995: 40). At another point, Camatte approaches this negation of class somewhat differently, although, again, by looking back to Marx's unpublished sixth chapter: 'We have reached the end of the historical cycle during which humanity ... moved within class societies. Capital has realized the negation of classes – by means of mystification' (1995: 60).

In fact, Camatte (1995: 58–9) now suggests the inherently reformist character of the working class: 'Doesn't Lenin's discredited statement that the proletariat, left to itself, can only attain trade-union consciousness, describe the truth about the class bound to capital?'. That is, the proletariat outside of society is, through struggle, progressively integrated: 'It succeeds, with the German Socialist Party, in forming a countersociety that is finally absorbed by the society of capital, and the negating movement of the proletariat is over' (1995: 59). Here, any appeal to parties, councils or other forms of working-class organization as leading the way to communism are jettisoned as mere 'coagulations of despotic consciousness' (1995: 57). The 'revolutionary reformism' of the period 1913–45 is also indicative of a decisive dimension of Marxism's failure – its implication in, even glorification of, a mid-nineteenth-century-onward 'wandering of humanity': that is, the notion of 'growth of productive forces as the condition *sine qua non* for liberation' (1995: 54). Given this, 'it becomes increasingly imbecilic to proclaim oneself a Marxist' (1995: 70). This lament about the folding together of the proletarian movement with the presuppositions of capital is later expanded upon as follows: 'the dichotomy of interior/exterior; the vision of progress; the exaltation of science; the necessity of distinguishing human from the animal, with the latter being considered in every case inferior; the idea of the exploitation of nature' (1995: 199–200). (As a parenthetical note, I would raise the issue here of Camatte's dating of this domestication and the despotism of capital. For a start, the periodization of the despotism of capital appears to be connected by Camatte [1995: 183] to the emergence of the new middle classes and what might be called the period of organized capitalism – social democracy, communism, fascism.[28] However, Camatte traces the tendency to the autonomization of capital much further back, in a cycle beginning with the Greek polis and ending with the fall of the Roman Empire (1995: 184). Even further than this, though, Camatte (1995: 237–8) evidently locates critical negative facets of the present much further back, pinpointing the advent of animal husbandry[29] with the Neolithic Revolution as the historic founding point of science [the treatment of other as object], patriarchy,[30] and capital.)

What, then, replaces the Marxian vision of and politics towards an emancipated life? Once again, the broad answer for Camatte (1995: 71) is to be found in the notion of Gemeinwesen: 'Our revolution as a project to re-establish community was necessary from the moment when ancient communities were destroyed'. This means a break from present domestication and is not at all, insists Camatte, in contradiction to reaffirming individuality (1995: 69).[31] This re-establishment of community necessitates a break with both humanism and scientism (1995: 88), as well as the transformation of technique – Camatte arguing that technology is not neutral but determined by the mode of production (1995: 67). It entails, too, crucially, a new relationship to nature: from domination over nature to reconciliation with and regeneration of nature – 'The naturalization of man and the humanization of nature' (1995: 66). This further implies the 'destruction of urbanization' in favour of multiple communities; the transformation (diminishment) of the transportation system; a changed division of labour and 'the suppression of monoculture'; the end to the 'mad' growth of population (1995: 66); and a 'new active and unfixed life', which will cure the 'somatic and psychological illnesses of present-day human beings' (1995: 67).

Anticipating objections, Camatte (1995: 88) maintains that his position does not lead to fatalism. And yet, I think it is clear that his own question – 'How can destroyed human beings rebel?' (1995: 85) – remains tricky for him. Here, Camatte is obviously looking to some of the content of the new revolutionary cycle that opens with 1968 (1995: 98). Clearly, though, those modern Leftist currents reinvigorated in that period are not what he has in mind and, instead, he mentions youth, who are not yet fully domesticated (1995: 109), as well as elements of the (third) world that 'have not yet fully succumbed to the despotism of capital' (1995: 128).[32] In terms of further materialist groundings for his revolutionary hopes, we have perhaps the pressures of environmental destruction – 'overpopulation, pollution, and the exhaustion of natural resources' – along with 'the monetary crisis' (1995: 92). However, the major underlying footing for communism appears to be an existential hope and appeal to a notion of human essence and refusal. Communism, here, is viewed as a 'necessity that extends to all people' (1995: 124),[33] and we have, above all, a moral appeal, a call or desire for a 'fracture through which, a new feeling, etc. all surge' (1995: 179): 'We must abandon this world dominated by capital, which has become a spectacle of beings and things' (1995: 170). This appeal is, for Camatte (1995: 179), grounded in an invariant:[34] 'What is invariant is the desire to rediscover the lost community, which will not be realized by the recreation of the past but as an act of creation.'

Concluding comments

As a concluding note, I want now to make a number of interpretative and evaluative suggestions. Here, I feel that it is best to proceed by placing Camatte's later work within a tradition of thought that has come to be known as primitivism or sometimes anarcho-primitivism – even if those grouped under the heading would often reject the label.[35] Primitivism becomes a fairly widely known and frequently controversial sub-tradition within the Left communist field of discussion and debate from around the mid-1980s to the mid-1990s, after which it is progressively overtaken and eclipsed by the anarchist-leaning alternative-globalization current, wherein some of its themes continue to be visible. The English-speaking wing of this current includes figures such as Fredy Perlman,[36] John Zerzan,[37] John Moore and David Watson,[38] and the leading papers/journals associated with primitivist positions include *Fifth Estate, Green Anarchy, Species Traitor, Anarchy: A Journal of Desire Armed* and *Green Anarchist*. For those involved, Jacques Camatte's pioneering work appears to be significant and influential,[39] as are elements found in the work of a variety of other thinkers – for instance, Lewis Mumford, Martin Heidegger, Jacques Ellul, Ivan Illich, the thinkers of the Frankfurt School and the Situationists.

There is a wealth of different emphases to be found across what might plausibly be described as primitivism, and this makes it difficult to summarize tightly and without provoking objections, but it is worth making some generalizations in terms of key idea clusters/ themes. Primitivists tend to erect a multi-stranded critique of hierarchical, domination-ridden civilization – private property, class and caste divisions, the state, patriarchy. We have, in a sense, fallen from the grace of hunter-gatherer existence,[40] which is often looked back on in admiring accounts, drawn from anthropological work – these 'primitive' social orders characterized by community, equality, mutuality/connectedness with the natural world, and psychological and physical well-being. This fall is often dated to the time of the agricultural revolution – the foundational moment for private property, patriarchy and the state. Central in this fall is a transformed epistemological and practical orientation to the now *other* natural world – separation, instrumentalism, abstraction. Tied up with this are questions of science and the development of technique, which are seen as far from neutral and as tending to become autonomous and enchaining of human beings. In turn, this technique problem is linked to the fragmenting division of labour and to a generalized disempowerment, as human beings come to be more and more infantilized and dependent. The advent of private property, patriarchy and the state are also linked to militarism, conquest and genocide, and, less drastically, but also destructively, homogenization/mass cultural conformity. The ill-effects of this civilization, megamachine or Leviathan apparently worsen as modernity moves forward, leaving damaged, controlled, spiritless and aggressive human material in its wake; generating mass murder and ecological devastation; multiplying unfreedoms, deadening conformity and dominations.[41] The alternative to current civilization is the construction of 'future primitive' social configurations – reconnection with the natural world, decentralization, self-sufficiency, autarchy; a simpler, less technologically mediated form of life; a spiritual-intellectual re-enchantment aligned with the natural world (Davidson, 2009; Kinna, 2005; Millett, 2004; Williams, 2007); a tiger's leap away from the 'interlocking armoured juggernaut' – capital, technology, state (Bradford, 1989: 50).

The affinities between this primitivism and the post-1968 development of Camatte's thought should here be clear. Undoubtedly, for the reader newly encountering these ideas, a number of problems, common to Camatte and primitivists more widely, will also appear quick to hand. And, indeed, right from the start, critics leapt upon the deficiencies of primitivist thinking – the quickest response the question, 'We are to return to the caves, then?' (Gordon, 2008: 127). It is interesting to note in passing that some of the retorts[42] echoed certain much earlier clashes between Marxism and anarchism.[43] What are the main lines of this critical response? One major objection is the apolitical character of primitivism, which offers a one-sided portrait of humanity's long and deep fall into decadence, but provides only moral convictions and nostalgia as a means of addressing the predicament. In Camatte and a number of English-speaking primitivists, we get a picture of a world of total domination, of humanity at large imprisoned by the powerful machine of capital, which is the only remaining agent in the story – a version of the 'capitalocentrism' found among some Marxist thinkers, where only a miraculous leap backwards or catastrophe provide any hope of remaking the world. Perhaps, some critics have suggested, primitivists simply leave us with faith in the individualized, rebellious, purely ethical gestures of *l'homme révolté*, given that there is no clear subject here materially propelled to become agent of a transformatory movement. This, I would suggest, seems a not illogical conclusion when faced with Camatte's (1995: 62) contention that capital has now run away, even conquering the very last, intimate bastion of the imagination. What we seem to be offered, then, is a quite violent oscillation between complete despair, residency in a new 'grand hotel abyss' (the 'ruin of the contending classes'?), together with the most incredible optimism, required to sustain commitment to the enormous tasks of leaving this world. Bey's (1995) and Smith's (2010) astute readings point to the distinctly purifying impulse within a strand of thought so often inattentive to the many possibilities in the present, which is read so one-sidedly as a time of absolute contamination.

Unsurprisingly, the anti-science, anti-Enlightenment mood of primitivism has come in for a fair amount of searching critique – often in line with Marxian critiques of post-modern thought. Thus, from the later part of the 1980s, Murray Bookchin (1995a) directed his increasingly vehement polemics at primitivists, charging them with a wrongheaded blame of technology *per se*, an apolitical withdrawal inwards and a retreat to anti-rationalist, personalist, mystical and even fascistic, misanthropic positions.[44] Here, in a debate that seems likely to return in some form, Bookchin sought to play the Habermas to primitivism's Foucault, urging a completion rather than an abandonment of the modern project.

One might be tempted to view the primitivist current through the lens of Jonathan Friedman's (1995) analysis of the identity consequences of the systemic crisis of the world-system after the 1970s – with multi-polarity and global turbulence generating a range of new dominating identity impulses, including traditionalist re-rootings (ethnos, nation, doctrine, place) and primitivism (the revolt against rational civilization, championing of the natural, the libido, creative energy). Perhaps this is more tempting still in the light of the shedding of more conventional Left communist commitments by some of these authors, after the dispersal of hopes that followed the political and counter-cultural surges of the 1960s and 1970s.[45] Here, Camatte's starting point, Bordigism, begins to look as if it may have travelled better with time, in view of the current revival of interest in Marx, the apparent return of history and the resonant critique of democracy mounted, say, by Alain Badiou (2003a; 2005b; 2007a).

And yet, despite the melancholic, un-dialectical ticks one finds within primitivism, combined with an undeveloped secret optimism (Jacoby, 1981), there might be some elements worth salvaging or at least meditating upon at length within this 'maximalist' critique of current technological civilization (Gordon, 2008). I think we could safely say that there remains a strong popular current of ambivalence about technological development – not only with respect to the uncertain and risky ecological consequences of such development, but also with regard to the suspicion that it might be bound up with waning solidarity, disconnection, infantilization, weakening authenticity and the like.

In particular, the existentialist and communal being-centred notes sounded by primitivism are, I think, due something of a comeback – in line with the widespread dissatisfactions with the predominant liberal suspicions of commonality, obsessions with growth, profit, competition and an individuality wholly conditioned by the market – and it appears that, here, a primitivist thinker such as Jacques Camatte still has something to offer us, after the prohibitions of the anti-essentialist and triumphant liberal moments. We cannot avoid, I believe, saying something about human flourishing and the content of the good life (Levitas, 2013), just as socialists cannot help but attempt to say something truly distinctive about ecological questions. Before consigning this singular wing of Left contestation to the dustbin of history, we should perhaps pause and remember how many surprising affinities and re-emergences are to be found in the realm of history of ideas, a caution perhaps especially in order in the light of Keucheyan's (2013) acute observation that ours is a moment of energetic theoretical rediscovery and hybridization.

6
Anarchism as the Contemporary Spirit of Anti-Capitalism?: A Critical Survey of Recent Debates

Introduction

Mikhail Bakunin's last few years – following his dynamic, productive anarchist phase, running from the mid-1860s to the early 1870s (Shatz in Bakunin, 1990) – were far from happy. In a letter to the *Journal de Geneve* in 1874, Bakunin wrote that he felt 'neither the strength nor, perhaps, the confidence which are required to go on rolling Sisyphus's stone against the triumphant forces of reaction ... Henceforth I shall trouble no man's repose; and I ask, in my turn, to be left in peace' (in Woodcock, 1962: 169), explaining to Élisée Reclus the following year that 'there is absolutely no revolutionary thought, hope, or passion left among the masses' (in Dolgoff, 1972: 354). This gloom was materially well founded: the tragic end and reactionary aftermath of the Paris Commune; the acrimony and intrigue between the Bakuninites and the Marxists, culminating in Bakunin's expulsion from the First International; the split with Carlo Cafiero (who ended his days in madness, obsessed with the idea that he might be consuming more than his fair share of sunshine), amidst charges Bakunin had mismanaged the Italian's inheritance; the unfortunate entanglement with the nihilist Sergei Nechayev; the participation in the chaotic, doomed Bologna uprising of 1874, possibly in the hope of salvaging something with a heroic death (Joll, 1979; Marshall, 1992; Masters, 1974; Woodcock, 1962). These unhappy final years aside, perhaps it is possible that, at the end of the epic Marx–Bakunin bout,[1] we might be compelled to declare the anarchist the winner. This, at least, could be the implication if we are to take the current publication purchase of anarchism as any sort of scorecard.

In this 'cottage industry' (in Franks, 2007: 127) of work since the pro-test events in Seattle at the 1999 World Trade Organization's Ministerial Conference, anarchism tends to be viewed as something like the spirit of contemporary anti-capitalism – see David Graeber (2011), for instance, speaking of Occupy Wall Street's 'anarchist roots'. Thus, Gordon (2008: 2) talks of a 'full revival of a global anarchist movement on a scale and on levels of unity and diversity unseen since the 1930s'; Purkis and Bowen (2004a: 5) view anarchism as being given a new lease of life by the newest movements (those associated with 'anti-globalization'), forc-ing overdue attention to 'the most idealistic, complicated and contra-dictory political philosophy to have emerged from the Enlightenment' (2004b: 213); and Newman (2011b: 314) declares that we are presently at 'an anarchist moment'. Thus, a host of anarchist-themed journals, events and books – often bridging, or seeking to bridge, an academic–activist divide – have appeared in recent years.[2]

Responding to an earlier phase of re-awakened attention to anarchism in the 1960s, a surprised Eric Hobsbawm read the phenomenon as an explicable outcome of the crisis of post-Stalin communism, student dis-content and the then bare revolutionary horizon, uncharitably suggest-ing that anarchism's intellectual primitiveness had proven a strength in the face of the rebellions of the late 1960s – 'an occasion when only the blind chicken was in a position to find the grain of corn' (1973: 87). In the 1960s Hobsbawm continued an earlier line that had interpreted early Spanish anarchism as categorizable together with a range of other forms of social organization of 'pre-political people who have not yet found, or only begun to find, a specific language in which to express their aspirations about the world' (Hobsbawm, 1963: 2). More impres-sive in social ambition than, say, social banditry, Spanish anarchism had produced little of intellectual interest beyond 'hedge-preachers' and 'village priests' and was, all-up, a modern mass millenarian movement, an outcome of modern conditions, but certainly no answer to them – he judged the history of anarchism, overall, as one of 'unrelieved failure' (1963: 83, 92).

I will return to a number of these issues (the relevance of the move-ments of the 1960s, Marxian 'failure', political and geo-political changes, and questions of class and agency) and to the persistent Marxism–anarchism debate, but what are we to make of this rather impressive revival of interest? In this chapter, I move from the anar-chistic inclinations of primitivism to anarchism more widely and conventionally understood, seeking to explore this new literature, and beginning by reflecting on the meaning of anarchism and on its major transformations, as a backdrop against which to consider our own 'anarchist moment'. I then turn to two affinities that are often appealed to as making anarchism relevant to activists and to academics: an affinity between anarchism and what has been happening 'on the streets' within the alternative globalization movement; and an affinity between anarchism and the post-modern thought that has been so influential in seminar rooms across the human sciences. These affinities, as well as the scope and energy of much of this literature, make anarchism worthy of greater intellectual attention. Nevertheless, I will argue that this work continues to demonstrate the fruitfulness of emphases more characteristic of the Marxian tradition and suggests the importance of, and interest potentially contained in, a new round of Marxian–anarchist dialogue in addressing central political and intellectual dilemmas.

Narrating anarchism – devices, unity and change

I want to begin by thinking about the ways in which anarchism is narrated and, first of all, with four common introductory framing devices, openings typical of both popular and academic treatments of anarchism. The first device is definitional, which often serves as a way of heading off the immediate association of anarchy with violent disorder; for instance, in Ward's (2004) gentle, concise introduction, anarchism is simply contrary to authority, the condition of being without ruler. We shall see soon that even this apparently straightforward launching point comes into question today among anarchist-leaning intellectuals.

The second device is what Newman (2010: 1) appeals to as the 'anarchist invariant'. This, again, can function to close down quick, negative assumptions, with the desire for a life without government posited as continually reappearing throughout history (Newman, 2010: 1). Thus, in Peter Marshall's (1992) mammoth survey, we find anarchist impulses, for example, in Taoism, Buddhism and Greek Antiquity. Once more, this device might be found wanting today, at odds with dominant theoretical emphases, because the assertion of 'anarchist invariance' appears to have a suspiciously 'essentialist' quality. A variant of this device is to insist that anarchism is always already here – as Ward (1988: 14) puts it, like a seed beneath the snow – wherever people are organizing together in ways that are voluntary, functional, temporary and small.

The third device, a 'difference device', has a post-modern taste to it, underscoring plurality, multiplicity, complexity. Thus, readers will often be reminded that we are speaking of *many* anarchisms rather than a singular anarchism. This multiplicity is perhaps especially important in the case of a tradition that has so often been associated with extreme individuation – bringing to mind William Godwin's suggestion that even participating in a musical ensemble might negatively affect creative self-direction.

On this note, the last device is an appeal to 'intellectual credentials' – partially in contradiction of the notion of anarchist invariance, and also of the frequent anarchist pride in being without commitment to a pantheon of professorial gods[3] – to a relatively systematic set of ideas found within a classical canon, founded by a small number of dead, white, males – for instance, Godwin (1756–1836), Pierre Joseph Proudhon (1809–65), Bakunin (1814–76) and Petr Kropotkin (1842–1921).[4]

Connected to these questions of definitions, locations, differences and canons is the question of what holds anarchism together as a family of ideas, a coherent set of practices or a culture. Rejection of the state has been the answer that looms largest here. As Klausen and Martel (2011) note, perhaps today this anti-statism seems less compelling, in the face of what many commentators describe as the withering of the state under the force of neo-liberal globalization. That is, one line of argument holds that, at this point in capitalism's trajectory, some variety of defence of the sovereign state, or at least of certain state-sponsored institutions, is the only progressive tactic for those on the Left. One possible anarchist response to this is to see the state as having been rendered completely irrelevant as a tool of even a mildly ameliorative politics and more and more a simple committee for managing the affairs of the ruling elite, with steeply escalating post-democratic and repressive (surveillance, political policing, incarceration) tendencies everywhere. On this score, in some contemporary anarchist literature the state is portrayed as looking, in certain ways, increasingly like it did in the period of anarchism's nineteenth-century emergence.

These important issues aside, the tendency in recent work has been to consider anarchism's unity as an intellectual-political formation in a manner that is more wide-ranging than anti-statism. For instance, for Jun (2012: 107) anarchism is, above all, a movement against 'representationalism'. I will return later to this problematic notion. More useful, I think, is Gordon's (2008) enumeration of three idea clusters to approach anarchism's stable core: the concept of domination; a set of commitments to direct action and prefigurative politics; and a commitment to diversity and open-endedness, an inclination, that is, to perpetual experimentation. The prevailing emphases attached to these idea clusters – direct action, consensus-seeking, grassroots alternatives, decentralization, spontaneity, diversity, flexibility, affinity, a concern with means, liberty and opposition to hierarchy, authority, domination (Epstein, 2001; Gordon, 2008; Grubacic and Graeber, 2004) – give us, I think, a helpful snapshot of anarchism as a tradition.

Unsurprisingly, when we examine the ways in which anarchism has played itself out over time, at its cycles and sequences, things become more complicated. One way of anchoring anarchism would be to set it against Marxism, and we have compelling material to work from here in Marx's confrontations with Proudhon, Stirner and, above all, Bakunin (see, for instance, Thomas, 1980). Yet, despite Bakunin's expulsion from the First International, the demarcations separating Marxists and anarchists were unclear for a long while (Cole, 1954), with the anarchists – Kropotkin, Landauer, Michel, Malatesta, Reclus, Nieuwenhuis and others – participating in the Second International between 1889 and their expulsion at the London Congress of 1896,[5] insisting that they, too, as socialists, should be involved (Braunthal, 1966; Foster, 1955; Joll, 1966; Woodcock, 1962). Despite the difficulties involved, however, already by this point a number of patterns and tendencies were discernable. One issue here is that of national specificity, because it has been the case that anarchism has flourished in certain quarters and not in others. Early on, Bakunin had particular success in Spain, Italy and Switzerland, and anarchism was to make its presence felt, at various points, in France, Russia, Latin America (Malatesta spent four years in Argentina, something, as Anderson [2005] points out, that would have been unthinkable for Marx or Engels), and to an extent, in China and Japan, while it was unable to penetrate significantly into north-western Europe (with the exception of Holland) (Hobsbawm, 1973). The most well-travelled explanatory route for this pattern relates to class – the more extensive industrial working class of northern Europe, the anarchist appeal to the artisan and the peasant, as well as the attraction the emphasis on individual freedom was to hold for writers and artists (particularly marked in France) (Anderson, 2005). So, for instance, the particular strength of anarchism in Spain has been linked to the slow industrialization, authoritarian politics and intense localism of that country at the time (Hobsbawm, 1973).

A second issue in considering patterns of anarchism involves three noteworthy tendencies, which crystallized in the late nineteenth and early twentieth centuries. The first and most persistent (the anarchist mainstream, according to Ward [2004]) – if not the most impressive in mass movement terms – is anarcho-communism. First mentioned in the mid-1870s by Francois Dumartheray, and adopted by the Jura Federation in 1880, anarcho-communism could be viewed as an evolutionary development out of Bakunin's later collectivist work and that of his close collaborator James Guillaume, the resemblance especially clear in the latter's 'On Building the New Social Order', for example (Dolgoff, 1972; Fleming, 1979; Pengam, 1987). It is most closely associated with Reclus, Malatesta and, particularly, Kropotkin (in *The Conquest of Bread*), while, in my memory at least, one of the most attractive and persuasive attempts at popularization was provided somewhat later by Alexander Berkman's 1929 work, *What Is Communist Anarchism?* This strand of thought combines systematic critique of state and capital, often bolstered with close attention to questions of anarchist/communist transition.

Concurrent with this is a second tendency – the notorious period and tactic of 'propaganda by the deed'. Arguably traceable to the Benevento affair of 1877, an uprising that Malatesta and Cafiero and a handful of others instigated or, alternatively, to stormy developments in Russia in the same period, this line of development must be viewed as an expression of the post-Commune intensification of capitalism, autocracy and imperialism; its recourse to targeted violence against authorities was viewed by its adherents as a tool that would intimidate elites and ignite the flame of rebellion among the popular classes (Anderson, 2005; Guerin, 1970; Joll, 1979). Blossoming after the close of the 1870s, this strand of anarchism is associated with names such as Duval, Ravachol, Vaillant, Caserio, Henry, Lucheni, Bresci and Czolgosz, with Italians playing a significant role; it drew support from central anarchist thinkers such as Reclus and Kropotkin, and achieved some spectacular successes – targets included royals, police chiefs and heads of state – as well as having the dubious honour of acting as a model for the nationalist assassins that were to follow (Anderson, 2005). As Anderson (2005: 4) notes, we can see these actions as an early form of suicide bombing by those who viewed themselves as 'acting for a world audience'.

The third tendency, anarcho-syndicalism, begins to take hold as the period of propaganda by the deed of the 1880s and 1890s receded (Cole, 1954), emerging and peaking in different places between the 1890s and 1940, a mass, more organized movement (van der Linden and Thorpe, 1990). With its emblem of revolutionary unions of workers as both fighting organizations and the basis of the new social order, emphasizing direct action and the general strike and rejecting, often fervently, state politics and reformism, this tactic was expounded by Fernand Pelloutier in 1895 and is seen, by some, as having been born with the unification of the Bourses and the CGT in France in 1902, to be followed, particularly significantly, with the CNT (1910) in Spain and the USI (1912) in Italy (Sonn, 1992; van der Linden and Thorpe, 1990). Achieving its high-point in France before the First World War, and elsewhere (the US, Holland, Germany and Italy) in the period 1916–23, anarcho-syndicalism re-emerged spectacularly in Spain, and particularly in Catalonia, in the 1920s and 1930s.

Defeat in the Spanish Civil War is frequently viewed as the final chapter of anarchism's heroic period. In most narratives, anarchism is depicted as confined thereafter to small – though this is not to say stagnant (Cornell, 2011; Sonn, 1992) – activist and bohemian pockets. However, as previously indicated, an anarchist quality was often identified in the upheavals of the 1960s – it was viewed either negatively, as spontaneous, lacking organization and direction, and hedonistic, or positively, as indicative of a libertarian break from the dominance of Bolshevism. This manifestation is captured, for instance, in Gombin's (1975) discussion of the flavour of the rebellions of this period in France under the heading 'modern Leftism'. The most well-known of the explicitly anarchist thinkers coming to prominence from this point are undoubtedly Noam Chomsky – relentless critic of US foreign policy – and Murray Bookchin, a prolific and combative public intellectual who developed an ecologically informed anarchist municipalist stance, which, despite its expansive, systematic and tenacious qualities, remained only modestly influential.

Today – in the streets and the seminar rooms

Today's anarchist revival, as mentioned, is sometimes linked to this 1960s New Leftism (Cornell, 2011; Epstein, 2001), often in terms of both intellectual tendencies and modes of political action. Here I want to return to those two affinities noted in my introductory remarks and explore some of the qualities of this revival of interest in anarchism, in the streets (more briefly) and in the seminar rooms, examining a number of difficult questions characteristic of our 'anarchist moment'.

Anarchism as alternative globalization

For a start, numerous commentators have noted the presence of something akin to an 'anarchist sensibility', a 'soft and fluid form of anarchism' (Epstein, 2001), within the alternative globalization movement or movements. Both Epstein (2001) and Grubacic and Graeber (2004), for instance, note that while participants in this movement seldom explicitly describe themselves in this fashion, a core of anarchist principles and impulses animate the thinking and practice of those involved. Important aspects of this are the prominence of non-violent direct action, smaller, autonomous (but sometimes flexibly linked) 'affinity' groups and consensus decision-making within the movement (Epstein, 2001). These emphases were visible, for example, in the highly planned, co-ordinated and successful activities around the Direct Action Network, in its attempt to shut down the WTO meeting in Seattle in 1999 (Gabay, 2010).

In related fashion, an anarchist sensibility is also evident in what Epstein (2001) describes as the 'morally charged and expressive politics' contained within the alternative globalization movement, connected to the very creative, sometimes playful, desire to put values into practice. Linked with the notion of prefiguration (living other-wise), the role of humour and 'carnivalesque dissent' (de Goede, 2005: 381) (for example, ironic slogans and chants, The Yes Men, revolutionary anarchist clowns), aspects of do-it-yourself culture (informational politics, becoming the media, for instance) and more existentially oriented contestations (activism around consumption) – all of these impulses have important anarchistic resonances and appear at some distance from more traditional Marxian modes of political intervention.

Equally distant from Marxian orthodoxy are the emphases on consensus and decentralization that many have detected within the newest movements. A key inspiration, here, has been the Zapatista movement, with Subcomandante Marcos explicitly rejecting vanguardism, denying he is leader of the movement, rejecting power seizure and emphasizing instead the participatory organization of society (Franks, 2010; Grubabic and Graeber, 2004; Lynd and Grubabic, 2008; Marcos, 2001). Apparently breaking from the Leninist dictum that there can only be 'one struggle ... one theory ... one leadership' (May, 1994: 21), we find emphases across the alternative globalization movement on participatory or high-intensity democracy (Santos, 2005b), pluralism and open structures, compromise and synthesis, and horizontal rather than vertical organization (Grubacic and Graeber, 2004; Santos, 2005b; Tormey, 2004).

In a similar way, we also see in initiatives – often most developed in semi-peripheral countries – linked to alternative globalization that attempt to organize another type of production, separate from neoliberal capitalism and statist socialism, and often centred around principles of democracy, solidarity, equity and environmental sustainability (Santos and Rodriguez-Garavito, 2006): variously – decommodification; alternative development schemes; re-localization; new forms of capital control proposals; co-operatives; movements for ethical consumption;

new forms of labour internationalism; and organization of marginal workers and other excluded groups. Again, such initiatives are frequently viewed as prefigurative and as reminiscent more of anarchist than of Marxian forms of action.

The many dilemmas and difficulties surrounding the alternative globalization movement have been the subject of extensive discussion, within and beyond the social movement literature. I now turn at greater length to consider the intimately connected questions around that second affinity I have mentioned, between anarchism and post-modern thought, especially contained in the notion of 'post-anarchism'. This is a topic of considerable interest, I suggest, a door to more detailed consideration of the distinctive character and claims of anarchism today and, because of its position with respect to other social theories and pressing theoretical issues – hegemony, universalism and particularism, essentialism, power – of great interest to those within the human sciences.

Rethinking classical anarchism

A persistent and foundational issue of contention within the contemporary academic literature might be captured as 'an inheritance in question' – the problem of the relationship between today's and yesterday's anarchism, an obstinate theme, for instance, in Rousselle and Evran's *Post-Anarchism: A Reader* (2011) and in Kinna's *Continuum Companion to Anarchism* (2012). On the one side are those who suggest that a simple return to the anarchist classics is out of the question, particularly in light of the developments (progress?) that have occurred in the world of social theory. Thus, Koch (2011: 39) claims that 'Post-structuralism offers a new opportunity to reformulate the claims of anarchism'. The most prominent contemporary thinkers to advance this position are Todd May[6] and, particularly, Saul Newman. For Newman (2010: 4), post-anarchism is a project that promises to radicalize and renew anarchism, a kind of deconstructive enterprise that works at the limits of anarchism. Insisting on the always 'heterodox' and 'diffuse' character of anarchism, Newman (2010: 1) nevertheless charges that certain predominant tendencies found within the anarchist tradition need to be decisively abandoned – the essentialism of the subject, the universality of reason, the dialectical view of history,[7] the positivism, the naive approach to power, the attachment to necessity in history and to the idea of progress – in short, an Enlightenment humanism that can no longer withstand the strong questioning provided by post-modernism. Indeed, a good case can be made, I believe, that across what is often called classical anarchism we find appeals to the authority of science and the notion of universal laws, to an understanding of human nature or society as organic (in opposition to the artifice of the state), to a fairly straightforward conception of the operation of power, and to a conception of history as unfolding in a progressive direction.

In opposition to such 'sins of modernist theorizing' (McLennan, 1996), Newman (2010) assembles a number of more contemporary theoretical tools and emphases to support the formulation of a recharged anarchism: from Stirner, a non-essentialist view of the subject; from Laclau and Mouffe, the emphasis on contingency, as against assumptions of the stability, coherence and systematicity of the social; from Foucault, a focus on micro-power, and an insistence that power is, and will remain, everywhere, unable to be exclusively, or in large part, reduced to state power; from psychoanalysis, an interest in the psychic attachments to power; from Balibar, an emphasis on 'equal-liberty' as anarchism's driving ambition; from Levinas, an an-archical ethical focus. I think it's worth examining some of this more closely.

To begin with, the use of Stirner already suggests possible doubts about certain kinds of post-anarchist claims about the flawed Enlightenment humanism of classical anarchism. Similarly, the appearance in this literature (for instance, Day [2005] or Gaarder [2009]) of Gustav Landauer's injunction that the state is, above all else, a *relation*, raises questions, as does Landauer's (1978: 54) impassioned appeals to spirit over the arguments of the 'scientific swindlers', his anti-productivism, his scepticism about progress (is 1908 really better than 1907, he asks). In like fashion, Emma Goldman might not mesh with post-anarchist contentions, given her Nietzschean enthusiasms, given the advocacy of 'ceaseless epistemological and political change' (Bertalan, 2011: 209) we arguably find in her work. There are even questions to be raised about Kropotkin – for instance, his insistence that anarchism was perfectly compatible with 'variety, conflict' (in Antliff, 2011: 161; Jun, 2011). And was Bakunin, in fact, naively optimistic about human nature – his assertion that anyone participating in government would change completely – and science – his emphasis on the imperfection of science, his doubts about Marxian appeals to science, his suggestion that, in some respects, art was a superior mode of knowing (Bakunin, 1973; Bakunin in Maximoff, 1953)?

Raising such doubts, Franks (2007: 128), for instance, maintains that post-anarchist discourse simply misrepresents classical anarchism,[8] that everything the former try to market as a new way for anarchism to forge ahead was always already there in what has, since its inception, been a very 'flexible constellation of principles, theories, discourses and practices'. In conclusion, post-anarchism is 'a variant' and 'not a transcendence' of classical anarchism (Franks, 2007: 128). On a related note, Jason Adams (2003: 1) has made the pertinent suggestion that we are reading things the wrong way around, in that post-structuralism was itself an expression of the anarchist-flavoured rebellions of the 1960s: the anti-authoritarian spirit of anarchism 'mutated into a thousand different miniviruses, infecting all of these critical theories in many different ways' (2003: 6). A similar but more controversial line is taken by Jun. Arguing the need to clear the 'detritus' of post-anarchism, Jun (2012: xiv) contends that anarchism calls into question the entire framework of political modernity – the 'state fixation', universal and transcendent solutions, normativity. Rejecting out of hand the idea of classical anarchism as 'mythical', Jun finds what he takes as the defining feature of post-modernity, the refusal of representationalism, spread evenly across anarchist thinkers from the nineteenth century, brought together, too, by their positive emphasis on immanence and vitality.[9]

Jun is clearly, I would suggest, 'bending the stick' too far. I just do not think these assertions – that, across the anarchist thinkers he mentions, there is a uniform *absence* of fixed views of human nature, of uncritical worship of science, of attempts to represent what is, of a conception of power emerging from a unitary centre, of universalization, and the like – stand up to scrutiny. More broadly, we might also wonder, placing post-modern *doxa* aside for a moment, why an appeal to the inherent goodness of people (co-operative, empathetic, uncomfortable with inequality and suffering), to the ordinary anarchism that operates here and now, is necessarily bad, at the least as a rhetorical strategy, given the omnipresence of the neo-liberal view that human beings are straightforwardly self-centred, competitive, acquisitive and aggressive. Does not this more optimistic humanist language still have plenty of political and moral purchase?

Politics today – hegemony, power, democracy, ethics

Another variety of response to post-anarchist arguments has been that it is *anarchism* that is in the position to draw attention to, and provide resources for amending, the various shortcomings of post-structuralist and post-modern thought (Antliff, 2011). This type of reply might be a signal of certain anti-intellectual, or – perhaps better – pro-activist, non-academic tendencies to be found within the new literature on anarchism. Thus, Gordon (2008: 43) dismisses post-structuralist anarchism as a mere 'intellectual preoccupation' that scarcely touches upon activist concerns, seeking instead, with his *Anarchy Alive*, to write an 'anarchist book about anarchism' (2008: 3), and closely tying theory to activists and their dilemmas. Thus, concern with the issue of co-optation is a major sub-theme in the rather academic-oriented Amster et al. (2009) anthology. Thus, we sometimes find a curiously apologetic tone from writers involved in activism but evidently concurrently pursuing academic studies, with numerous nervous disclaimers and uncomfortable situatings of self – 'Male, young, white, university graduate, precarious worker, activist' (de Rota, 2011: 139).[10] On a related front, one mode of critical retort to post-anarchism has been to draw attention to its supposed Eurocentric and masculinist biases, biases against which anarchists are urged to respond with 'unlearning' and a thoroughgoing commitment to decolonization (Jeppesen, 2011: 152). Here, while mobilization around marginalized indigenous groups and related questionings of Western-centred forms of knowledge have clearly been important within the alternative globalization movement (Santos, 2005b), I believe that the fitting together of anarchist universalism with assertive status group identity politics[11] remains a tricky and unresolved problem.

One way of reading this question of particularism and universalism is that it is an issue of articulation and hegemony. Indeed, part of what appears to be taking place in discussions of post-anarchism is congruent with debates around post-Marxism, where problems of unity amidst diversity loom large. In fact, in thinking anarchism today, a number of commentators are explicitly or implicitly drawing from Laclau and Mouffe.[12] This is true, for instance, of Simon Critchley (2009) who says he has gone in the direction of anarchism as a result of frustration with Marxism and who, in his recent book, *Infinitely Demanding* (2007), brings together a range of resources, which include, very prominently, emphases from the authors of *Hegemony and Socialist Strategy*: insisting on the current multiplication of subject positions, against the Marxian notion of the progressive simplification of class structure; speaking of the contingency of capitalism and of interminable dislocation; and arguing for the centrality of the notion of 'hegemonic universality'. In like fashion, Mueller (2011: 77) finds anarchistic resonances in Gramsci's notion of creating 'sustainable communities of resistance'.

On the other hand, Day (2005; 2011) seeks to contest the 'hegemony of hegemony', the assumption that significant social change can 'only be achieved through the deployment of universalizing hierarchical forms, epitomized by the nation state, but including conceptions of the world state and other globalized institutions as well' (2011: 96).

Day's argument is that the terrain on which radical politics operates has shifted with the failure of the new social movements to prevent the progress of neo-liberalism, and with the rise of the novelties within the alternative globalization movement (visible, say, in the practices of the Zapatistas, Indymedia and Food Not Bombs). There has been a shift, he maintains, away from the attempt to create a new power around a hegemonic centre towards a 'politics of the act' (rather than that of the demand) – an affinity-based, direct-action politics, which is beyond both reform and revolution (in its prefigurative emphasis) and 'challenges', 'disrupts' and 'disorients' hegemonic politics (Day, 2011).[13] In a similar way, remarking on the affinities between post-anarchism and the work of Laclau and Mouffe (a wider conception of domination, for example), Newman (2010; 2011a) notes and contests the underlying centralism (connected to the importance lent to the notion of representation) of their thought, the prominence of leadership in Laclau's analysis of populism, and Mouffe's capitulation to a conservative cynical realism in her attempt to work from the materials provided by Carl Schmitt.

In social theory and political philosophy in recent years, and under the influence of post-modern anti-foundationalism, a number of efforts have been made to rethink politics or 'the political' – Laclau and Mouffe's post-Marxism being one particularly influential version. This rethinking has frequently been of a rather abstract, meta-theoretical type, characterized by attempts to rid political reflection of essentialism, determinism and teleology, and it has tended to emerge in analyses close to Claude Lefort's argument about the distinctly modern emptying of the place of power. And there is certainly a strong flavour of such lines of argumentation in post-anarchist discussions – for instance, in Critchley, Newman, Jun and May – which is often coupled with more familiar political theoretical themes – power, the state, democracy – again, though, examined under post-modern lights.

Arguably, the most defining theme of anarchism has been its equation of power with the state and with unfreedom. After Foucault, though, a more nuanced appreciation of power has apparently become necessary, evident in Gordon's (2008), and others', re-specification of anarchist objections as opposition to domination. Here, anarchism is sometimes touted as more in line than other radical traditions with Foucauldian subtleties, because of its early advocacy of decentralized resistance, its awareness of the ills of multivalent hierarchy and its attachments to a range of prefigurative, here-and-now and processual political actions (Bowen, 2004). In particular, these anarchist themes are said to contrast sharply with a 'day-of-the-great-sweep', revolutionary, strategic and centralized Marxian political focus.

Once again, the rhetorical intent here is to proclaim the contemporariness of anarchism – for instance, in its affinities with the apparent convergence of 'radical feminist, ecological, anti-racist and queer struggles ... in the late 1990s' (Gordon, 2008: 31). It can also be seen as again recalling Landauer's focus on the state as a relation rather than a solid entity (Graeber, 2004). I think, though, it is worth remarking here on what I would argue is the obvious awkwardness of attempting to combine anarchism and its historical attention to the state with a Foucauldian desire to jettison outdated analyses of sovereign power for a focus on the ubiquity and micro-quality of contemporary power – a course that might be seen as even more difficult for anarchists than for Marxists to take. A related disjuncture appears to be created when gestures to Foucault, micro-power and the necessary break from the simple-minded classical anarchist opposition between state and society are combined, say, in Newman (2010: 29-30; 2011b), with assertions about a contemporary situation of 'naked power' in which democratic states are increasingly becoming 'authoritarian police states'. Having said this, the opposition to normalization and the attention to governmentality apparently works well with anarchism, as do the Deleuze and Guattari tropes such as excess, lines of flight, overcoding, nomadism, antagonistic desire and becoming-other (de Rota, 2011; Heckert, 2011).[14]

The argument, then, presented by those seeking to bring anarchism together with post-modern thinking is that, at their best, anarchists help us grasp the autonomy of the state, teach us that, today, there is no Winter Palace to storm (Beilharz, 2005b) (the state, now, as 'dispersed and differentiated'), remind us to be permanently suspicious of all forms of authority and demonstrate that power is everywhere and, as Foucault put it, 'everything is dangerous' (Newman, 2010: 169, 63). What might contemporary anarchism offer us in thinking about democracy? A common historical line has been to raise scepticism about mere state forms and to appeal to some more genuine democracy but, alongside this, we might appear to be transported to some place *other* than democracy with the persistent anarchist focus on individual freedom, the emphasis on direct action, and the commitments to decentralization and consensus. This clearly remains a very difficult and sometimes embarrassing question, which, I think, is rather lightly and ineffectively dealt with in this new literature. Newman (2010), for instance, equates post-anarchism with a politics of autonomy, equates this autonomy with democracy and, at the same time, apparently means by democracy Derrida's 'democracy to come' or, in another formulation, the 'democracy of singularities'. This reluctance about institutions can certainly seem solidly anti-vanguardist, and it sensibly refuses rigid blueprints of the future, but is it helpful? Similar are Simon Critchley's (2007) appeals to the young Marx's (by way of Abensour) notion of 'true democracy'. For Critchley, at least for now, there is no path beyond the state, which is insinuating itself into ever more areas of life. Given this, the most promising response, says Critchley, is to attempt to create spaces at a distance from the state ('interstitial distance') within state territory by way of such true democratization. This democratization is understood, following Rancière, as a disturbance of order and consensus, here and now, upon the 'terrain on which we stand, live, work, act, think' (Critchley, 2007: 114).

This may all seem unobjectionable for the already converted, but it clearly needs some meat added to its bones. One way in which Critchley and others have sought to provide this flesh is by turning to ethics – Critchley (2009: 8), for instance, summarizing anarchism as, above all, a 'set of ethical concerns with practice'.[15] For Critchley, Day (2005) and Newman (2010), the work of Emmanuel Levinas can help us, here. The attraction of Levinas resides, at least in part, as an alternative to a too-libertarian anarchist conception of the subject and of freedom, in favour of a 'relational and communal' (Newman, 2010: 55) understanding of liberty. In addition, the prerogative given by Levinas to ethics appears to offer a brake that might prevent the dangerous inflation of politics to everything. Critchley's (2007) account is the most developed, seeking to prioritize responsibility over the old imaginary of unlimited freedom, a responsibility based on our encounter with the other, an encounter that 'dividuates' us from ourselves, showing us our limited self-mastery, inauthenticity and ridiculous failures. The ethics of commitment that this Levinasian anarchism promises, Critchley (2007: 7) hopes, might allow us to 'face and face down the drift of the present'.

One reply to such Levinas-influenced accounts is provided by Žižek (2005) and Badiou (2001) who charge that such an intellectualist ethics is completely inoperative – one part of their assault on what had appeared to be a new academic-theoretical commonsense around human finitude, limits, responsibility, post-secular tolerance and human rights moralism, the so-called 'ethical turn' in social thought (Garber et al., 2000).

Post-anarchism, radical academia, the disciplines and Marxism

At this juncture, it seems relevant to deal with the ways in which post-anarchist discourse has intersected with the radical thought that has succeeded post-structuralism and that might provide resources or competition for anarchism's bid for attention – especially the work of Hardt and Negri, Badiou and Rancière. Here, Newman (2011a: 52) argues that despite a 'general and somewhat perplexing silence about anarchism', there are a number of important anarchist themes in the work of these thinkers: variously – a break from the industrial working class as privileged agent of change; a wider focus on domination; the notion of a politics without parties; and a thoroughgoing opposition to the state. With respect to Badiou, both Newman and Critchley see the notion of the 'Event' as too rare and grandiose, an 'implicit vanguardism' (Newman, 2011a: 53) that discounts the possibilities alive in ordinary events and politics; and Newman argues that both Badiou and Žižek dangerously and reactively respond to liberal concerns by fetishizing revolutionary violence. In the case of Hardt and Negri, Newman (2011a: 57) sees the concept of the multitude as 'a dressed up version of the Marxist theory of proletarian emancipation' and rejects their 'immanentism', which posits emancipation as an automatic result of the unfolding of capitalism. We have seen, finally, that Critchley draws on Rancière (as do May [2009] and Newman), and Rancière (2008) himself notes the ties between his thought and historical anarchism. Certain kinship connections are indeed suggested by Rancière's emphases on the presupposition of equality, dissensus and anti-vanguardism, and by his focus on current forms of opposition rather than future-oriented programmes. However, it seems to me that Rancière's commitment to anarchist-inflected forms of political action are unaccompanied by anything like an anarchist *vision* of an emancipated future, a world free of police.

Arguably, the literature surveyed above furnishes us with at least some of the important elements of a reconstructed anarchist political-intellectual orientation and, here and there, this is combined with some attempts to trace the shape of an explicitly anarchist academic theory. Graeber (2004), for instance – though underscoring the need for low (around immediate questions linked to political action) rather than high theory (Grubacic and Graeber, 2004) – very imaginatively sets out a number of key *problematiques* for an anarchist anthropology. These would include an analysis of the state as a relation between a utopian imaginary and a messy reality of flight and evasion, elite action, etc., a proper theory of wage labour, an ecology of voluntary associations, a theory of political happiness and an attention to uncovering the already extant counter-powers to state and market across space (against Eurocentrism) and time (questioning, after Latour, the solidity of our modernity).[16] In like fashion, Purkis (2004) provides a Bauman-esque critique of sociology as being in the business of modern knowing, ordering and controlling, and he identifies a number of tools useful in the construction of an anarchist sociology:[17] Feyerabend's 'anarchist epistemology'; post-colonial critiques of Eurocentrism in the social sciences; the feminist questioning of objectivist methodological precepts; and chaos theory (especially its critique of hierarchical, predictable and generalized theories in favour of non-linear, non-determinist, non-reductionist emphases).[18]

In these kinds of proposals for an anarchist presence in the disciplines, an obvious point to make is that anarchism has not had the success of Marxism in the academy (Graeber, 2004; Purkis, 2004). This could be either a source of pride or resentment among anarchists: pride, in that this could be explained by anarchism's predominantly practical, down-to-earth, worldly and activist character; or resentment, in that anarchism deserves as much credit, can compete on the same terrain, is every bit as intellectually rigorous and morally compelling and so on – although unburdened by Marxism's authoritarianism and dogmatism. It is evidently timely to return to this long-postponed issue – Marxism versus anarchism.

Frequently, an important rhetorical step in the contemporary anarchist plea for reconsideration is to represent the contemporary political field as marked by the resolute and final defeat of anarchism's major historical competitor on the Left. Marxist failures are posited as manifold and crushing: for instance, its notion of a single antagonism (class), against an increasingly complex and contingent reality; its productionism, set before looming ecological catastrophe; its naivety about the state as a tool of emancipation; its vanguardism; and its indifference to ethical reflection, all in evidence in Stalinist totalitarianism (Critchley, 2007; Newman, 2010; Purkis and Bowen, 2004a). However, as Evren (2011) notes in his introduction to *Post-Anarchism: A Reader*, the emblem of Marxist failure is no argument for or against anything, especially as anarchism can hardly contrast this with a history of anything that could reasonably be counted as 'success'. The relentless hostility to the Marxian tradition often found in this new body of anarchist re-thinking can be perplexing, especially as this tends to stand cheek by jowl with emphases on pluralism, experimentation and tolerant, pragmatic attentiveness to other modes of thought and ways of being.

Of course, this unsympathetic boot has very often been on the other foot, as indicated by my earlier reference to Hobsbawm (1973) – the British historian limiting anarchism's entire worth to a rather back-handed compliment about its sensitivity to spontaneous elements in mass movements. Far too seldom have Marxists remarked on, let alone analysed at length, the frequent instances when they and the anar-chists were at least roughly on the same page. This convergence can be seen, for instance, in the concerns within the Third International around 'anarchist' tendencies, such as those represented by *Marxian* currents attached to names such as Pannekoek, Bordiga and Luxemburg (Hobsbawm, 1973).

The polemics on both sides are unhelpful, as well as frequently wildly inaccurate: on the one side, Marxism versus anarchism as a story of authoritarianism, vanguardism and statism versus liberty, spontane-ity and autonomy; on the other, a story of organization, intellectual clarity and persistence versus shambolic, capricious and individualistic politics. Thankfully, there are contemporary voices speaking to a move beyond such simplifications. For instance, the conversation between Lynd and Grubacic (2008) involves discussion of the 'Haymarket syn-thesis', the periodic coming together – for example, in Chicago in the late nineteenth century, then again with the Wobblies (IWW) – of Marxian and anarchist emphases. Similarly, reflecting on the alternative globalization movement, Santos (2006; 2008) suggests that the current period is neither anarchist nor Marxist, but instead the moment of the making of a new global Left.[19] This global Left has at its educative and strategic disposal a rich and variegated socialist tradition, and – while, within this Left, people will certainly continue to emerge from and lean towards particular socialisms rather than others – for reasons of changing generations, and in the hope of making inroads, a clear-cut segmentation of socialist currents seems both unlikely and of little help today (Epstein, 2001; Santos, 2008).

Concluding comments

There is a good argument to be made, I think, that, both in terms of political life and the orientations within the human sciences, the old is dying but the new cannot yet emerge. This in-betweenness presents us with an experimental, promising moment (Badiou, 2008a), both in pol-itics and social thought. It is a virtue of this new anarchist literature that it straddles both, that, in its efforts to retrieve a much neglected radical tradition of thought, it positions itself at the intersection between recent contestatory social movements and contemporary theory and political philosophy.

Despite this promise, I have suggested a number of problems or issues, still unresolved, within this literature – in particular, some potential concerns about a strong post-modern line of influence. Here, it seems to me that a too-tight set of post-modern strictures – against totalizing, determinism, universalism and in favour of difference, contingency and complexity – would undermine central basic dimensions of theoretical reflection (McLennan, 1996; 2006). Tied to this, I have also maintained that a more embracing, interlocutory approach to Marxism would be one way forward in this literature. This, as noted, is encouraged by the situation of these newest movements at present. That is, it seems likely and important that anarchistic impulses will continue to be strong in such a new global Left: opposition to a range of forms of domination (including the contemporary managerialism linked to flexible capitalism); intransigence towards and bypassing of conventional political forces, stages and modes of action; suspicion of vanguardism; emphasis on prefigurative politics and direct action; concern with the equation of means and ends (Purkis and Bowen, 2004a and b). It is equally probable and vital that we will find affinities with more conventionally Marxian emphases and strengths – equality and solidarity, organizational discipline, the ambitious expansion of networks and institutions, attempts to systematically theorize the social transformations occurring and a renewed focus on the question of work.

Developing further reflections in all of these directions is important. In particular, I would mention, in closing, four pressing and recurrent sub-themes and dilemmas, all of which are in evidence, to greater or lesser extents, in the new anarchist literature – work and class, prefigurative politics, violence, and science and technique.

On the first issue, one of the apparent strengths of anarchism *vis à vis* Marxism is to be well equipped to think about identities and contestations that require wider resources than merely those associated with class analysis. However, I think it is clear that no radical politics today can do without vigorous analysis of the changing character of work, reconfigurations – both within nations and in the international division of labour – of class composition and various attempted 'fixes' by capital. This work is clearly being done, but more could be added to this literature.

Second, prefigurative political impulses have been important across socialism's traditions, and especially to anarchism and Left varieties of Marxism. The frequent sense that the older reform–revolution debates and transformatory strategies are, today, of diminished relevance, because of transformations such as globalization and neo-liberal post-democracy, make this focus of renewed importance. It is surely time for more intensive reflection on the socialist history of the construction of alternative institutions and on unearthing and reclaiming the everyday reality of mutual aid. Workers' councils, anarchist efforts at alternative educational principles and institutions,[20] and the multi-form socialist assembly of cultures within cultures are significant examples, but new forms are needed, and already being established, as modes of living otherwise, as responses to urgent needs and as new sources of meaning-making.

It seems likely, third, that such institution-building will be faced with the prospect of violence, as it always has been, and here some re-exploration is in order, too. Beyond corporate media representations of the irrational and criminal character of anti-globalization activity (Gabay, 2010) and the fetish sometimes made of anti-violence and the uncritical use of liberal discourses of totalitarianism and limitation in Left academic circles, a nuanced global Left discussion of violence is in order. Relevant topics here include reflection on the violence already in play in apparently peaceful situations, the contemporary repressive turn by states – coercive accumulations by dispossession, intolerance of dissent, new developments in surveillance and law – and the emergence and the strengthening of violent reactionary forces (the Greek Golden Dawn organization being a contemporary, outer-limit, example).

Last, from anarchism in particular we have an important strand of thinking that has raised questions of size, technique and nature, which has run from nineteenth-century figures such as William Morris and Kropotkin, to a more recent anarchist thinker such as Bookchin and, at its farthest reaches, to the work of the anarcho-primitivist thinkers discussed in Chapter 5. Even if it is easy to conclude that this latter strand is out of step with present realities like no other socialist tradition, anarcho-primitivism raises again, in the most striking fashion, questions about authenticity, consumption, alienation, knowledge, domestication and community. These questionings deserve a serious hearing today.[21]

Such discussions, involving Marxists and anarchists, drawing on a range of paradigms and practical experiments to live otherwise, are of great and pressing interest to social scientists and to anyone concerned with the shape and direction of our current world-system.

7

Reflections on Wallerstein: The Modern World-System, Four Decades On

Introduction

Four decades have now passed since the 1974 publication of Immanuel Wallerstein's *The Modern World-System I: Capitalist Agriculture and the Origins of the European World-Economy*. In many ways, the startlingly ambitious project launched by this book, world-systems analysis, must surely be deemed a thoroughgoing success story. *The Modern World-System I* was instantly recognized as pressing, challenging, even game-changing – so that a critic as apparently resolute as Theda Skocpol (1977: 1075, 1089) still described it as 'a splendid undertaking', concluding that there was 'no intellectual project in the social sciences ... of greater interest and importance'. World-systems analysis was institutionalized as a section of the American Sociological Association, at Binghamton from 1976 with the establishment of the Fernand Braudel Centre, since the mid-1990s in the *Journal of World-Systems Research* and through the disciplined and creative work of a cohort of talented researchers, taking the world-systems approach in an array of new and interesting directions.[1] On this score, Therborn (2008: 104) comments that Wallerstein's 'academic entrepreneurial acumen and achievements have had only one comparable Marxist parallel – Max Horkhiemer'. And Wallerstein was president of the International Sociological Association (ISA) from 1994 to 1998, has been senior research scholar at Yale since 2000 and is an altogether obvious inclusion in the recent *Wiley-Blackwell Companion to Major Social Theorists, Vol. II* (Ritzer and Stepnisky, 2011), alongside the likes of Elias, Foucault, Bourdieu and Habermas.

This success, I think, is clear and well merited, but, at the same time, there is perhaps also a strong sense of world-systems analysis and of Wallerstein himself as a figure of largely *historical* importance and interest in the world of social theory, as overtaken by new realities and more fashionable theoretical paradigms. For some, already in the 1970s, Wallerstein's modernist 'sins' (McLennan, 1996) – functionalism, teleology, determinism and so on – were revealed by critics such as Skocpol; and as post-modern thought exercised ever more influence from the 1980s, world-systems thinking could appear increasingly antiquated, a totalizing modernist metanarrative unable to compete in a new knowledge environment. In related fashion, as Marxism and Third Worldism, which provided the foundational co-ordinates for world-systems thinking, came unstuck from the late 1970s, the stubborn continuation of a basically unaltered Marxian development sociology could look more and more out of time. And, in more recent years, as globalization and post-colonial thinking gained traction in the 1990s, world-systems thought seemed, to many, less a still relevant forerunner and competitor than a now entirely replaceable relic of a lost world, confined to nostalgic Marxian intellectuals refusing to acknowledge that things had moved on.

If the anarchism I surveyed in the previous chapter has been reinvigorated by the discontents of our 'global' moment, it is timely as well, I think, to offer a broad-ranging reconsideration of the origins, trajectory and questions around Wallerstein's world-systems analysis. Beginning with a broad characterization of the background to and major theoretical-historical axioms of Wallerstein's project, I will move to consider issues that have been debated in the fields of economy, politics and culture – or what Wallerstein would characteristically parse into three as the international division of labour, the interstate system and the geoculture. Here, at each point, I want to argue the continuing relevance, despite some pressing issues, of Wallerstein and of world-systems theory – its scope, boldness and still lively and important research programme. Above all I suggest that, after the post-modern and globalization moments, and in the face of current global turmoil, it is worth returning to Wallerstein, admitting that we must now renew 'our tolerance of what Lyotard called "grands recits" ... to learn once again to tell large stories, and to tell them better' (Palumbo-Lio et al., 2011: 9).

Theorizing the world-system – formation, concepts, substantive claims

Before treating the basic conceptual moves of world-systems analysis, it seems important, in line with Wallerstein's own constant efforts at historicization, to situate world-systems thinking. There are a number of relevant and enlightening efforts at this. For a start, Bergesen (2000) places Wallerstein's enterprise firmly within the tradition of the 'Columbia social essayists' – thinkers such as Daniel Bell, Lionel Trilling and C. Wright Mills (one of Wallerstein's teachers at Columbia). In particular, Bergesen (2000: 212) underscores the 'triple hegemony' in operation during Wallerstein's crucial period at Columbia (1947–71) – the US, New York and Columbia University. This, he suggests, underpinned Wallerstein's confident moral authority, the daring to offer absolute judgements about the essence of things – 'the sense of intellectual entitlement to conceptualize the world as a singular system, and to pleas for its democratic and egalitarian transformation'. Wallerstein, in common with his fellow Columbia intellectuals, Bergeson (2000: 211) points out, excelled at the essay form as 'mid-wife' to 'concept formation' through a wide historical scope of enquiry. In another contribution from the same festshrift, Goldfrank (2000) emphasizes three *places* as formative for Wallerstein's thought: sub-Saharan Africa (with Wallerstein's work of the early 1960s dealing with African independence movements, his encounter with Frantz Fanon in 1960 [Wallerstein, 2009]); the cosmopolitanism, radicalism, diversity and very visible power structures of New York; and Paris (the influence of and interchange with Braudel, his French rather than English political leanings – Rousseau over Mill, Wallerstein's preference for 'vigorous' politics over compromise).

Further, we can see in the development of world-systems analysis the intertwining of a number of important influences and events: the core–periphery conceptualizations coming out of the Economic Commission for Latin America (ECLA) from the late 1940s and developed by the *dependistas* – erected in opposition to modernization theory's internalist approach to the problem of development – built around an emphasis on the constitutive importance of colonialism and imperialism, and developed against a backdrop of Third World rebellion against the First World; the Annales insistence on total history and the *longue durée*, against event-focused historiography; German historical economy – for instance, the existence of business cycles, the role of status groups; and Marxism – the central role of conflict between social groups, totality as crucial optic, the importance of accumulation and the dialectical insistence on the priority of contradiction in social change (Chase-Dunn and Inoue, 2011; Goldfrank, 2000; Wallerstein, 2005a).[2] Above all, perhaps, Martin (2000; Goldfrank, 2000) is right to insist on the structuring role of what Wallerstein has called the 'world-revolution of '68'. This moment signals both the high-water mark of the power of the 'antisystemic movements' (social democracy, communism and national liberation) and the appearance of fundamental challenges to them (and to American domination of the world-system) – decolonization, the student movement (in which Wallerstein participated at Columbia), opposition to the Vietnam War and the flowering of movements on behalf of those 'left out'.

Much of this background can be read into two major contributions of 1974 – the first volume of *The Modern World-System* and the long article, 'The Rise and Future Demise of the World Capitalist System: Concepts for Comparative Analysis', originally published in *Comparative Studies in Society and History*. In these texts, Wallerstein (1974; 1980b) begins with a critique of ahistorical and reifying social sciences, of the modernization attempt to outline a series of universal stages of development and, of particular importance, of the assumption that national societies are the appropriate unit of sociological analysis. Wallerstein's alternative unit of analysis is that of totalities, especially the 'world-system' (Goldfrank, 2000). Wallerstein suggested here the existence of three historical types of totalities: mini-systems (simple agricultural or hunter-gatherer orders); world-empires (characterized by political centralization and the forcible extraction of tribute); and world-economies (multiple cultures joined primarily by trade and a division of labour). The focus of the first volume of *The Modern World-System*, of course, is the origins of the modern capitalist world-economy. Here, Wallerstein challenges the characteristic sociological narrative of modernity's emergence in a 'long nineteenth century' by way of intertwining industrial, intellectual and political revolutions (Pitts, 2012). Instead, he contends that capitalism emerges in Europe from around 1450, in the wake of the crisis of Western feudalism, a crisis that is pinned to a number of explanatory factors (including population decline, disease, peasant rebellions [Wallerstein, 1974; 2010b]). This capitalist world-economy appropriated surplus on 'a more efficient and expanded productivity ... by means of a world market mechanism ... and with the ... assistance of state machineries' (Wallerstein, 1974: 38).

A number of points, then, to remark upon at this juncture. First, Wallerstein, in common with the structural-functionalist thought that, in other respects, he so vehemently seeks to break from, is deploying systems language, a social system defined by the existence within it of a division of labour (Wallerstein, 1980b: 5), its dynamics of development being largely internal (Wallerstein, 1974: 347). At numerous points Wallerstein (1980b: 23) is clearly and unabashedly deploying functionalist explanation – for instance, in terms of the role of the semi-periphery in preventing polarization between core and periphery.

Second, Wallerstein (1974: 15) is clearly positing the world-system as above all a world-*economy*, contending that the 'basic linkage between the parts of the system is economic'. He is later to emphasize, in particular, the systemic imperative of the endless accumulation of capital (for instance, Wallerstein, 2005a). Third, as noted, Wallerstein is challenging the common story of the advent of modernity – Enlightenment, Industrial Revolution, French Revolution – and pushing the modern break back from the eighteenth century to locate the origins of *capitalist* modernity in the Iberian expansion of the fifteenth century. In some part, he is emphasizing, in making this claim, the shift from trade in luxuries to 'basic bulk goods' (Wallerstein, 1974: 20), as well as the emergence of capitalism as a means of dealing with the crisis of feudalism (Wallerstein, 1980b: 25).

In Wallerstein's view, capitalism emerges in a first phase that he calls 'the long sixteenth century' (1450–1640) and we should reject parsing capitalism into merchant and industrial phases. Wallerstein (1980b: 16) instead characterizes the first phase as 'agricultural capitalism' – a single division of labour, a world market and production for sale and profit. The world-economy in this long sixteenth century encompassed North West Europe, the Christian Mediterranean, Central Europe, the Baltic region, certain regions of America and some enclaves of Africa (Wallerstein, 1974: 68). Within this world-economy, crucially, certain tiers can be identified and are of decisive importance. Here, Wallerstein develops the *dependista* focus into a threefold division: the core (North West Europe – strong states, increasing variety and specialization in production, profitable production processes, monopolization); the periphery (Eastern Europe and Hispanic America – weak states, tending to monoculture, producing lower ranking, less profitable goods); and the semi-periphery (Mediterranean Europe, for instance – in-between forms, such as sharecropping [Wallerstein, 1974; 2005a]). And Wallerstein (1974; 2005a; Goldfrank, 2000) is insisting, unlike the *dependistas*, on the relational and dialectical aspects of the core–periphery pairing, and on a sort of circulation of elites between these different tiers.

One central point to raise here is that Wallerstein (1980b) shifts from the Marxian focus on industrial labour as a defining feature of capitalism and insists instead on a range of modes of labour within capitalism – tenancy, slavery, coerced cash-cropping – with different modes characteristic of different tiers or geographic units in the overall division of labour. On this note, still placed within the Marxist tradition, Wallerstein emphasizes the important role of class (exploitation and inequality) within the division of labour (Boli and Lechner, 2009), but status groups are, right from the beginning, given significant weight as 'elements' in the system (Wallerstein, 1974: 351), connected to the struggle within the world-economy for power, wealth and status. It is important to note that, for Wallerstein (1989), the working class is not 'liberated' as an actor until around the 1830s in Europe, but that for him, classes and status groups are not, in any case, 'eternal essences' but are social creations, constantly forming, dissolving and re-forming (Wallerstein, 1991a; 2011a: 166), in 'constant movement' (Wallerstein, 1980b: 224), and that, contrary to many Marxian analysts, status groups are not seen as in decline but, in fact, as of growing importance within the world-economy (Wallerstein, 2005a). Another point of note is the Marxian focus on the extraction of surplus, not only from the labourer, but also across the tiers of the system by core states and through unequal exchange, with Wallerstein looking to the work of Arghiri Emmanuel. Further, and connected to this Marxian thrust, the state is read as a 'means of assuring certain terms of trade in economic transactions' (Wallerstein, 1974: 16) in the battle between different owner-producers in the world-economy (Wallerstein, 1980a: 114), despite being lent a 'certain autonomy' (Wallerstein, 1980b: 20). And Wallerstein (1974: 136; 1999a) charges that we see the growth of state power from this long sixteenth century – bureaucratization, protection of private property, monopolization of the means of violence, the creation of legitimacy, and the homogenization and keeping in check of subject populations.

Vitally, within this system of states, Wallerstein (1980b: 31) is, from the beginning, mentioning the pivotal importance of hegemony. Hegemony, which is key for the stability of the system, is later glossed by Wallerstein (2005a: 58) as follows: the hegemonic state is 'able to establish the rules of the game in the interstate system, to dominate the world-economy (in production, commerce, and finance), to get their way politically with a minimal use of military force (which however they had in goodly strength), and to formulate the cultural language in which one discussed the world'. This hegemony, while necessary, is temporary – because it is expensive and abrasive, because others tend to catch up (innovations and monopolies don't last) and because of struggles within a fundamentally conflictual system (Wallerstein, 2005a). Historically, for Wallerstein (1974; 1980a), there have been three hegemons within the world-economy: first the United Provinces, rising in the last half of the sixteenth century, and dominant from about 1625 to 1675; then, after a struggle for hegemony between Britain and France, Britain, decisively from 1815; then, after a further struggle between America and Germany, America from 1945.

At the start of the second volume of *The Modern World-System*, Wallerstein (1980a: 26) notes the importance of secular trends and cyclical rhythms in approaching the question of social change within the system. He notes that in this next overlapping period, 1600–1750, which is characterized as one of 'calming down and cooling off', of slowdown and consolidation in the world-economy, the boundaries changed little, with a B-phase of contraction felt across the system. Here, Wallerstein (1980a; 2005a) draws on work around Kondratieff waves of expansion and contraction of around 50 years in length, and on Simiand's notion of longer periods/waves of approximately 250 years, which are bound up with transformations in hegemony.[3] In the next volume, covering the period 1730–1840s, Wallerstein (1989) notes the incorporation of a range of 'external' zones (such as the Indian sub-continent and the Ottoman Empire), which are peripheralized until, by the close of the nineteenth century, the entire globe is inside the world-economy. From 1873, we see the slow decline of Britain and the rise of new contenders for hegemonic status within the world-system and, eventually, America arrives at a position of unquestioned dominance following the Second World War.

As well as emphases on secular trends (geographical expansion, commodification, mechanization of production, proletarianization and bureaucratization) and cyclical rhythms (caused by overproduction) (Goldfrank, 2000), and attached to these closely, Wallerstein notes a series of contradictions in operation within the system, which, as well, push in the direction of systemic transformation. These contradictions, other than supply and demand, are given more weight in Wallerstein's analysis of the late eighteenth century onwards, with the French Revolution given pride of place as a symbolic opening. Again, Wallerstein (1989; 2011a) rejects the common interpretation of the French Revolution as a bourgeois revolution, insisting that this was simply the moment when the ideological-political superstructure caught up with an already transformed base, and arguing that the Revolution was less important solely for France than is often imagined (having vital global implications). It is at this point that we see the creation of a geo-culture (broadly shared and dominant ideas, values and norms) across the world-system – the third major part, alongside the international division of labour and the interstate system of the world-economy, and the focus of Wallerstein's recent fourth volume of *The Modern World-System*. From the French Revolution we see, first, the emergence of the three big ideologies – conservatism, liberalism and radicalism/socialism. Centrist liberalism – conscious, intelligent reformism, with the strong state as the instrument of this reform, clothed, though, in the language of individualism; themes of rationalism, science and economic progress (Wallerstein, 1995; 2005a: 61; 2011a: 6, 9) – emerges triumphant, the defining feature of the geoculture, so that both conservatives and radicals became, over time, variants on the centrist liberal theme. We see, second, the Revolution stimulating the emergence of the historical social sciences. These sciences sought to comprehend 'what generated normal social change in order to be able to limit the impact of popular preferences' (Wallerstein, 2011a: 220); they split into 'two cultures' (science and humanities), and the social sciences, pulled between these cultures, divided into disciplines – economics (the market), political science (the state) and sociology (civil society). Finally, the French Revolution sets in motion (releasing 'the genie out of the bottle' [Wallerstein, 2005a: 51]) the anti-systemic movements – social democracy, communism and national liberation – which come onto the political stage with the 'world-revolution of 1848'.[4]

Outside of the four volumes comprising his major contribution to historical sociology, Wallerstein has focused particular attention on the changes within the world-system since the 1960s and the prospects that might lie ahead, and I will spend a moment here outlining, again in broad brushstrokes, his major theses. First, Wallerstein (2000c) charges that the world-economy has, since the late 1960s, entered into another B-phase of stagnation and chaos, an 'age of transition'. A central part of this is that, from around this point, we have been witnessing the unstoppable demise of America as world hegemon, and the jockeying for position of a number of core and semi-peripheral countries – ours, then, is a time of relative destructuring and multipolarity within the world-system (Wallerstein, 1998b; 2001b; 2003a; 2003b; 2006a). Even the demise of America's Cold War rival, the USSR, is viewed by Wallerstein (2006a) as only hastening this decline. In this period, we have also seen the demise of the anti-systemic movements, especially after a period of their remarkable success (construction of welfare states, decolonization and indigenization of personnel, and socialization of the means of production and planned economies) from 1945 to 1968 (Arrighi et al., 1989). In particular, the world-revolution of 1968 offered these movements a number of fundamental challenges from which they have not recovered: charges that they had not transformed life as they had promised, that they had been co-opted and themselves become agents of oppression and exploitation, and that they had left certain crucial people out (Arrighi et al., 1989; Wallerstein, 1990a; 1991b; 1991c; 2002a; 2010a). In a similar vein, from that second world-revolution, we have also seen the steady decline of liberalism as the governing geoculture – the end of developmentalism, the rise of neo-liberalism and the Washington Consensus, a loss of faith in the state and, for the first time since the arrival of the world-economy, a decline in state power (Wallerstein, 1995; 2005a).[5]

Alongside and connected to this, we see fundamental shifts in the realm of knowledge structures, with a number of crucial challenges to science in general and to the social sciences in particular, a veritable 'crisis in the sciences' (Wallerstein, 1991b: 113): complexity analyses, cultural studies, post-modern thought, feminism; questioning of the ideas of 'laws' of science, linearity, rationality, progress, inevitability and Eurocentrism; and interrogations of our common assumptions about time (Wallerstein, 1991b; 1991c; 1995; 1997a; 1997b; 1998a; 1998c; 1999a; 1999c; 2000b; 2004b). Here, for some time, Wallerstein (1999c; 2000a; 2000b) has been calling for a re-organization of the sciences, and urging an acknowledgement of and commitment to the ineradicable intertwining of reflections on the good, the true and the beautiful. In terms of the future prospects of the world-system, Wallerstein has tended to be, as Chase-Dunn and Inoue (2011: 407) suggest, 'apocalyptic and ... millenarian', boldly predicting that a number of secular trends are reaching asymptotes that are exacerbating the crisis tendencies of the system. These include the deruralization of the world and the impossibility of running away from growing workers' power; the growing cost of inputs – for instance, ecological exhaustion, with Wallerstein (2011c) emphasizing present environmental chaos and the possibility of future 'supercalamities'; the rising infrastructure bill; and the burdensome costs associated with growing democratization (health, education and guaranteed life-time income) (Wallerstein, 2000a; 2005a). In a number of articles, Wallerstein (2000c) has suggested that a bifurcation out of our transitional age is likely in the next 25 to 50 years, demanding a species of reflection he designates 'utopistics'.[6] The likely paths into the future are designated 'the spirit of Davos' or 'the spirit of Porto Alegre'. Wallerstein suggests as strategic measures along the way to the latter (an updated emancipatory socialist alternative) the establishment of de-commodified economic structures, defensive electoral tactics, a move beyond the old two-step strategy and democratic centralism as modes of oppositional organization towards open debate, anti-racism and 'forcing the pace of liberalism' (1998a; 2000c; 2002a; 2002b: 20; 2004a).

Evaluating Wallerstein I – the international division of labour

Obviously, one of the still very striking things about Wallerstein's work – perhaps even more striking today, given the pervasive sense of limits installed by the post-modern moment (Beilharz, 1994) – is the enormous scope and ambition in play (a framework, that is, for the understanding of nearly everything), which can be, variously, for commentators, a major strength and a profound weakness. Here, I want to begin turning to the broad types of critical commentary raised in challenge to world-systems thinking, crudely moving from questions of economics or the international division of labour to politics or the interstate system and, finally, to culture or, as Wallerstein would have it, questions of the geoculture. While a number of these assessments raise important questions, none of them, I believe, proves fatally damaging to the research agenda and basic postulates of world-systems analysis. In this section, I focus on central contentions around capitalism, class, global inequality and the challenge offered by globalization discourse.

A first stop, given Wallerstein's prioritization of economics, is the international division of labour and here an early and predictable objection was made to Wallerstein's dating of the genesis of the capitalist world-economy and to the terms of his comprehension of capitalism. Robert Brenner's 1977 article in *New Left Review* was an early and comprehensive salvo fired from the more orthodox Marxian camp. Brenner's basic complaint was that evidence of barriers to capitalist expansion (persisting underdevelopment, that is) had led a number of Marxists such as Wallerstein to abandon a focus on class relations and follow Adam Smith's 'individualistic-mechanist presuppositions' (Brenner, 1977: 27). For Brenner, Wallerstein focuses incorrectly, and in un-Marxian fashion, on the trade-based division of labour and exchange relations, thereby excluding an adequate explanation of the unique dynamism of capitalism. Proper explanation demands analysis of class, commodication and exploitation – the real sources of the exchange relations that Wallerstein attends to – and such an analysis would also have the effect of undermining Wallerstein's periodization of capitalism. That is, the more standard Marxian focus on the qualitative break represented by the Industrial Revolution correctly foregrounds the generalized separation of labour from means of production, the appearance of capital and labour as commodities.

There are a number of significant issues here, and a first has to do with Wallerstein's dating of capitalism and/or the construction of a world-economy. As mentioned, Wallerstein (1989: 33; 2010b; 2011a) is profoundly sceptical of the notion of an Industrial Revolution, viewing it as 'misleading', suggesting that we should focus on the world-economy developing over time rather than on sub-units within, and insisting on the continuity of ruling families in the transition to capitalism, rather than the appearance of a new bourgeois class.[7] This is, unsurprisingly, a vastly complicated debate,[8] and, even within the field of world-systems thinking, there are significant differences of opinion here. Thus Arrighi (1997) contends that the how and why of transformation is the 'missing link' in Wallerstein's schema, and that his own world-systemic insistence on the earlier period of Italian city-state activity provides the answer. Here, the suggestion is that we need to break from Wallerstein's surprisingly state-centric focus and look at the interstices that connected larger territorial organizations to each other and other worlds – the growth of capitalism between worlds – as well as giving more weight to the military factor. I will come back to some of this in the following section.

Another major argument within the world-systems school concerning the dating of the emergence of the world-economy led to a growing separation between Wallerstein and Andre Gunder Frank. Frank's (2000) contention was that his earlier dating of the world system to 1492 and Wallerstein's continued deployment of 1450 needed to be pushed back some 5,000 years. We find a world system and capital accumulation far beyond and before these dates and this necessitates, argued Frank, both a break with the feudalism–capitalism–socialism sequence (on this last term, Frank increasingly found the notion of future systemic transformation unlikely) and from what he charged was Wallerstein's Eurocentric neglect of Afro-Eurasia. A robust research programme has emerged around such contentions within the broad world-systems school.[9]

A second, connected set of issues relates to the problem of class. We have here not only questions about the emergence of the capitalist class but, very crucially for any analysis within the Marxian field, questions of working-class designation, struggle and unity. Brenner's charge was, of course, that Wallerstein 'displaces' class relations and structures, and others (for instance, Martin, 2000) have insisted that class struggle does not really play an important enough role in Wallerstein's work, given the emphasis on system dynamics and the prioritization of First World–Third World exploitative relations.[10] And, indeed, it can be reasonably suggested that a close attention to class structures is largely non-existent in Wallerstein's work – for instance, the almost total absence of this variety of conflict until volume four of *The Modern World-System*. Here, though, Wallerstein's flexible model of classes as constantly in formation rather than as permanent, static and unchanging categories, as well as his insistence on the diversity of labour forms, could be deemed an advantage against static conceptualizations that fail, in any case, to attend closely to troublesome but urgent problems of class consciousness and class action. It seems advantageous, too, to be focusing, as Wallerstein does, both on interstate and intrastate processes of class domination and struggle (So and Hikam, 1989; So, 1990). These are underscored, for instance, in Chase-Dunn's (1998: 41) consideration of the historic achievement of a situation of relatively protected labour by core workers, forcing a certain socialization of the state by way of their skills and organizational capacity, of 'relative harmonies' between classes, while also insisting on bolding the global and historical dimensions to these achievements. And, within the field of world-systems analysis, Arrighi and Silver have sought to pay more attention to class, offering large-scale but still nuanced accounts of transformations and ambiguities of class formation, conflict and dissolution.[11]

It is, in the end, I think, quite misplaced to accuse Wallerstein of ignoring class, even if he has leant in a less than orthodox, division of labour-centred direction and has not focused in detail on such dynamics. In fact, it is more reasonable to seriously consider suggestions that class remains too prominent and the analysis is too reductive on this front. Thus Wallerstein (1980b: 230) calls class struggle the 'fundamental political reality' of the world-economy, though this is softened by his contention that this constantly changes form and that objective class status only becomes a reality when it becomes a subjective phenomenon. It could, that is, be charged that while giving status groups an important (equal?) place as elements or institutions within the world-economy, these status groups are, in the end, reduced to class realities. Sanderson (2005: 185), for instance, contends that conceptualizations of racism and sexism within world-systems analysis are reduced largely to 'epiphenomena of the capitalist world-economy'. Thus, Wallerstein (1980b: 224) says that class and status are 'two sets of clothing for the same basic realities' – classes as 'objective categories', but status groups as 'constructed peoples' (Wallerstein, 1991a: 84). Here, status groups are understood as modalities of the struggle to alter the distribution of goods and privileges by way of organizational cohesion and the manipulation of cultural symbols, with racism on one side and the struggle by disadvantaged groups to equalize their life-chances on the other (Wallerstein, 1980b; 1991a).

These objections, I believe, are misplaced. Despite a sense one gets at times of a 'capitalocentrism' at work in Wallerstein's analyses, where the only real actor is the capitalist world-system and its imperatives and objective contradictions, he has consistently underscored the successful and system-transforming role of the anti-systemic movements, understood in terms of class, that is, the capitalist world-economy, even if he has been equally insistent on the systemic constraints facing them.[12] And he has steadily emphasized status groups as a continually vital set of dynamics, which should not be, he maintains, considered outside of the antagonisms within the international division of labour. Overall, then, here I think it is fair to say that an orientation to the 'processes by which groups (and institutions) are constantly recreated, remoulded, and eliminated in the ongoing operations of the capitalist world-economy' (Arrighi et al., 1989: 22) remains a justifiable orientation, provided this is, at some point, backed by more nuanced analyses of the dynamics and contradictions in play across different spatial and temporal moments. This approach is perhaps particularly pertinent in a period that has witnessed such dramatic reconfigurations of the international division of labour (for instance, de-industrialization in the former industrial centres and the creation of industrial working classes outside of the core), especially when set against attempts to map out static class structures and then assume consciousness and action as consequent upon these objective class co-ordinates or, on the other side of this, the more common trajectory of abandoning the still pressing question of class.[13]

I will return to the question of class and socialism in a later section, and will now turn to further questions around economic issues in Wallerstein, primarily what we might label problems of the post-*dependista* moment. Right from the start, a number of Marxian critics found the dependency sociology of development field too rigid in dealing with the failure of certain expectations stemming from Manifesto-Marxism. Was underdevelopment really indispensable to capitalist development (Brenner, 1977)? Were the categories core, periphery, semi-periphery really adequate to the job of thinking world-capitalism? Here Sanderson (2005) charges that these tiers induce very reified forms of analysis, and a focus on global inequalities would do a much better job as the analytical starting point. Did these dependency thinkers not provide too static and pessimistic an account of the transformations of the capitalist mode of production? By 1973, and within the Marxian field, Bill Warren, for instance, was already asking some very sharp questions here, noting a number of significant cases in which capitalism had not permanently developed underdevelopment. The implication of these sorts of questions was that more nuanced conceptual tools and detailed empirical work were needed to determine causes of stagnation and backwardness and possibilities for modernization and growth, against the undifferentiated and reified contentions of dependency sociology. The obvious anomalous cases early on were the newly industrializing countries (NICs) and, clearly, in the past four decades, since the beginnings of Wallerstein's world-systems analysis, a number of countries have changed tiers. Did these developments, then, not significantly limit the purchase of world-systems thinking?

A significant part of this question often touches on the degree to which exogenous factors are given too much weight in world-systems analyses. However, as Chase-Dunn and Inoue (2011) affirm, Wallerstein's point is not to deny the importance of endogenous features and unevenness or specificities within national spaces, but to question this very exogenous–endogenous distinction, and to urge analysts to move beyond the nation state as unquestioned unit of analysis, as independent, self-contained systems. That Wallerstein (1974) is attentive to unevenness within nations and to different path possibilities and movement within those broad tiers is clear from the start, in the notion of a circulation of elites between categories. Nevertheless, these questions raise the rather counter-intuitive question of whether, in fact, world-systems analysis is too state-centric and has been left behind by the post-1970s thickening and extension of world connectedness and by the globalization literature that has attended to these apparently novel processes. For a start, does a category as large and internally heterogeneous as 'semi-periphery' do any justice to the empirical variants on the ground, when this concept encompasses such varying capitalisms as, say, Pakistan, Brazil, Egypt, South Africa, and New Zealand? This is the old charge that this category, particularly, is simply residual, lacking any real specificity (see Snyder and Kick, 1979, for instance), but that the heterogeneity, here, has become even more marked in the contemporary globalizing period. Here, newer work on multiple capitalisms, modernities or civilizational analysis might be deemed a more adequate starting point (see, for instance, Therborn, 2000a). Moreover, but connected, Sanderson (2005: 189) charges that much of the capitalist periphery has been disappearing over the last 30 or so years, and that those nations that have remained peripheral, with sub-Saharan Africa as the prime example, are much better approached in terms of endogenous factors – such as 'predatory' state structures – than through world-systems analysis with its external bias. What we have in the case of Africa, says Sanderson, is growing marginalization in terms of the world-economy, and we have to question the idea that capitalist penetration continues to produce underdevelopment. In addition, charges Sanderson, China's recent growth seems to favour a more straightforward modernization reading than the one pioneered by Wallerstein. These sorts of assertions also intertwine with objections to Wallerstein's persistent immiseration thesis (see, for instance, Wallerstein, 1980; 1990b; 2005b), which Sanderson (2005: 196) argues should be buried 'in shame' – whether we judge according to per capita GDP, life expectancy or a range of other measures of global inequality, those at the bottom have, over time, been lifted up.

For some, the main issue is that globalization as a distinctive phase needs to be acknowledged as marking a necessary break from dependency perspectives. In contrast, Wallerstein has absolutely refused to acknowledge its distinctiveness, charging that globalization is an essentially meaningless term, better situated in the realm of ideology,[14] and that such globalization has, in fact, been a persistent tendency of the world-economy since its fifteenth century inception, a periodic cyclical trend. In a sustained and compelling analysis, Robinson (2011a; 2011b) charges that this 'traditionalist' line will just not do, given novel contemporary phenomena: the wild expansion of financial flows; new productive processes (networks, 'spaces of flows') that render a territorial conception outdated (see also McMichael, 2000); other transnational processes that complicate a simple international division of labour–interstate system analysis (for instance, what some have called the pluralization of power today); and the emergence of transnational rather than primarily nationally based class divides (a transnational capitalist class, the denationalization of elites). In short, globalization is a new epoch, characterized by the liberation of capital from the nation state, an 'incipient transnational state apparatus', the erosion of the core–periphery distinction, and, especially, an increasingly social rather than national polarization process (Robinson, 2011b: 349).

In defending Wallerstein in the face of these contentions, a number of points are in order. Again, world-systems analysis does not in the least rule out the importance of national specificities and structures in thinking about paths and prospects, but insists that a global political economy focus always be present in analyses. The analysis of the dramatic upward mobility of a number of Asian nations, for instance, is unthinkable by way of a focus on endogenous factors alone (Therborn, 2011). The world-systems approach does not, either, deny movement within and across the different tiers of the world-economy: obviously,

America represents a particularly remarkable example of upward mobility (Chase-Dunn and Grimes, 1995). And both Chase-Dunn (1998) and Arrighi, for instance, have attempted to address the rise of East Asia on the one side, and the 'African tragedy' on the other – the 'bifurcation of Third World destinies' (Arrighi, 2002: 5). Further, against some of the wild globalist rhetoric that imagines a flattening of the world, a completely transformed, transnational economy and the demise of sovereign nation states, it is well to remain sceptical. As Michael Mann (2013: 357, 410) – no great supporter of world-systems thinking – has recently noted, nation states and transnational capitalism have expanded together. States remain 'entrenched regulators', 'transnational institutionality' in the shape of the IMF or the WTO continues to look like economic imperialism, led by Northern states, and a transnational capitalist class is nowhere (outside of finance) a plausible contention. And still, says Mann (2013: 410), the vast bulk of life chances (60 per cent plus) are dependent on '[t]he luck of where you were born'. Further to the charge of the very static quality of world-systems analysis, Wallerstein's vocabulary after the mid-1980s of commodity chains encourages more detailed attention being given to transnational processes and he, of course, recognizes historical transformations in terms of leading products within the world-economy – textiles, for example, were once but are no longer a monopolized core product (Wallerstein, 2005a). Finally, on the question of immiseration/polarization, clearly this is a hugely complex debate (see Held and Kaya, 2007). An immiseration and polarization argument, though, still holds ground in such debates (for instance, Pieterse, 2005; Wade, 2007), especially as the relative rise of two profoundly populous nations – China and India – has skewed world income distributions. Here, in support of world-systems' contentions, we could note the following: that the richest, almost exclusively Northern, 10 per cent have gained distance on the poorest 10 per cent (Mann, 2013); that there were growing inequalities between and within many countries, 1980–2000; that recent rises in the fortunes of the BRICS nations, development across Asia and even Sub-Saharan Africa, and equalization measures in Latin America are plausibly connected to the growing multipolarity characteristic of a phase of hegemonic decline and restructuring (Mann, 2013; Therborn, 2011; 2012) and are not, in any case, necessarily permanent trends, given the possible impact of the recent recession; that there is good evidence for a major concentration of capital to the advantage of Northern companies from the period of the Washington Consensus to the present (for instance, Nolan and Zhang, 2010); and that there continue to be massive gaps between nations, however we choose to measure this. That is, the core–periphery schema as problem and hypothesis (Jameson, 1989) and polarization contentions continue to make sense, in terms of older and more recent work within (Chase-Dunn and Grimes, 1995; Snyder and Kick, 1979) and beyond the world-systems camp.

Frequently, what we have in many of the objections raised against world-systems analysis is something of the order of the oft-repeated post-modern-inflected assertion about the grey of theory versus the green of the world, although as McLennan (2006) notes, such gestures to particularity and contingency are incoherent: when can we ever be particular enough? We cannot, that is, escape a certain abstraction – this is what theory is: tools that guide and organize research that would otherwise be faced simply with a mess of unorganized and infinite empirical phenomena (Mann, 1993). And there is, in fact, no way to theorize contingency (McLennan, 1996). On a related note, the turn to the language of multiple modernities, civilizational analysis and the like can be read as having had the effect of returning us to the language of modernization, of obscuring the still driving effects of capitalism (Jameson, 2002), of contesting discourses of cultural inferiority at the expense of disguising 'the severe political, social, and economic hierarchies that continue to structure the world' (Palumbo-Lio et al., 2011: 9). In short, there is nothing – including assertions about the new shift to finance[15] or complexified networks of production and distribution – about contemporary 'globalization' that seems resistant to incorporation within and treatment by world-systems thinking. World-systems analysis, though, has the advantage of keeping before us not just a warning against chronocentrism, but also the structuring fact of capitalist imperatives of accumulation, class and inequality, of the priority given to profit, growth and competition, which today, arguably more than ever, must remain central to any sociological thought that seeks to say something about the configuration of the world.

Evaluating Wallerstein II – the interstate system

Rather similar counter arguments are often in order when we turn to questions of the interstate system. Here, I will focus, in particular, on issues around the autonomy of the political realm, the question of hegemony, the role of the military in the capitalist world-system and the problem of contemporary state power. Again, these issues are seminal and stem from the 1970s, very clearly articulated, for instance, in Skocpol's early critique of Wallerstein. Alongside Skocpol's queries about the origins and sources of dynamism of capitalism, she raised questions about Wallerstein's treatment of the political realm. A number of Skocpol's objections trace a familiar Weberian versus Marxian arc of debate around issues of economic determinism and teleology, including her contention that Wallerstein neglected geopolitical and military factors, and had trouble dealing with the relationship between state structures and status within the different tiers of the world-economy. On this last question, Skocpol, in common with other critics, suggests Wallerstein is circular and inaccurate in his assessments of the strength of core states. There is undoubtedly some substance to this objection, given Wallerstein's initially sketchy formulations but, arguably, over time Wallerstein's (2011c) efforts to tighten his conceptualization and the emphasis on the core states as those able to prevent internal fragmentation and outside interference have travelled rather well. In terms of her charge of Wallerstein's disregard of political factors, Arrighi (1997) suggests that Skocpol may get things the wrong way round in that there is perhaps an over-emphasis on states, given that the United Provinces, imperial Britain and continental America cannot easily be characterized in the same way. The military question, meanwhile, is an important one too, and, as Arrighi (1997) notes, well within the potential ambit of world-systemic reflection, which he and more Weberian thinkers such as Skocpol and Mann (1988) have underscored as an intermeshed and central dynamic in the modern world-system.

Here, Chase-Dunn (1998; Chase-Dunn and Grimes, 1995), in particular, has sought to incorporate military competition as a consequential dynamic within the world-systems paradigm, with ebbs and flows that are intelligible in terms of the cycles of capitalism, such as moments of K-wave upswings and periods of transforming hegemony. In a similar manner, Galtung (1971) and Snyder and Kick (1979) provide support for a world-systems approach, though by deploying more multi-factorial contentions, with Galtung considering five types of imperialism (economic, political, military, communication and cultural) and – backed both by rigorous argumentation and empirical support – exploring the various intertwinings and multiple spin-offs and spillovers, along with the impact of a 'feudal interaction structure' between peripheral nations. While this sort of work adds to the broad variety of world-systems research, it nevertheless moves from the problematic of 'relative autonomy' towards a model that starts to eclipse the distinctions between Marxian and Weberian paradigms. That is, it is not at all clear that Wallerstein is unable to lend political and military factors, say, a genuine level of relative autonomy. For instance, in his commentaries on contemporary affairs, say the neo-conservative-led US military interventions of the past decade or so, Wallerstein (2006a) is obviously suggesting a significant degree of causal power for political, ideological and military factors – though these are never fully detachable from questions of accumulation. We have a similar autonomy lent to political factors in Wallerstein's insistence on the significant concessions achieved by the anti-systemic movements, 1945–68 (the relative social re-embedding of the economy). This, of course, will not satisfy more Weberian thinkers like Mann, who are unlikely to find the notion of relative autonomy convincing, but surely it is incorrect to accuse Wallerstein of pure and simple economic determinism, of necessitarian, pure-system logic argumentation.

In terms of the charge of state-centrism, we might respond positively to Wallerstein's continuing insistence on the importance of states in the face of globalist rhetoric – national boundaries and states still matter, and we might appreciate world-systems analysis as a still productive and open research paradigm, able to innovate in the face of challenge to incorporate thinking, say, on the at times leading role of military competition and its intertwinement with the international division of labour. Wallerstein (1995; 1999a), as noted, has suggested a first-time reversal of the trend of growing state power.[16] However, it seems right not to go with the flattening approach that imagines an irreversible movement in the direction of a transnational state apparatus, beyond the 'Westphalian' system as articulated, say, by Hardt and Negri (2000), by McMichael (2000: 687) who suggests we are seeing a shift from citizen-states to global-states, geared to 'securing global credit, and circuits of money and commodities, and usually legitimated by "consumer citizens"', or by Robinson (2011a and b). Here, again, Wallerstein's emphases are supported by thinkers outside of the world-systems camp who argue that states remain the hegemonic political form in the world, that Northern states (despite significant attacks on social citizenship) have only increased their levels of spending and have maintained welfare states, that these states – along with East Asian development states – have not been wide open to global forces at all, that public employment remains high (10–12 per cent of world employment), and that many weaker states lack sovereignty not because of novel global forces but as a result of a long-standing trend in peripheral areas (Mann, 2013; Therborn, 2011)

Last, we might take up questions around hegemony. Wallerstein has tirelessly insisted that we are witnessing the secular decline of the current hegemon, America, and Arrighi (2010: 384) seems to go even further in claiming that we have already arrived at a situation of 'domination without hegemony'. But critics will, of course, contest this. For instance, with respect to the globalist contention about declining state power and globalization, Therborn (2011) asks rhetorically whether the present is not, in fact, a moment presided over by the most powerful state in human history, America. Similarly, Marxists such as Petras and Veltmeyer (2001) read the period of globalization as a renewed surge of American imperialism, and Harvey (2005) and others have convincing claims to make on this theme, as part of a wider turn back to the language of empire (Therborn, 2008). In a somewhat similar vein, fellow-travelling world-systems thinker Samir Amin (1994; 2003) sees the contemporary period as distinctive in terms of the question of hegemony, as true hegemony in the cases of the United Provinces and even Britain is questionable, whereas American hegemony after the Second World War is completely singular. And, also from within the field of world-systems thought, Arrighi (2005a; 2005b; 2010), while adding the hegemony of Genoa to Wallerstein's list, foresees a rather different future scenario ahead, with the possible succession of China as hegemon, unlikely to be unaccompanied by military dominance, which America may continue to exercise. In Arrighi's reading, the likely future prospects are quite different from those suggested by Wallerstein (2010a) who speaks of the coming end of the world-system, which will issue in something like socialism or something like barbarism. Clearly, there are no easy answers to such questions, other than to suggest that, at the very least, Wallerstein's version of continuing state power, declining hegemony,[17] and possible bifurcated futures remains a very arguable, supportable set of propositions – it is still a contender for serious attention in interpreting our moment, against a globalization literature that often issues in repeated clichéd paradoxes, explanatory unclarity and inconclusive or weak empirical substantiation.

Evaluating Wallerstein III – the geoculture

Once more, we encounter some significant argumentative congruencies as we move from political to cultural questions. Here I will explore questions around the structures of knowledge – ideologies, science, world culture and socialism – before bringing some of my assessments together in conclusion. Again, central objections revolve around the alleged determinism of the world-systems schema, this time against the tide of a cultural turn, or what might be called the post-modernization of knowledge, that has washed across the human sciences in the last couple of decades and that looks relentlessly unaccommodating to thinking of the scale proposed by Wallerstein and company. In these objections, the usual charges against the various 'sins' of modernist thinking – universalism, functionalism, determinism, teleology – are again raised (McLennan, 1996), either as long-standing problems we have finally got wise to or as concepts no longer defensible given the extensive changes that have taken place within the richest countries.

While this is not in any way a new complaint, it is well to begin to approach this issue by way of a fascinating collection, in which a number of distinguished humanities scholars 'committed in one way or another' to 'the study of culture' (Palumbo-Lio et al., 2011: 11) lucidly draw together a number of familiar criticisms in order to reflect on the contemporary relevance of Wallerstein's work – published, interestingly enough, in the same year as Wallerstein's fourth volume of *The Modern World-System*, which deals explicitly with such cultural questions. The problems with world-systems analysis for humanities-centred scholars seem clear enough – above all, perhaps, a 'bigness' problem in Wallerstein's work, which is, to say the least, 'somewhat unfriendly to the humanities' (Palumbo-Lio et al., 2011: 4). That is, the world and long historical scope, theorized in a way which can appear to lend the system 'almost theological omnipotence' (Palumbo-Lio et al., 2011: 10), would seem obviously incompatible with the characteristic humanities emphases on culture, subjectivity, difference, agency, the local and so on. More generally, has not everything that has been happening across the human sciences since the beginning of the post-modern turn moved in completely the opposite direction to the path taken by Wallerstein? For instance, as Robbins (2011: 57) notes, in the last couple of decades, humanities scholars have often asserted that 'what must be blamed is, precisely, thinking systematically', that perhaps, today, there is, after all, no system at all, just a disorganized tangle of multiple processes and events with unpredictable consequences. Here, as Balakrishnan (2011: 227) comments, only a few years after the end of the Cold War, 'world-systems theory already seemed to belong to a bygone era of upheaval', part of a now largely eroded rhetoric of denunciation (Boltanski and Chiapello, 2005) – not only in terms of changing theoretical emphases, but also with respect to the apparent distance separating the 1970s from a post-communist 'modernity of liberal democracy, markets, and human rights'.

For those underscoring the 'irreducibility of culture', there seems an immediate and obvious 'resistance to Wallerstein' (Robbins, 2011: 46). As Moretti (2011: 70) notes, world-systems thinking 'brusquely reduces the many independent spaces ... to just three positions', a challenge to the drive for specificity and nuance so often found, say, in literature studies. And, of course, compounding this, is that in Wallerstein's now less than fashionable emphasis on system, priority is given to the economic dimension (Robbins, 2011: 45). This systemic and economically reductionist optic seems to threaten an automatic blindness to struggle, the active making of history, contingency (Palumbo-Lio et al., 2011; Robbins, 2011): events, actions and movements, says Robbins (2011: 54, 55), 'tend not to appear on Wallerstein's screen as more than blips'; 'Everything is (or threatens to become) system'. And, of course, this sort of issue has been commonly registered from within sociology. Thus, in the aforementioned festschrift, Touraine (2000; see also Therborn, 2000a) appears to take an oblique swipe at world-systems thinking by emphasizing the need today to reach actors as autonomous beings, agents of transformation and creators of imaginary worlds more effectively – a return to the subject to be found in other important contemporary sociological thinkers such as Michel Wieviorka and Luc Boltanski. This return to the subject, a more culturally leaning sociology, multiple modernities contributions, a complexity-influenced globalization discourse seeking to attend to contradictory deterritorializing and reterritorializing processes (Brenner, 2011: 130), or pluralistic and pragmatic borrowings from a range of theoretical and empirical approaches (Moretti, 2011; Wigen, 2011) – all of these seem, today, much more sociologically in vogue.

Another important dimension to Wallerstein's cultural analyses involves his explicit commentary on the disciplines. In a gently probing piece on Wallerstein's reflections on the social sciences, Lee (2011), for instance, focuses on Wallerstein's embrace of the scholarly signs of the collapse of the liberal consensus (the questioning of rationality, determinism, progress, objectivism, modernity, linear explanations, Eurocentrism and so on). The implicit question obviously concerns itself with the compatibility of Wallerstein's enthusiasm with the thrust of the entirety of world-systems theory. All of these 'problems' seem integral to everything Wallerstein has done over the past four decades, making his welcoming of complexity and post-modern talk seem, to say the least, awkward. Therborn (2000a: 270) levels a similar charge in noting Wallerstein's attempt to combine a sympathy for the post-modern with a modernist orientation to the future. In a quite antithetical reading, meanwhile, Robbins (2011: 56) notes a central commonality between Wallerstein and the humanities, in an 'anti-progressive impulse' – a compelling issue about which more could be said.[18] A related issue is that of Wallerstein's commitment to anti-Eurocentrism. For instance, taking on Wallerstein and the mainstream of post-colonial thinking, Gregor McLennan (1998; 2006) contends that a number of problems appear in the charge of Eurocentrism, one significant effect of which has been to create a moralistic and irrationalist climate of debate: the genetic fallacy – the impossibility of separating ourselves from universalist aspirations, from the quest for truer, more objective knowledge (the need to keep questions of the true and good somewhat separate), from secular humanism and progressivist politics has to be recognized if we are to have the type of politics and also theory that are indispensable to Wallerstein's enterprise. In short, Wallerstein's strictures here are just not compatible with the intent of world-systems thinking, and his characteristically subsumptionary moves issue simply in antinomies.

Despite the presence of the abovementioned varieties of question and reservation in the Palumbo-Liu et al. collection (2011), the predominant attitude across the contributions is warm towards the potential contribution of the world-systems approach. Wallerstein (2011b: 225) himself is less receptive in his chapter, which appears towards the end of the book. In a pointed anecdote, he notes the typical anthropological seminar response to broad treatments of the situation of the South – 'But not in Pago Pago!'; and he restates the need to *explain* the *capitalist* world-system: 'It has its history, its structure, its contradictions, its prospects. I try to study this directly. Others study it implicitly. I think it might help us all if the latter reflected more openly on what it is they are really doing' (Wallerstein, 2011b: 226).

Wallerstein's obduracy, here, will be seen as matched by his own treatment of culture in the same year in that fourth volume of *The Modern World-System*, which is likely, again, to be interpreted as rather too schematic and broad-brush. Undoubtedly, many readers will be quickly dissatisfied with the characteristic three-way divisions and grand generalizations in play in terms of ideologies (reducing conservatism, liberalism and radicalism down to 'centrist liberalism'), with his congruent reading of the social sciences and with his treatment of the rich variety encompassed within the label 'anti-systemic movements'. And even in a world-system thinker more oriented towards the study of culture such as Jonathan Friedman (1995; 2000), the analysis flies very high. There is something to displease just about everyone in these cases but, once again, one important line of defence is to remind ourselves about the function of social theory in the first place – as a set of tools that enables us to organize our inquiries (Mann, 1993) rather than as an aspiration to create to-scale maps of the territory we seek to cover.

As McLennan (1996; 2006) notes, explanation requires those various 'sins' of modernism, and the social sciences are indispensably in the business of explanation, something that is significantly downgraded in much of the subject-centred, complexity-oriented and post-modern-influenced human scientific work of the past few decades (McLennan, 2006). Rough and ready though Wallerstein's judgements can appear, these are not only bold and striking hypotheses, but provide the scaffolding around which more nuanced, elaborative arguments can be and have been built. This is social theoretical abstraction as cognitive map, a point I will return to in conclusion.

A last stop – and perhaps one that runs best across the three substantive sections I have divided this chapter into, rather than being located narrowly within the cultural field – is the question of socialism, undoubtedly, the central political-moral nodal point of Wallerstein's entire intellectual career. There are a number of ways into these issues. A first problem concerns Wallerstein's treatment of the anti-systemic movements and of liberalism. For a start, as Pitts (2012) argues in a review of the latest volume of *The Modern World-System*, one could contest Wallerstein's portrait of liberalism as incomplete (restricted to France and Britain, devoid of attention to its global character) and coarse, missing liberalism's own liberatory and frankly contradictory moments. In like fashion, subsuming the entirety and variety of strong anti-systemic movements as mere variants of this liberal centre is likely to raise strong objections from thinkers of the Left still attached to the achievements and impulses of these movements.

Here, Wallerstein (1991b) is clearly attached to a more Left communist political tradition, to non-Leninist, anti-statist (councillist, syndicalist, anarcho-communist and so on) positions, than some of those other world-systems and dependency thinkers, such as Frank (early on) or Samir Amin. Wallerstein, that is, critically reads social democracy as a kind of social capitalism in the advanced economies, Real Socialism as a strategy of national development in the semi-peripheries and national liberation as a catching-up effort in peripheries and in semi-peripheral areas. At the same time, there is also a sense in Wallerstein that the way in which these movements played themselves out was the only feasible option on the Left agenda at this point (see, for instance, Wallerstein, 1991b: 96) and those achievements are still deemed considerable – 'magnificently successful' (Arrighi et al., 1989: 56). However, it is clear in Wallerstein (1991c; 1995; 2002b) that we are now in an era beyond statism, nationalization and developmentalism, and the democratic centralist modes of organization and naïve scientism of these movements and, looking into the future, we are the better for it. Here, we could again expect robust replies from a still trenchant Leninist Left, including recent defences of the real achievements of socialism in the twentieth century by the likes of Badiou and Žižek (see, for instance, Budgen et al., 2007). In related fashion, Sanderson (2005) contests the world-systems reading of 'really existing socialism' as truly part of the world-economy or as market-based, arguing that these orders cannot be conceptualized as state capitalist.[19]

From another angle, though, Wallerstein's continuing attachment to socialism is itself a major problem and, as mentioned, within certain of those world-systems thinkers – Frank and to a degree Arrighi – this attachment or hope had already waned significantly in their later years. One forceful version of what is at stake here is put forward by Sanderson (2005: 204) who argues that it is time to put away such 'foolish things'. Incorrectly criticizing Wallerstein for defending unrealistic autarchy, Sanderson (2005: 184) charges that a replacement socialist global system would 'likely descend into rent-seeking and become the most repressive and authoritarian state known to history', socialism now, on the balance of evidence, being discredited; Sanderson cites *The Black Book of Communism* as evidence, and raises the familiar argument about human nature presenting an unassailable barrier to socialist dreams (Darwin trumps Marx, humans by nature being status, wealth and power seekers). We are, of course, in the realm of endless warring gods and substantive rationality here, but for me, unsurprisingly, Wallerstein has firm ground on which to stand, given the various devastating problems of 'really existing capitalism', and given the reinvigoration of Leftist contestation and thought in recent times. To my mind, it is contentions such as Sanderson's that are increasingly beset by reality problems, centred as they are on an oblivious liberalism that accepts the broad shape of neo-liberal promises, radically truncates the possible for a jaundiced realism (what we have as the least worst alternative), or simply relies on a lazy anti-totalitarian set of 'prohibitions on thinking' (Žižek, 2001a).

Concluding comments

Contemporary judgements, then, of Wallerstein and world-systems analysis can be read as rather mixed. On the one hand, a range of contemporary researchers continue with the world-systems programme, producing a wealth of rich analyses,[20] and Wallerstein is widely and firmly positioned as a grand old figure in the world of social theory.

On the other hand, world-systems can be read as a paradigm largely surpassed by globalization-, post-colonial-, and complexity-oriented analyses, or as a theoretical project, at the very least, in need of 'prompt medical attention' (Sanderson, 2005: 206).

As I have noted throughout this chapter, my own sense is that much of the hesitation around world-systems analysis can be viewed as driven by an opposition to its broad-ranging and definitive statements, within a period that has been marked by deep hostility to totalizing thought and determinism of any stripe. But it is this very quality – the 'daring questions and provocative statements' (Therborn, 2000a: 266) – I think, that is remarkable and will last beyond the post-modern moment. Here, it is good perhaps to follow Jameson (1989) and ask why it is that at certain moments the category of 'totality', once thought fundamental for any analysis seeking to liberate us from the immediacy of common-sense, suddenly becomes prohibited, connecting this, paradoxically, to a moment at which capitalism has become more totalizing than ever. Following Jameson (1984a) once again, we can see this totalizing in Wallerstein as a powerful modality of 'cognitive mapping', a way of not being overwhelmed by the apparent complexity and detail that contemporary perspectives on 'global transformations' often foreground. There are undoubtedly a number of areas in which world-systems thinking could be thickened – for instance, the exploration of the periods in which military or ideological factors appear to lead – or questioned – for example, the compatibility between Wallerstein's project and post-modern modes of thought. But there is not, I have insisted, any reason why the broad conceptual tools forged by Wallerstein and other world-systems analysts cannot incorporate many of the observations of apparently novel processes and complexities in play in the present. Many of the trends suggested by Wallerstein – commodification, proletarianization, acceleration of technical change, growth of firms, for instance – are confirmed in the contemporary period (Chase-Dunn and Grimes, 1995), while other contentions remain respectable, and of use in arguing against much of the globalization literature. I would suggest that, today, it is most productive to read these contentions and conceptual contributions as problems and hypotheses rather than as complete solutions (Jameson, 1989), as spurs to further elaboration, argumentation and research. Finally, there is a sense in which, at this moment of intensified global chaos and suffering, Wallerstein is even more significant for us, as a break appears to be occurring in the history of the world-system, as new anti-systemic movements seem to be emerging, and as mounting contradictions lean on more and more people. Following this line, Balakrishnan (2011) suggests that the shift from something like a 1990s 'end of history' moment to the current moment of world turmoil vindicates the global and *longue durée* lenses that Wallerstein has so stubbornly worn. On this issue, Wallerstein (2004b: 189) has admitted that, in the end, there is no escaping macronarratives and that 'The only question is whether we are putting forward a defensible macronarrative'. Armed with a strong set of concepts and theses, in possession of a lively research agenda and equipped with an enormous scope of inquiry and weighty normative force (Anderson, 1983), Wallerstein's own macronarrative is arguably one of the few on the Left that is in a position to compete for attention with those fluent and encompassing narratives of reaction – triumphant globalism, the end of history and the clash of civilizations.

8
Narrating Socialism – Four Voices

Introduction

One of the notions I find most delightful and compelling within the Marxian tradition, especially among Trotskyists and ultra-Leftists,[1] is the idea of the 'balance-sheet'. In Marx's time, the balance-sheet appears to have been just that: balance-sheets from the minutes of the First International detail various contributions, costs for books and stationery, rent and gas, refreshments to delegates at conferences and so on. But, within later Leftist currents, there's a shift from the 'balance-sheet' as designating that very capitalist task of rationally accounting for profits and losses, and the term is appropriated and transformed into a minor Marxian theme – a drawing up of the situation, an assessment of the forces in play, the results of struggles and the prospects for socialism. From 1933, the 'Midnight of the century', *Bilan* ('Balance-sheet') was, for instance, the 'Theoretical Bulletin of the Left Fraction of the PCI [Italian Communist Party]', the exiled Bordigists, within which a sustained attempt was made to 'draw a balance-sheet of the post-war events ... to establish the conditions for the victory of the proletariat in all countries' (ICC, 1992: 70).

What sort of socialist balance-sheets might we draw up today? Reflections on the life and times of socialism have, I think, entered a new cycle, after post-socialism, after the end of history, post-post-modernism. As Lucio Magri (2008: 48) notes, a good many of the attempts, socialist and non-socialist, to offer answers immediately after the collapse of 'really existing socialism' came 'in a highly superficial, self-interested form: denial or amnesia'. Since the middle of the 1990s, as I have suggested in earlier chapters, we can detect a general shift in pitch, with a number of key Left thinkers offering important, thoughtful, sometimes surprisingly personal considerations on socialism. We have, here, a highly productive moment involving a real A to Z – Samir Amin (2006) to Slavoj Žižek (2009) – of socialist luminaries. How is socialism being narrated in such accounts? What are the broad intellectual patterns of this narration, thinking the past, present and future prospects of this family of ideas and practices, following all that has happened since the mythical '1968', a point at which Massimo Salvadori (1968: 1-2) could enumerate a highly impressive – for him, threatening – list of socialist accomplishments and conquests, way beyond those attributable to a mere European spectre? Four grand socialist voices – Perry Anderson (b. London 1938), Antonio Negri (b. Padua 1933), Regis Debray (b. Paris 1941) and T. J. Clark (b. Bristol 1943) – formed politically at about that point, 1968, can here serve as an entry into this chapter, and as contrasts to those voices to be examined.

First, Perry Anderson's pessimism of the intellect. Setting out the tasks before *New Left Review* into the new millennium, Anderson (2000: 9) notes that the environment in which the journal took shape – the Soviet bloc, socialism as widespread ideal, Marxism as dominant Left culture, Labourism – has 'completely passed away', leaving most socialists opting for accommodation or consolation. Against this, Anderson (2000: 14, 16) calls for an 'uncompromising realism', a 'lucid registration of historical defeat'. This realism means acknowledging the absence of significant opposition within the 'thought-world of the West', the collapse of a collective agency that might match capital and the complete ideological supremacy of neo-liberalism (Anderson, 2000: 17). In a later survey of the world-historical situation, Anderson (2007: 9) sticks with his cool – some would say, conservative – withdrawal to the socialist watchtower, noting the 'widening and deepening grip of capital', American hegemony at the head of a new 'Concert of Powers', the continuity of neo-liberal dominance (eased mildly by a shift from 'disciplinary' to 'compensatory' neo-liberalism) and a deep world cultural acceptance that there is no real alternative, flanked by sputtering contestatory efforts.

Towards the close of his later essay, Anderson turns to a number of competing narratives about Left prospects, and one of these is the thoroughgoing contrast, the immensely popular optimism of the intellect, offered by Hardt and Negri (2000; 2004; 2009). Here, of course, we have a fluent, seductive theoretical synthesis, which details a transformed capitalism, and exuberant talk of the 'irrepressible lightness and joy of being communist' (Hardt and Negri, 2000: 413), underpinned by an updated workerist contention that capital follows, and is really subordinate to, the creative, deterritorializing resistance of the Multitude, who are constructing counter-Empire before our eyes. In this story, as Turchetto (2008: 308) rather mercilessly interprets it, 'Empire shall fall, is about to fall, it is falling, has already fallen!'.

Third, in an account that seems to uncertainly pitch between detached description and bitter regret, Regis Debray (2007: 5) seeks to analyse the eclipse of socialism, 'the great fallen oak of political endeavour', as an expression of an epochal mediological shift. Socialism's life-cycle runs from 1831 to 1968, closing with the advent of the videosphere, the new age of the image, which triumphs over those great invisibles (God, History, Progress) of the past. Book, newspaper, school – these crucial co-ordinates of socialist culture cannot survive the major videospheric transformations: in terms of group ideal (from all to each); vector (from future to present); canonical generation (from adult to youth); spiritual class (intelligentsia to media); legitimating reference (the ideal to the effective); driving force (law to opinion); status of the individual (from citizen to consumer); identifying myth (hero to celebrity); symbolic authority (legible to visible); and subjective centre of gravity (consciousness to body) (Debray, 2007: 26). The thought-networks of the videosphere, Debray concludes – is his tone blank or full of foreboding? – are fatal for socialist culture.

Finally, one-time Situationist International member, more recently art historian and member of the Bay Area collective Retort, T. J. Clark's (2012: 57) provocative recent piece, 'For a Left with No Future', which entreats a deeply defeated Left to make 'Many and bitter' sacrifices. Calling for a 'tragic' perspective on politics to think 'our catastrophe', 1914–1989, including a recognition of 'the human propensity to violence' (2012: 66), and 'an abstention from futurity' (2012: 71), Clark insists the Left re-think its hesitation about the term 'reform': 'To move even the least distance out of the cycle of horror and failure ... will entail piece-by-piece, assumption-by-assumption dismantling of the politics we have' (2012: 73). Clark (2012: 75) concludes his essay – consciously seeking a Left occupation of typically conservative ground – in a resolutely melancholic key:

> There will be no future, I am saying finally, without war, poverty, Malthusian panic, tyranny, cruelty, classes, dead time, and all the ills the flesh is heir to, because there will be no future; only a present in which the left (always embattled and marginalized, always – proudly – a thing of the past) struggles to assemble the 'material for society' Nietzsche thought had vanished from the earth.

These balance-sheets, I think, contrast nicely with the four accounts I will treat here, where there is no chilly withdrawal, bitterness, blankness, despondency, giddy sanguinity: Lucio Magri – PCI member after the 20th Congress of the CPSU (Communist Party of the Soviet Union), expelled in 1970 as part of the *Il Manifesto* group, only to rejoin again in 1984, as part of the Proletarian Unity Party for Communism, before the PCI was disbanded in 1991 and he took up a leadership role in *Rifondazione Comunista*, finally deciding to wind up the revived journal *La Rivista del Manifesto* in 2004; Alain Badiou – ex-Maoist, disciple of Sartre, Althusser, Lacan, combatant, unyieldingly faithful to the Events of the Algerian struggle for independence, May '68, and the 1965–8 phase of the Chinese Cultural Revolution; Goran Therborn – part of the *New Left Review* stable, product of the radical 1960s, too, and particularly the structuralist moment (in bold, expansive early contributions on science, ideology and the state [1976; 1980]), more recently turning his impressive historical and theoretical gaze on modernity and contemporary shifts in social thought; and Peter Beilharz – Antipodean co-founder and editor of *Thesis Eleven*, turning, like Therborn, from capitalism to modernity, but importantly formed by the outsider Marxism of Castoriadis, Heller, Bauman.

In this chapter, then, I will explore the narrations of socialism across these four balance-sheets, the big questions running, I think, as follows: Whose was the twentieth century? What was 1968? What is the meaning of the three decades running from 1980 to the present? What remains of Marx and Marxism? What can we say about the traditions and future of socialism? What are the situation and tasks of social theory? In doing so, I want to attempt to make these very different but important, compelling balance-sheets from apparently more orthodox socialist directions – Leninist and social democratic – collide with each other across these urgent issues and with a Left communist sensibility I have focused on in the previous chapters. I continue to favour that Left communism but, nevertheless, find it interrogated, impelled in crucial ways by these accounts. These four voices, then – and voices like theirs – insist upon being part of any dialogue around a new global Left.

Yesterday – whose twentieth century?

Eric Hobsbawm's (2003) memoir is significantly sub-titled *A Twentieth Century Life*. Whose was this century? Was it the Soviet, socialist, liberal, totalitarian, mass, American century or something else entirely? Lucio Magri's (2011) *The Tailor of Ulm* significantly takes up such questions, and many others, in a modest, grave and resolute voice. At the close of his 'Parting Words', on the occasion of the 2004 suspension of the journal *La Rivista del Manifesto*, Magri (2005: 105) announced the need for 'a differentiated analysis, a counter-factual history of the communist tradition and its overcoming'. Doubtful at the time that he had the ability or strength for such a task, Magri nevertheless suggested that he 'would not want to free [himself] ... from that burden' and that, at the least, it would promise 'excellent mental gymnastics'.

The Tailor of Ulm sees Magri accepting this task, and, while the sub-title of the work – *Communism in the Twentieth Century* – is somewhat misleading (because it is more a history of post-War Italian PCI com-munism than of communism more widely in the twentieth century), it is nevertheless an enthralling work, full of sparkling interpretation, bold, wide-ranging evaluation and subtlety – even, I think, for those not inclined towards Magri's particular variety of Marxist commitment. In addition, the Italian socialist scene is so very fascinating and peculiar – a relatively open, mass-movement official communism, alongside a range of off-beat and well-subscribed-to varieties of Leftism – that these reflec-tions are of significant interest to anyone on the Left.

On the question of the century, Magri is clearly torn, adamant, in some respects, that everything noble and right-headed in the century (say, anti-fascism, and movements and institutions of equalization and recognition) was ultimately communistic and entwined with the self-movement of the masses, but too honest and solemn – Hobsbawm described the work as 'shrewd and despondent' (in Hellman, 2012: 198) – not to register the scale and consequences of Left failures. Magri's disposition, his orientation to the complicated task he sets himself, is signalled in the choice of title, drawn from a Brecht poem, referred to at a meeting in 1989 to consider a name change for the PCI. In making the reference, Pietro Ingrao attempted to link the apparent failure of com-munism with the tailor's failed attempt to fly – human beings did, in the end, despite various flops and fiascos along the way, manage to fly. As Magri glosses it, if capitalist modernity's path was far from a story of linear, smooth progress, why should communism's path be otherwise?[2] Magri's determination to bravely and clear-headedly face both the good and the bad, as well as the many unrealized possibilities, are clear in two further probing questions he, in turn, responded with at the meet-ing in question: if the tailor had not been killed would he have got up and tried again, and would/should his friends have attempted to stop him?; and what contribution, in fact, did the tailor make to the finally successful efforts to fly?

Magri (2011: 188), as I have indicated, is unwavering on the need to confront all questions, no matter how difficult: as he says, what has been left out and ignored is just as important, in a person's life and more widely, as what is faced and accomplished. And the book is full of probing analyses, frequently operating by way of counter-factual thinking – his constant refrain, 'could it have been otherwise?' – developing a smooth, uncluttered narrative, often reliant on his own recollections (I am 'a living private archive' [2011: 17], he says), older and newer documents, and the memories of those involved, all woven together in a careful and sombre voice. This austerity – a still vibrant but grave, if not pessimistic, intellect – is at work throughout, a dedication to writing in a 'spirit of truth' (2011: 10).

Setting out with a sweep over the early phase of the consolidation and subsequent undulations of capitalism and the socialist movement, we arrive at a first major question, the meaning of the Russian Revolution. Hostile to the contemporary consignment of communism to the category of 'calamity', a mere 'heap of ashes', Magri's (2011: 382) accounting for the weakening of the soviets, restrictions on liberty and so on in the time of Lenin has a familiar ring to it – civil war and foreign intervention, the failure of revolution in the West – though he does refreshingly note three fundamental errors made by Lenin: the obsession with the 'correct line' within the Third International (a particularly relevant issue for the PCI); the decision to go for rapid industrialization and collectivization in the countryside; and the decision to portray centrism as the major enemy within the workers' movement.

Trenchantly noting the role of communism in the spread of democracy, the Allied appeasement of the Nazis in the hope of turning Germany Eastwards, and underscoring the central role of the communists in the defeat of fascism ('Communists did not create a river of blood, they shed their own' [Magri, 2011: 36]), the terror of the 1930s is, to my mind, very lightly treated (read as a voluntarist and subjectivist distortion). There is more than a glimpse here of a defensive and less than brutally self-critical cast of mind, apparent at various points in the book – for instance, in Magri's (2011: 79) refusal to 'demonize' Stalin's 'whole record', finding the last five years the worst. This is, to say the least, a thorny issue and one the Left communist tradition, with its remorseless criticism of socialist orthodoxy (as essentially state capitalist), helps us approach. Magri, born in 1932, entered the party after the 20th Congress of the CPSU, was expelled in 1970 for attempting to respond creatively to the contestations of the 1960s, rejoining as part of the PCI leadership in 1984, and fighting to the last against the decision to disband 'an army that had not yet dispersed' (2011: 16). This remaining attachment to the Soviet Union and communist orthodoxy limits certain reflections. A good part of this seems an effect of the 'Gramsci genome', the desire to be with the masses in a significant party rather than in a small but 'uncontaminated' sect, the determination that Italy would make its own particular road to socialism, between Leninism and classical social democracy. Here, despite the ups and downs, Magri's narrative reinforces throughout his early insistence that the PCI was something else than either a middle-of-the-road social democratic force or a simple echo or puppet of the USSR. And, despite the limitations bound up with this, we should also see, here, and perhaps see *appreciatively*, that which, in Perry Anderson's (2011: 111) estimation, makes Magri unique, 'the only significant revolutionary thinker of his time whose thought was inseparable from the course of the mass movements of the decades through which he lived'.

Even for the most sceptical far-Leftist – who would read such an understanding of Gramsci as inevitably heading in the direction of Eurocommunist accommodation with some type of more or less social capitalism – there are plenty of reading rewards from Magri's stance. We get a close, intelligent insider's view on the various important periods in the life of the PCI: from the central moment of Togliatti's return to Italy in 1944, to the brink of the Third World War (driven exclusively by the West, in Magri's firm estimation), to the response to the secret speech, Poland and Hungary, and the China–USSR split. Here, Magri's counterfactual approach is often fascinating, deeply informed, and remarkably concrete: for example, what room may Togliatti have had to move in a more positively socialist direction in the delicate period 1945–8? How else might the PCI have responded in the wake of the Hungarian events, between uncritical support and potentially dangerous condemnation of the Soviet invasion? What was lost in Khrushchev's insistence on capitalism versus socialism as a question of economic results rather than on socialism as another sort of society? Nothing perhaps better sums up Magri's (2011: 129) understanding of the century until the 1960s shift than the very Gramscian notion that 'There are many ways of manning a barricade'.

Alain Badiou's (2007a) *The Century* confronts the questions of the century's meaning and ownership much more directly, urgently, bracingly. *Fidelity* – to political, artistic, amorous and scientific truths, which are tied to events/ruptures, are universal and infinite, as well as historical and situated, and which induce a subject (as opposed to the mere animality of our usual existence as individuals) (Badiou, 2010a) – is a crucial part of Badiou's orientation, and he has remained unbent from his early *gauchisme*. Two examples of this continuing militancy: responding to journalistic accusations of anti-Semitism, Badiou (2008a: 4) states that, as a partisan of direct action, he'll respond with a slap rather than take legal action; well into *The Century*, Badiou (2007a: 126) pauses to ask us to spare a thought for Ulrike Meinhof and Nathalie Menigon (of *Action Directe*) – 'Say what you will, these women had "the passion for something illegal and savage"'. And so the book runs – a startling, controversial, exciting, occasionally bewildering trip. Badiou's short twentieth century runs from 1914 or 1917 until the early 1980s, and it belongs to communism. Its prologue is provided by the two remarkably creative decades between 1890 and 1914, and the century, says Badiou, was faithful to the excitement and rupture of these decades. Centrally, what the nineteenth century announced, dreamed, promised, the twentieth century sought to realize, to achieve, to fashion (Badiou, 2007a: 15, 31, 32). The 'passion for the real' is key to understanding the century, and this passion made it both creative and lethal, violent, inventive, a century of radical commencement, seeking to 'break the history of the world in two' (2007a: 16). Rejecting the widespread post-modern condemnation of the twentieth century, a century that makes us turn our backs on modernity's metanarratives, Badiou urges us to recognize and embrace its heroic, epic qualities – the creation of the new person, the will to compel history, the necessity of terror to accomplish this destiny, the image of the last war, the omnipresence of scission (one must decide): 'the century's subjectivity, prey to the passion for the real and placed under the paradigm of definitive war, stages a non-dialectical confrontation between destruction and foundation, for the sake of which it thinks both totality and the slightest of its fragments in the image of antagonism, and posits that the cipher of the real is the Two' (Badiou, 2007a: 39).

This passion for the real explains the century's obsession with semblance, ideology, mask, misrecognition; it explains, too, its suspiciousness – is the real truly real?; and it explains the omnipresence of purging or purification. The Act – a central variety of which is revolution – is linked to this, also, as the 'defeat of defeats' (Badiou, 2007a: 58). One can witness all of this in the artistic avant-garde: its commitment to rupture, victory, its announcement 'we begin' (Badiou, 2007a: 135), its breaks and purges – Breton and Debord are heroes in this regard.

Praising the century's insistence on greatness ahead of happiness, Badiou (2007a: 93) emphasizes also the fervent desire for fraternity expressed through that short century – the 'we' against competitive individualism. Against more recent returns to emphasize unique individuality, Badiou (Badiou, 2007a: 99–102) looks back to the structuralist problematic – the modifiability of the individual, the individual as lacking essence, a nothing to be dissolved into a 'we-subject', the rejection of 'formal freedom' for fraternity as the real manifestation of the new world and the new human being. This anti-humanism is, in turn, linked to the century's desire for the infinite over the finite: the infinite *we* over the finite individual; the party as indestructible, that which is 'always and forever' (Badiou, 2007a: 129). On this score, Badiou has long crusaded against the contemporary intellectual predominance of post-foundational emphases on finitude, limits, particularism, rights.

For Badiou (2007a: 108), the great weakness of the century's thought, on the other hand, was its representational conception of legitimacy against the 'presentation of the real'. This is to italicize politics against democracy, politics as a 'collectively recognized break' (2007a: 150) or, as he puts it elsewhere, 'organized collective action, following certain principles, and aiming to develop in reality the consequences of a new possibility repressed by the dominant state of affairs' (2008a: 11). For Badiou (2006; 2008a: 31–2; 2011), in contrast – and in stark contrast, too, to our other three socialist narratives, but reminiscent of Bordiga (see Chapter 5) – democracy is indifferent to any content, principles and convictions, and is simply a matter of numbers, universal suffrage having produced numerous abominations – Hitler, Pétain, the Algerian War.[3]

What of the century's cruelty, the spectre of the hangman, the weight of the shared, the human consequences of the attempt to bend history and the passion for the real? Badiou (2007a: 63) is unmoved by such questions. In the quest for a free politics, in the search of total emancipation, we will find an overwhelming 'enthusiasm in the absolute present'. This is beyond good and evil: 'Extreme violence is therefore the correlate of extreme enthusiasm, because it is in effect a question of the transvaluation of all values' (2007a: 63).[4]

Both Badiou's and Magri's connections to and defences of certain domains and inheritances of official communism – as singular and stimulating as they are – are an entire world removed from what might be called the 'warm socialism' of Peter Beilharz's *Socialism and Modernity*. The title's second substantive term is already an indication of a distance of emphasis and interpretation that separates this account from Magri's and Badiou's, with Beilharz (2009: ix) noting the shift in the discourse of radicalism over his lifetime from socialism to modernity, from Marxism to critical theory. This is no simple renunciation of socialism though. We remain, says Beilharz (2009: 42, xvi), creatures of traditions, and he places his own formation within a plurality of socialist currents – German and Scandinavian social democracy, council communism, Western Marxism, Fabianism, English ethical socialism.

This pluralism is key, against the rather negative connotations it carries for Badiou and Magri, Beilharz underscoring the plural against some Marxist and socialist attempts to override difference and, at the same time, insisting on the plurality of socialism, of Marxism, of the various socialist and Marxist sub-currents, and even of Marx (Beilharz [2009: 180], for instance, identifying five separate images of utopia in Marx). Pluralism is, too, the reason that modernity replaces capitalism as analytical object, Beilharz influenced by Feher and Heller's early work on modernity as the complex intertwining of three logics and, more recently, leaning towards multiple modernities and civilizational analyses.[5]

Such a shift from capitalism to modernities clearly entails certain dangers/renunciations (?) for socialism (Jameson, 2002). This pluralism means that socialism remains inescapable, as the alter-ego or counter-culture of modernity, that Marxism, too, continues to matter, but Beilharz (2009: 1, 27) clearly will not award the twentieth century to them. Whose century is it? One gets the sense with Beilharz that Marxism, socialism, America, liberalism, the unpredictable unfolding of democracy – they will have to share the century. The twentieth century was also, importantly, a totalitarian century – the 'age of disaster', the age of 'Behemoth and corpses' (2009: 113). It is little wonder, says Beilharz (2009: 113), as if answering Badiou, that after this century people celebrate the individual, worry about cruelty, feel compelled to go with liberalism. Beilharz finds unacceptable the 'Deutscherist' position – closest, here, perhaps to Magri – that, despite all, the twentieth century was the Soviet century. This line is wrong-headed, partly because of the unthinking anti-Americanism it often encloses – when so much of our modernity is American or looking towards America, including socialist alternatives – and partly because the attempt to defend the Soviet experience in the last instance, as its abominable acts were committed in the name of noble ends, is morally indefensible (2009: 136, 139). Here, Beilharz makes a move absolutely rejected by Magri and Badiou,[6] aligning the extremities of Left and Right as totalitarianisms (2009: 122). For Beilharz, they connect in the 1930s, at least, by way of hostility to parliamentary forms and through their common enthusiasms for planning (2009: 122). This totalitarian connection, though, is made not via the Cold War liberalism of Talmon, Friedrich, Brzezinski and company, nor by the French paths of New Philosophy, revisionist approaches to revolution or post-structuralism/post-modernism, but instead by way of the ultra-Left-inspired work of Castoriadis, Heller and Bauman. The last, in particular, has come to be ever more pivotal to Beilharz over the past decade or so. And Bauman is perhaps the central presence in Beilharz's (2009: 167, 177) book, occasionally explicitly – such as when Beilharz makes the compelling suggestion that we see *Legislators and Interpreters* as Bauman's companion volume to *Modernity and the Holocaust*, a kind of *Modernity and Communism* – but mostly, and deeply, I think, implicitly, as an interlocutor, inspiration, guide, consort.

For Beilharz (2009: 198), then, the Nazi and Soviet experiences are 'appallingly similar'. In a related vein, Marx provided an anti-political utopia (2009: 187), wrongly and dangerously imagining an end to history; and Marxism did end up a mirror of production (Baudrillard) and a partner with capitalism in the fantasy of unlimited rational mastery (Castoriadis) (2009: 138). This is not, though, a one-sided *post*-Marxist move, because, again, a thoroughgoing pluralism reigns; Beilharz wants to remind us that socialism and Marxism remain with us somehow, and his socialism is too warm, too generous and embracing to countenance merely casting thinkers and traditions into the dustbin of history. For instance, in a chapter on Australian communism, he asks 'Where have the communists gone?' (2009: 91). The communists generated zealot and administrator character types, but also good citizens. These good citizens weren't big on pluralism, we can't, in the end, be nostalgic about the ruinous Cold War, but they made a choice, and their commitment to strong Stalinist-communist norms and values looks positively far removed from the 'flatulent self-indulgence of the 1990s' (2009: 91).

Here the overriding impression is that Beilharz's (2009: 188) approach is to attempt to hold together and keep in tension Enlightenment and Romantic sensibilities, keeping at analytical and historical arm's length a third, Revolution (Badiou's master current). The century 1880–1980 is partly about the social question, citizenship, economic integration, the public, the nuclear family (2009: 105). All this is going and, on the one hand, some of this has to be viewed as loss, because it opens new undergrounds, and the new world is getting built on new barbarisms but, on the other hand, Weber was right – the Soviet experience set socialism back a hundred years (2009: 93). In the end, for Beilharz, to face all this, Enlightenment and Romanticism, social democracy and liberalism, these remain part of our modernity, colliding and rubbing against each other endlessly, while the old rhetoric and politics of the 'day of the great sweep' appear no longer available or defendable (2009: 188).

In some ways, Therborn seems, with his social democratic leanings, closest to Beilharz rather than to Magri or Badiou, despite the distance of intellectual influences – the *NLR* folk apparently don't want anything to do with Castoriadis, Bauman, Heller. Therborn's hugely ambitious brief is a survey of current Left political thought and practice, against the Marxism of the previous era but often it is modernity rather than capitalism that is highlighted and latterly Therborn (2000a; 2003) turned his attentions to the notion of multiple modernities and the theoretically consequential advent of a decisive new imaginative space, globality. Like Beilharz, Badiou and Magri, Therborn acknowledges a radical end to and shift from the twentieth century: 'the century of total industrial war, communist revolution and dictatorship, fascism, anti-fascism, working-class hopes for socialism, and welfare-state capitalism ... has drawn to a close' (1995: 89); 'the socio-economic, the cultural, and the geopolitical spaces of the twenty-first century are radically different from those of the twentieth' (2008: 57). For Therborn (2008: 111), the twentieth century was socialist more than liberal, and the role of Marxism stands out – the twentieth century was also the 'century of Marxism' (2008: ix). Marxism was importantly alone in acting as 'Her Modern Majesty's Loyal Opposition' (Therborn, 2008: 66), uniquely reconciling a view of modernity as simultaneously emancipatory and exploitative, progressive and catastrophic (Jameson, 1984a). This Marxism outstripped its competitors, none of which 'had a comparable reach and persistence' (2008: 94) and, from the 1880s until 1980, it was unique in existing as the main intellectual culture of two social movements, the labour movement and the anti-colonial movement.

In drawing his balance-sheet for this century, 1880–1980, Therborn's (2008) reminders of big Left successes are welcome and important: the discrediting of racism and the fall of colonialism; the victory in arguments about the welfare state; the advances of the forces of 'irreverence' from the 1960s; the impact of feminist contentions. In terms of defeats, these are also pretty weighty: the 'missed rendezvous' (2008: 23) between the '68ers and the labour movement; the Right's capacity for violence; the implosion of 'really existing socialism'; and the partial rewards that have emerged from neo-liberal policies (say, new opportunities opened by globalization, control of inflation).

We have four different balance-sheets of the twentieth century, then, though there is some agreement that a closure happens somewhere between the 1960s and early 1980s. From this point onwards, certain currents and ideas appear to have been – to use Badiou's (2006) term – 'saturated'. I like Fredric Jameson's (1984a) insistence, in the face of the generalization of the new post-modern cultural logic, and the sometimes unthinking Marxian retorts, that it makes little sense to moralize a historical epoch – we have to keep assessing things as progress and catastrophe all at once. This is in order to avoid confusing transformation with decline, in part, to sidestep the danger of analysis lapsing into a 'generational lament' (Mann, 1995: 113). But, of course, we still need to register the real losses in what has passed away, like that great generation of self-educated communist good citizens of the Cold War period (or, more appositely for the focus of this chapter, the problem of replacing the generation of intellectuals radicalized between 1956 and 1977, now in their 60s, 70s, and 80s [Keucheyan, 2013]); and we need to face the intellectually and emotionally demanding task of thinking what might be retrieved or re-worked and what is now ashes and dust. In terms of awarding victory in the twentieth century, it's hard not to be pulled this way and that by the accounts before us, to be swayed by each of these distinct paths, headed to four quite different places: 'defiant humility', and a loosely carried, alert and open Marxian and socialist orientation for Therborn (2008: 181); a pluralistic, social democratic search for the wisdom and strength still to be drawn from socialist history in Beilharz (2009: 141); a Gramscian determination in Magri (2011: 10, 17), to confront in a 'spirit of truth' the entirety of the socialist tradition, to painstakingly consider 'what could have been done, or might yet be done'; an insistence on courage, endurance in the impossible, but also faith in the miraculous, reconfiguring Event in Badiou (2008a).

One response would be to confront each of these narrations with the valiant, doomed ultra-Left. These Left communists, to my mind, mounted the best critiques of Soviet totalitarianism, without ever giving up on revolution, without submitting to what Žižek (2001a) correctly criticizes as the pessimistic and misanthropic blackmail of much of the liberal analysis of totalitarianism. They also took social democracy to task for its lack of socialism and democracy, forging a robust critical and utopian path still worth engaging with. From these far-Left vantage points, the narrations under observation could be set upon for their defeatism and capitulation, for their confinement to socialisms now in discredit – residual social democratic tinkering, Leninist voluntarism and substitutionism, ponderous Eurocommunism, merely ethical socialism. At a certain level, this is good medicine in light, say, of Badiou's (2010b: 101) insistence that the creative decade from 1968 belongs to the 'Maoist current, the only true political creation of the sixties and seventies', his appropriation of the Paris Commune (exactly along the lines but without mention of the ultra-Left) as a politics beyond party and state, his avoidance/lack of acknowledgement of most of this Left communist current, other than anarchism, which he very casually dismisses again and again. At the same time, the quality of these four narrations can equally tune us in to the failings of that communist Left: an extremism that very often unfolded as *attentisme*, revolutionary waiting and withdrawal, or as tremendous unrealism with respect to revolutionary prospects, sometimes coupled with the worst adventurism, or a purist damnation of the old world, hand in hand with a void of political thinking and subtle cultural analysis about how that world might be left behind. These four balance-sheets show us just how much wealth and life – analytical, theoretical, strategic, utopian – remain in those rather complicated but more orthodox socialisms.

And the contemporary period? – of events and sequences

What of the contemporary period? If socialism at least partly owned the past, what happened? What went wrong? How and why did socialism's grip loosen? Of course, '1968', as shorthand for the contestations running from the mid-'60s to the early/mid-'70s, has been viewed as a moment of special significance in narratives of socialist fortunes and misfortunes into the contemporary period; 1968 is, for instance, the point of the advent of the videosphere for Debray. The world-systems theory reading, meanwhile, has this 'world-revolution' as expressing the beginning of the end for American hegemony in the world-system and the close of the variety of opposition articulated by the 'anti-systemic movements' – communism, social democracy, national liberation (Arrighi et al., 1989; Wallerstein, 2002a). In a somewhat related way, Fredric Jameson (1984b: 207) reads the sequence 1967–1973 as a momentous dialectical combination of liberation (that has Third World beginnings) and domination (capital's penetration and colonization of 'the last vestiges of Nature'). For Badiou (2008a), '68 remains an Event to which he must show fidelity, and a nodal-point in a period of vast communist contestation of the old world, which runs from 1966 to 1976.[7] In a similar vein, Therborn insists that the radical generation of the 1960s, of which he is part, has refused to surrender; he laments, as noted, the missed connection between the culturalist and materialist contestations of the 1960s – what Boltanski (2002) calls the artistic and social critiques; and, in thinking about a re-articulation of socialism, he clearly looks back to the utopian and revolution-of-everyday-life registers of that period, which might be re-discovered in new ways in the present.

The battle for the 1960s, and '68 in particular, began almost immediately – Hobsbawm (1973: 234) noted that by the end of 1968 at least 52 books about the French events had appeared. This struggle for meaning and ownership, in the French case, is treated beautifully by Kristin Ross (2002) in her *May '68 and its Afterlives*, and many of her observations could be expanded to the wider period of contestation. For Ross (2002: 3), May '68 has 'been buried, raked through the coals, trivialized, or represented as a monstrosity'. What was significantly a workers' movement, with a strong Third Worldist dimension (the Algerian War as its prehistory, opposition to American imperialism and the Vietnam War as animating referents), whose thrust was, above all else, equality – this is all transformed in a vast process of social amnesia, stripped of violence, represented as a mellow, poetic generational revolt, a necessary moment towards cultural modernization, centred on the emancipation of the individual, and so on. Those two vital figures of 1960s contestations, the worker and the colonial militant, are soon replaced by the New Philosophers, by 'the pleb' and 'the dissident' and here, and then more widely, the language of totalitarianism and the Gulag inaugurates a retreat from politics to morality, a war against Marxism (totality = totalitarianism) and a shift from militant Third Worldism to the representation of those in the poorer countries as victims, desperately in need of humanitarian assistance and human rights, to be delivered by the West (Ross, 2002).

However we code '68 – what did it mean? Victory, defeat, watershed? When did it begin and end? – by the 'fateful 1980s' (Magri, 2011: 324–47), for all four thinkers, the twentieth century appears to have closed, in a 'seismic shift', in Goran Therborn's (2008: ix) reading, in line with the direction noted and lamented by Ross. For Therborn, since the close of the 1970s, we have seen transformations across states, markets and what he calls social patternings of actors. Against wild globalization analyses, states continue to be able to do their thing, provided they can compete on the world market, and the welfare state remains standing. On the other hand, major power changes have followed upon the 'neoliberal tsunami' (2008: 113): privatization, deindustrialization, the concentration of capital, the growth of markets – what Beverley Silver (2005: 176) calls 'the de-socialization of the state' – and a tilt away from North Atlantic world domination, together 'narrowing' the Left's cultural space. In this phase, too, the 'irreverent collectivism' (Therborn,

2008: 19) of the working-class movement peaked, weakened, then reversed; we have seen the decline of progressive academic culture, the depoliticization of students, the failures of secular anti-colonial nationalisms; and, more ambiguously, we have also witnessed the rise of other movements and the emergence of a new type of (media/image-centred) politics, with new fields of irreverence opening up.

As we will see, for Therborn (2008: 116), this means that 'the old cartography of "roads to socialism" has lost its bearings', that the terrain of Left thought and politics has been transformed. Turning to the contemporary Left 'repertoire of positions' (2008: 151) across two poles, one theoretical (Marxism/non-Marxism), one political (socialism/ capitalism), we see a real pluralization effect: post-socialism (Giddens, Beck); the non-Marxist Left (Bourdieu, Unger, Sennett); Marxology (Derrida, Carver); post-Marxism (Laclau and Mouffe, Castells, Bauman); neo-Marxism (Žižek, Hardt and Negri). Left-wing intellectual creativity, then, has not ceased, even if – in a revealing but disappointingly unelaborated moment – Therborn (179) declares that its 'greatest moments may have passed'.

I will return to this shortly, but the pluralization Therborn emphasizes and appears to endorse is again echoed by Beilharz, though with a different inflection. The 1980s, again, might be read as crucial in this pluralizing transformation: *Thesis Eleven* is founded in 1980; the Australian Communist Party closes up shop early in 1984; labourism and Labour in the Antipodes are reconfigured, as Antipodean Labour Parties lead the neo-liberal, modernizing charge; Feher et al.'s *Dictatorship over Needs* appears in 1983, Bauman's *Interpreters and Legislators* in 1987; the Berlin Wall falls in 1989. This 1980-onwards pluralist turn is centrally implicated by Beilharz (2009: 15) in the collapse of Marxism as a key presence in social theory: the void is filled by the return of methodological pluralism and 'the rediscovery or re-negotiation of democracy via liberalism'.

If Therborn's assessment of the contemporary period, especially the sequence from the close of the 1970s, is in a somewhat declinist register, Beilharz's is cautiously welcoming. These changes, a lucid registering of epistemological and political limits, are understandable and laudable in a sense, after the brutal twentieth century. And yet, 'anything goes' post-modern pluralism, bereft of the will to reform, a liberal sensibility content with simply saying no, unaccompanied by a socialist conception of action[8] – these things just aren't enough. We continue to need socialism; socialism continues to demand a hearing. But to what extent, in the end? The question to be posed to both Beilharz and Therborn is, are they not engaging in a rather dramatic scaling back of socialist transformatory ambitions, to socialism as merely one of an array of diagnostic tools, or of rather vague ethical, cultural or counter-cultural impulses? I will return to this soon.

Magri's early attention to, and fluency with, the 1960s-onwards transformations taking place in Italy and more widely are the subject matter of perhaps the most rewarding chapters in *The Tailor of Ulm*, and make evident the still considerable excitement and coherence achievable by a refined mind placed firmly within the Marxian orbit. The 1960s and 1970s are, for Magri, real turning points for a party that was by then mature and equipped with impressive electoral support, a very large, active membership, and a genuine cultural presence, but whose decline can be traced from that moment, too. First, Magri is very interesting on Italy's 'economic miracle' – based upon an idiosyncratic mixed economy, a quick Fordist burst and its extension to new sectors and forms of production and consumption, culminating in a comeback for the large industrial and financial capitalist class and, very importantly and temporarily, predicated early on upon a labour surplus and very low wages.

That miracle was soon followed by an impressive labour revival and a robust student revolt. It is here that Magri (2011: 223) finds the PCI particularly disappointing, showing itself to be bereft of 'ideas, inspiration and energy', unable, in the face of both trade union combativeness and the emergence of new struggles, to take up a leading role parallel to the one it had played in the Resistance. One of the issues here is that a situation of surprising openness and toleration of dissent within the PCI gives way, under the weight of the urgent new questions – the party's 'protected democracy' (2011: 185) being not up to the task of responding to these necessary rethinkings. The purge of the *Il Manifesto* group, of which Magri was a member, is one instance of this, when such questioning could have genuinely contributed to PCI reinvigoration and perhaps answered, in part, the problem of the party's growing inability to attract young people into its ranks.[9] Importantly, Magri also finds Togliatti's death in 1964 particularly untimely (one of a number of 'strokes of divine malignity' [Anderson, 2011: 116]), at a point at which the latter was attempting some important innovation (the need for an accommodation between China and the Soviet Union, a deeper reading of Gramsci, a nuanced response to the Catholic question).

These opportunities slipping away, the 1970s see obstacles to capitalist restructuring cleared, a new international political climate created and a new neo-liberal capitalist phase becoming visible (globalization, technological changes, alterations in class composition) alongside Berlinguer's disastrous 'historic compromise',[10] where the PCI ended up 'legitimating the quasi-monarchical right of the DC [Christian Democrats] to govern the country' (Magri, 2011: 272). Italy's resulting 'downward miracle' is followed by the 1980s, designated 'fateful' – although Magri insists the PCI were not, at this point, a spent force. Here, in a piece from 1987, Magri surveys the changes taking place from the 1960s, to which he had, at the time, been keenly attentive (Anderson, 2011), demonstrating his great perspicacity in raising early and with great lucidity and eye for detail many of the changes and challenges that were to confront Left thought – mass media, globalization, finance, precarious employment, democracy without hegemony, de-industrialization, ecological questions and more.

The feeling of dissatisfaction with the present – deeply marked in Magri's introductory summation of our situation,[11] more muted but still registered somewhat in Beilharz – is unsurprisingly hearty, some might say absolute, in Badiou's trenchant narrative. What we have had since 1980 amounts to straightforward *Restoration* (a time akin to that of 1815–1840 [Badiou, 2012b]). The present is judged as lacking on a whole range of measures when compared to that short twentieth century. Ours is a pacified and moralistic rather than political age; we see a conservative return, back from the radical questionings of the previous century, to 'Money, Family, Elections' (2007a: 66); we have today an 'artificial individualism' replacing the 'we-subjects' and schemes for a new person of the previous century's endeavours (2007a: 93); in place of the constructivism and future-orientation of that century, we have today a paradoxical 'stagnant feverishness' (2007a: 106); in place of the demonstration, we have celebrations (2007a: 107); in place of politics – the new – we have the return of the religious and of human rights (man above all as a pitiable animal) (2007a: 175); we have now a dialectic of fear and war (2008a: 15); we have a situation where 'culture' is replacing art, 'technology' is replacing science, 'management' is replacing politics and 'sexuality' is replacing love (2003b: 12). Ours is a time of defeat, then, but more, too – a time to rethink, but what to rethink and how?

Into the future – Marxism, socialism, social theory

Marxism, socialism, critical social theory – what might the future hold, here? Will our future be post-communist, post-socialist, post-Marxist? Are we moving beyond 'the social', beyond the old modality of theoretical comprehension and critique, which, for some, has 'run out of steam' (Boltanski, 2002; Boltanski and Chiapello, 2005; Latour, 2004; Rose, 1996)?

Sadly, Magri has the least to say on these questions, other than hints – caught between cautious optimism (a 'turn has taken place' [2011: 6]) and doubts ('The outlook [ahead] is not auspicious' [2011: 8]). The final chapter of *The Tailor of Ulm* deals with the end of the PCI. Here, one might expect more detailed reflection on the possibility of a different road, a new communist-inspired movement that might have emerged, or that might still appear, as a response to the many contemporary challenges, theoretical and practical, underscored with such skill and sceptical foreboding in the introduction. This was not to be. As Magri notes briefly, movingly, the period between the completion of the previous chapter and the return to this one was marked by the death of his wife, Mara Caltagirone, which he describes as 'like an amputation that will never heal, making my mind opaque and my will sluggish' (2011: 368). Having promised her he would complete the book, Magri draws things fairly abruptly to a close, appending a text he had written in 1987 as some indication of an answer to the problem of communist futures, which, as Hellman (2012) notes, is both more combative than the rest of the book and of doubtful relevance in terms of guidance on the way forward today. In November 2011, his promise to his wife fulfilled, Lucio Magri chose an assisted suicide in Switzerland (Anderson, 2011). Despite this sad finale, which leaves those questions of other roads into the future unanswered, Magri delivers a searching, intelligent reminder of the best of that disappearing communist generation, the insistence on the unity of theory and practice (Anderson, 2011) and the importance and fertility of re-opening the critical debate about communism. Perhaps Magri's evaluation of the outlook and tasks ahead are best summarized in this characteristically nuanced and intriguing formulation at the close of his introductory remarks: 'The "old mole" has been burrowing away, but being blind he is not sure where he comes from or where he is going; he may be digging in circles. And those who cannot or will not trust in Providence must do their best to understand him, and help him on his way' (2011: 17).

Thankfully, Therborn is able to address these questions, but he is interestingly unclear on some of them. Up front, Therborn (2008: ix) raises three toasts to Marx, as a still 'maturing' and 'stimulating companion': first, as a proponent of 'emancipatory reason'; second, for the historical materialist approach to social analysis, which Therborn reads, rather minimally, as a 'broad directive' to pay attention 'to living and working conditions of ordinary people and to the economic and political materiality of power'; third, for his sensitivity to contradictions and conflicts. I like this a great deal, and these continuing strengths should make us uncomfortable about assertions of a post-Marxist condition: not only is the broad Left still intellectually creative, but the neo-Marxian Left still has plenty of gas in the tank in terms of contemporary discussions of world politics and broad logic-of-the-social analyses,[12] when placed side-by-side with its post-Marxist competitors.

Therborn (2008: 108) seems to acknowledge this, at one moment speaking in the present tense and declaring Marxism 'without rival among modern conceptions of society', and it appears that, regardless of whether Marxism is an ascending or declining research programme, Therborn would continue to prefer to remain intellectually housed somewhere in this camp. However, at the next moment, Therborn notes that the 'parameters of the political field ... have shifted' (2008: 25), and that the 'Marxist triangle' – historical social science, philosophy of contradictions, working class, socialist politics – has been broken, class is unlikely to regain its centrality (2008: 57) and any future socialism is unlikely to be Marxist (2008: 119). Therborn is, here, strangely opaque on the reasons for these declared endings. For instance, it seems strange that he avoids the route taken by Fredric Jameson (1996) in the latter's insistence that as long as capitalism remains, Marxism will continue to flourish in new and surprising ways, keeping pace with the novel twists and turns of capital.[13] Part of the issue, for Therborn, is clearly the shifting significance of class. In a more recent piece, for instance, Therborn (2012: 5) designates the twentieth century the 'age of the working class', but deindustrialization in the West has shifted the parameters and today, while intra-nation inequality grows and class remains pressing, an apparent 'universal aspiration to middle-class status' (2012: 15), the division, defeat and demoralization (2012: 20) of the Western working class, and the changing international division of labour promise us a number of non-canonical possibilities ahead: 'globalized middle-class consumerism; middle-class political rebellion; industrial class struggle ... with its centre in East Asia; and heterogeneous mobilizations of the popular classes' (2012: 26–7). Here, it is hard not to be surprised by the absence of a detailed encounter with the sorts of sophisticated and more Marxian arguments put forward by the likes of Beverley Silver (2005) about the continuing centrality of class.

Further to current Marxian marginality, Therborn (2008: 60) mentions that Bolshevism 'turned out to be an unsustainable modernism'. In addition, post-modernism appears important, this turn producing 'a rift in cultural social thought ... which has not been overcome' (2008: 127). And yet, the post-modern 'avalanche' (208: 29) is viewed, above all, and dismissively, as 'a manifestation of ex-leftist exhaustion and disenchantment' (2008: 30). Might this be turned around? Therborn (2008: 125) notes that by the 1990s, modern social theory's 'belief in the future had been fundamentally shattered'. But has this lasted? Will it last? If so, why and with what cultural-political effects? Post-modernization and those big emphases over the past decades on pluralism, culture, ethics and complexity have certainly transformed social theory, and elsewhere Therborn (2000b) suggests that on those three crucial theoretical issues of social cosmology, social direction and mode of cognition the dominating answers have shifted fundamentally between the mid-1970s and now: from antagonistic structure, emancipation, and consciousness and science in the 1970s, to strategies, contingency, and understanding and discourse today. The outer edges of these shifts look decidedly non- or anti-Marxist, non- or anti-socialist: networks and associations rather than structures and systems; contingency rather than progress, evolution and determinacy; understanding and discourse as modes of cognition rather than big-S science aspirations; description rather than explanation and evaluation; the decentring of the world against classical sociology's Eurocentrism – in short, a drift to a 'post-social' theoretical universe – for instance, in thinkers such as Latour (2004; 2005), de Landa (2006), Rose (1996) and Urry (2005). On this score, Therborn detects a number of new Left theoretical turns: the post-secular European turn (for example, Badiou, Negri, Žižek); a new American utopianism (Jameson, Olin Wright, Wallerstein); displacements of class; shifts away from state theory (political philosophy, globalization, civil society); the return of sexuality (Butler and queer theory); a shift to networks (Castells, Hardt and Negri); and new political economies (Blackburn, Brenner, Arrighi).

This all seems to cry out for more evaluation and reformulation than Therborn is prepared to engage in, as some of the shifts appear inhospitable to or awkward for socialist theory and politics. Therborn, as noted, avoids erecting a defence of Marxism, declining to carefully assess these moves for their compatibility with a Marxian framework, but he appears attached still, at the same time, to some sort of Marxism – though Marx, Marxism and socialism are residual at best in his recent, attractive, big-scale sociology primer, *The World: A Beginner's Guide* (2011). What Therborn (2008) does instead is to shift his attention to politics, predicting continuing struggle and transformation, and speaking of a future 'trans-socialism'. This 'trans' is partly an acknowledgement that

Marxism was a 'profoundly European movement' (2008: 61), and it signals a shift beyond the familiar strategies and institutions of socialism, beyond the centrality of the working class and beyond the notions of public ownership and large-scale collective planning of industry (2008: 61). Such suggestions are ambitious and, clearly, detailed discussion of them is beyond the already large scope of his book; Therborn opts to single out four quick points or issues as particularly salient. First, capitalism continues to provoke contestation. Second, Therborn points to the importance of vigorous movements of marginalized ethnic groups. Third, he acknowledges the growing importance of moral discourse, especially around human rights and violence. And, finally, he suggests this trans-socialism will/should tap into a 'commitment to universal pleasure', returning to the ludic spirit of the 1960s, towards a 'universal society of fun and enjoyment' (2008: 64–5).

Therborn's (2008: 110) positive comment about the 'return of socialism from science to utopia' also underscores the contemporary proximity of the 1960s, Therborn imagining a revival of interest in Ernst Bloch. Beilharz would likely appreciate the broad shape of Therborn's trans-socialism and Beilharz, too, emphasizes the positive socialist journey from science to utopia, but this utopia is thought experiment, diagnosis and critique, *norm* rather than *place*. In his introduction, Beilharz (2009: 138) appears to acknowledge, too, a continuing attachment to Marxism and says, later in, that it is hard to imagine modernity without Marxism. Socialism also, as counter-culture, remains with us. But in which particular ways?

At times utopia, socialism, Marxism seem to have a more historical presence in Beilharz's narrative: too much has perhaps happened; complexity, pluralism, differentiation are obviously here to stay. In terms of Marxism, for instance, those old illusions about the authoritative, hard scientific status of historical materialism are decidedly over, but Marxism, like Freudianism, is part of our commonsense now – the critical spirit after the death of the body, to paraphrase Castoriadis, the widespread acknowledgement that economy rules if we let it. Beilharz has no nostalgia either for the highly abstract, empiricism-hostile theoretical production characteristic of some of the Marxian tradition, and he takes a much more deflationary approach to theory, much closer to the lighter touch of Bauman, or perhaps someone like Michael Mann (1993) for whom theory is simply and pragmatically a collection of tools to help us deal with 'a mess'.

The same thing applies to socialism. Beilharz acknowledges the influences of Bauman and Bernard Smith, socialists who travelled from politics to culture; and after the end of the Soviet experiment – which is variously judged to be 'pre-modern' (2009: 29) or another modern civilizational project (2009: 108) – socialism itself is relocated to cultural and ethical realms (see also Beilharz, 2003). Socialism remains because there will be no end, contra Marx, to the master–slave dialectic and here Beilharz's civilizational turn has clearly Benjaminian connotations – civilizations as always built on barbarisms and undergrounds – as well as certain post-colonial resonances. Given this, the materials and riches provided by the vigorous and plural socialist tradition are worth returning to but, in the end, only some specific strands and not others because, above all, Beilharz is interested in looking back to the social democratic and Fabian traditions to excavate useable materials. Demonstrating the plurality of the Webbs' utopia, with its separate realms and economy of mixed property forms (2009: 45–9), Beilharz's real sympathies lie – despite the past influence on him of the radical council communist current – with the pre-1914 German social democrats: socialism as norm rather than goal, the future as complex and differentiated, citizenship, acknowledgement of the limits on knowledge and action, a kind of Weberian Marxism, 'which is politically realistic, takes ideas seriously, and embraces a post-Faustian future' (2009: 38).

Beilharz is here infinitely more 'realistic', some will say 'defeatist', than Badiou, but surprisingly perhaps there is at least something shared between them – something like a fidelity to socialism. For Beilharz, this fidelity sees socialism as a humane, gentle but often positively unsettling presence that should continue to orient us, to remind us about the necessity of struggle, reform, values (2009: 114), an ethical urge that we 'act as though freedom and dignity remain possible' (2009: 141), in opposition both to a post-modern withdrawal from truth, judgement, critique, and to a liberal rejection of utopia and reluctance about the social.

Badiou's (2008a) considerably more violent fidelity to the 'communist hypothesis' is fully on display in his trenchant and controversial *Meaning of Sarkozy*. This communist hypothesis, which seeks 'to move beyond capitalism, private property, financial circulation, the despotic state, and so on' (2008a: 39), has appeared in two great sequences – 1792–1871 and 1917–1976. Between these two sequences lay 40 years of reaction, and we find ourselves in a similar position after 1976, a situation 'dominated by the enemy' (2008a: 113). Here, the absence of nostalgia in Badiou is perhaps surprising. There is, Badiou insists, no returning to the second sequence. Marxism,[14] the workers' movement, mass democracy, the dictatorship of the proletariat,[15] Leninism, the proletarian party, the classical dialectic,[16] the socialist state – these twentieth century inventions will no longer serve us. We are, in fact, closer to the nineteenth century than we are to the twentieth and its problem of achieving and maintaining victory: 'All kinds of phenomena from the nineteenth century are reappearing: extraordinarily widespread zones of poverty, within the rich countries as well as in the zones that are neglected or pillaged, inequalities that constantly grow, a radical divide between working people – or those without work – and the intermediate classes, the complete dissolution of political power into the service of wealth, the disorganization of revolutionaries, the nihilistic despair of wide sections of young people, the servility of a large majority of intellectuals, the determined but very restricted experimental activity of a few groups seeking contemporary ways to express the communist hypothesis' (Badiou, 2008a: 116–17). The point now, for Badiou, is to make this hypothesis exist in a new way. There are some glimpses in Badiou's (2006; 2007a; 2008a; 2008b; 2008c; 2012a; 2012b; 2013a) more recent writings of what this might mean (and often, to my mind, resonant, for all their differences, of elements in Ernst Bloch) – discipline, courage, holding on to a point in the impossible against the rule of the service of wealth, fidelity, the Idea, Truth and the Real over reality, a return that is somehow new, the construction of time and places absolutely independent from Capital – and perhaps there is a sense that Badiou's militancy (rather than social democratic retrieval and excavation) is currently on the right side of history, with his fast-growing oeuvre coinciding with Occupy, the Arab Spring, the harder Left contestation in Greece and elsewhere, with his unusual but somehow timely combination of structuralist (events can't be made, anti-humanism, the prioritization of universality and infinity – the we, the body-of-truth, the Idea) and existentialist (incorporation into a truth procedure is about choice, will, decision) gestures.

In general, and by way of final thoughts, first up, a Left communist optic encourages us to take issue with aspects of all four of these balance-sheets: for instance, the rather residual ethical or cultural presence of socialism in Beilharz; the ambivalence and hesitation around socialism and Marxism into the future in the case of Therborn; the lingering problems of socialist orthodoxy – the Maoism of Badiou, the Eurocommunism of Magri. Here, these narratives urgently require a more elaborate interchange with Left communism but, equally, the warm socialism of Beilharz and his and Therborn's expansive, intelligent vistas of socialism past and present; the rhetorical daring and inventiveness of Badiou; the solemnity and eye for detail in Magri's effort to take socialism as a whole, as a family affair full of both proud and shameful moments; the manner in which all four thinkers are directing our socialist attentions to the undergrounds, to new and not so new forms of social apartheid (Žižek, 2009); the identification, across these accounts, of numerous contemporary points on which socialists might focus their energies – in all of these ways and many, many more, these voices and voices like them must clearly be part of the discussion of a socialism of the future, reminding us of just how many tools and how much wisdom is bequeathed to us by our multiple socialist traditions.

9
Concluding Comments

There is no uncomplicated way to conclude these reflections, across a range of thinkers, traditions and issues. I hope to have demonstrated both something of the wealth of contemporary socialist thought *and* the interest in and relevance of engagements with Left communism, given the times we are living through. As I have said, these times appear to be marked by a paradoxical combination of features. For a start, the historic achievements of the broad socialist and labour movements remain in evidence – in large belts of anti-sexism, anti-racism and emphases on the sovereignty of those in the poorer parts of the world (anti-imperialism); in the continued currency of egalitarian and irreverent sub-currents within the wider culture; in institutions such as the still-extant welfare state, employment laws and anti-discrimination measures; and, in more radical form, within movements connected with globalization and its discontents.

At the same time, neo-liberalism, despite its now apparent variegation and contradictions, continues to be the dominating modality of governance today – profit, growth, competition – and a liberalism of individual consumer freedoms and inalienable rights, a libertarian current prizing atomistic freedom and self-interest above all else, notions about the sanctity of private property and the like, appear to be, in the many pessimistic readings of our moment, unassailable dimensions of commonsense. Even more dispiritingly, for some, post-political tendencies afoot in many countries – declining citizen participation in the formal political sphere, party convergence and the widespread absence of genuinely Left electoral alternatives, scandal and spectacular informational politics, a shift to the rhetoric of technical problem-solving governance (rather than politics as popular sovereignty), a resurgent Right-wing populism and large pockets of religious chauvinism – make socialist prospects seem rather dim.

Amidst this, though, I have sought to explore what I see as mounting attention to socialist arguments and emphases today, visible in the currency of many of the thinkers and ideas I have dealt with in this book. Why is it that Slavoj Žižek is probably the most well-known philosopher today, crossing the academic–popular cultural divide, that Alain Badiou is currently the most translated French intellectual, that a work as singular and strange as Negri and Hardt's *Empire* has garnered so much attention and that, more broadly, the publishing purchase of works around socialism, Marxism and anarchism has grown so steadily over the last decade and a half? To me, all of this is some evidence that we are, indeed, at a point of a re-opening of history, the re-invigoration, after a period of substantial eclipse, of socialism, anarchism, communism, the Left that, at the least, 'the experience of defeat is beginning to be superseded' (Kouvelakis, 2008: 37).

It is plain, I think, that the broad socialist tradition is equipped like no other with a wealth of resources, intellectual, political and affective, that provide us with some significant help in mapping the world as it stands and imagining another way of being, as well as uncovering and constructing the means by which we might move from one to the other. While none of the thinkers and currents dealt with here are self-sufficient guides – remedies to everything – they provide us with plenty of glimpses, suggestions and energies towards these tasks. To put this simply, what I am advocating is an open, experimental and dialogic Leftist stance, attentive particularly to what I have called Left communism but not, for all that, ignoring the riches still offered by more orthodox strands of Marxism such as social democracy and Leninism, in order to think critically about where we are and where we could and should go.

I would very quickly and partially summarize the help that might be sought from these communists as follows. Post-Marxism undoubtedly encourages us to approach social change seriously, stimulating us *not* to think within closed, sealed-up traditions and urging us to imagine how we might productively stage conversations between apparently incompatible modes of thought, re-imagining politics as primary, history as open and history and politics as shaped by a range of emancipatory projects. Castoriadis, for instance, belongs within this post-Marxist field and while he offers us a rather severe diagnosis of the present (which we might, in any case, choose to read not as resignation but as a prompt to action) he also continued to make one of the most implacable, compelling cases, tied to the historic line of council communism, for a direct, participatory democracy, towards autonomy. The return to

Lenin, charted by the likes of Žižek and Badiou, meanwhile, taking a psychoanalytic, savvy popular-cultural and existential direction, has consistently thrown all sorts of unexpected, and often dazzling, confronting light on our predicament, our current moment of ideological hegemony, while attentive to the small breaks and to the Events that might rather quickly reconfigure the terrain on which we stand. In a different cultural Marxist register, Debord and the Situationists, while contributing an important negative lesson with their legacy of vituperative sectarianism, still have plenty to impart in the realm of a cultural politics, a cultural politics quite other than the rather paralyzing and tame post-modern doxa that provides the commonsense across much of the human sciences, and a politics whose teeth remain sharp when confronting an ever more spectatorial politics and an increasingly aesthetic economy. From another Left communist direction, Hardt and Negri chart an often curious and enchanting post-secular optimism of the intellect, retrieving those dynamic materials from Italian workerism, to both map the present and imagine a set of forces that are always already taking us beyond the ills of actually existing capitalism. In forcible contrast, reflections by figures whose filiations are more with social democratic or Leninist currents of thought – Beilharz, Therborn, Magri – remind us of what is being lost as the generations raised in these traditions age and disappear, and of how much sober diagnostic, tactical and strategic wisdom can still be generated from the resources bequeathed by this socialist ancestry. Contrastingly, again, in the return to anarchism many have detected in anti-globalization and its successors we have a significant challenge to those who think predominantly from the Marxian tradition, a demand that old prejudices might need to be set aside in the face of an emerging Global Left that is clearly drawing from or resonant with anarchism, in thinking domination widely, turning to something like prefigurative politics and often expressing a light-hearted, warm and idealistic reading of human beings and everyday life that quite urgently deserves rediscovery. This humanistic quality is to be found in the singular case of Jacques Camatte, whose path from Bordigism to primitivism, while likely to inspire all sorts of hesitations, is also suggestive of a host of still attractive appeals – the critique of 'really existing democracy', the emphasis on communal being, the strong note of existentialist refusal, the opposition to thought and life founded on an imaginary of growth, progress, control. Finally, also sceptical about the progress represented by Western-dominated modernity, the work of Immanuel Wallerstein displays the impressive constancy and expansiveness of vision characteristic of the best of the

Left, the synthetic fluency, daring and unwavering emancipatory persistence in speaking about everything at once, in imagining the world and its transformation as a whole, undaunted by five decades of peaks and troughs, aware of the interminability of struggle and the ineradicable uncertainties of knowledge and politics, but determined still to stick at it as long as he can 'last it out' (Wallerstein, 2011a: xvii).

To my mind, the thinkers, ideas, currents treated here mark out a crucial orientating constellation deserving of attention from all those on the Left at present. They raise profound questions about values and institutions, in both a critical-explanatory and utopian sense – forcing us to think democracy beyond liberal democracy, to join positive and negative freedoms, as well as freedom and equality, to imagine a revaluing of our notions of the economy, work, value and worth. They pull us this way and that, providing dynamic, unstable materials, but in colliding with and rubbing up against them, we are surely going to be better for the immense tasks at hand.

Notes

Introduction

1. Throughout the chapters, my comments on utopia are reliant on the work of Ruth Levitas (1990; 2003; 2005; 2007; 2013). Defining utopia in a non-restrictive manner, as the desire for a better way of being, Levitas has long argued that utopianism is everywhere, across popular culture, political debates, social thought, and she has insisted on utopian analysis as an indispensable method (as archaeology, ontology and architecture) for the human sciences. See, in particular, Levitas (2013).
2. In 1977 Althusser (1978) declared a 'crisis of Marxism'. See Keucheyan (2013) for an analysis of the period of Left defeat, 1977–1993.
3. For an insightful, accessible, mordant Gramscian analysis of the various 'Princes' before us at this moment – anti-globalist/Occupy, nationalist, religious, austerity/re-asserted neo-liberal – see Worth (2013).
4. For proximate treatments of this current, see, for instance, el-Ojeili (2003); Prichard et al. (eds) (2012); Rubel and Crump (eds) (1987); Schecter (1994; 2007). Schecter (2007), for example, brings together a range of thinkers and traditions – Marx, Western Marxism, critical theory, syndicalism, council communism, guild socialism, anarchism, the surrealists and the situationists, Italian workerism, and Foucault and Deleuze and Guattari – drawing out elements from each as a way forward for a reinvigorated Left that must combine a critique of political economy with a critique of everyday life and bio-power.
5. As just one instance of this partial quality, we might remark upon the absence from this map of 'impossibilism'. For a discussion of impossibilism, see Coleman (1987). Similarly, guild socialism, and its major thinker G. D. H. Cole, might have been included. For efforts to push a renewed 'libertarian socialism' centred on this guild socialism, see Wyatt (2011) and Dawson (2013): Wyatt centres his critique of the present on commodity fetishism, alienation and oligarchy, and suggests 'new economic democracy' (centred on guilds and councils) as an alternative to both state socialism and liberal capitalism; Dawson sets out to demonstrate in convincing detail that this variety of socialism is both compatible with the individualism and pluralism of late modernity and equipped with the analytical and normative resources to undermine neo-liberal positions. Fotopoulos (1997) and Albert (2004) provide other recent examples, from the libertarian socialist/Left communist direction, of work that combines an extensive critique of the present with detailed socialist institutional alternatives.
6. For a discussion of the varieties of anarchism and some good efforts to diagrammize these, see Kinna (2005: 15–26).
7. For extensive critiques along these lines, see, for instance, Harvey (2007) or Dawson (2013).

8. See Levitas (2013) for an extended critique of neo-liberalism and, especially in Chapter Ten, for a poignant defence of socialist values and institutions. See also Dawson (2013).

1   Post-Marxist Trajectories: Diagnosis, Criticism, Utopia

1. See, for instance, Wood (1986), Geras (1987, 1988), Sivananden (1990), Cloud (1994) and Ebert (1995).
2. For instance, Docherty (1996) and Tormey (2001a; 2001b).
3. For instance, 'Perhaps it is time to admit that Marxism is beyond revision, either as a method or body of principles … and that all that remains [in post-Marxism] is a *nostalgia* for the ideal it appeared to be offering' (Sim, 1998: 9); 'post-*Marxism* marks not a new beginning, nor a way out of a theoretical cul-de-sac, but the recognition of defeat' (10).
4. Including Laclau, Mouffe, Negri, Badiou, Rancière, Castoriadis, Lefort, Heller, Bauman, Spivak and Hall.
5. For similar sentiments, see Butler et al. (2000a: 13–14) and Said (2001: 129, 195, 465, 467).
6. For instance, for Mouffe (2000: 85–6), 'What we are witnessing with the current infatuation with humanitarian crusades and ethically good causes is the triumph of a sort of moralizing liberalism that is increasingly filling the void left by the collapse of any project of real political transformation. This moralization of society is in my view a consequence of the lack of any credible political alternative to the current dominance of neo-liberalism'. See also Butler (2000b).
7. A 'prohibition against thinking', for Žižek (2001a: 3).
8. Castoriadis (1997b: 47), it should be noted, was deeply unsympathetic towards the post-moderns, perhaps surprisingly, given his association of autonomy with the rejection of the vision of history as progress or liberation, the rejection of the notion of a single, universal reason, and an emphasis instead on the instituted, historical, political and specific.
9. See, for instance, Castoriadis (1991: 5–12).
10. For further discussion of this, see McLennan (2006).
11. There are multiple examples of this. See, for instance, Rorty (1997; 1999); Bourdieu (1998); Wallerstein (1998); Rawls (1999); Harvey (2000); Hudson (2003); Levitas (2003; 2005; 2007; 2013); Jacoby (2005); Jameson (2005; 2009); Santos (2005a; 2006; 2008); Bell (2006); Tamdgidi (2007); another instance would be the work led by Eric Olin Wright around 'real utopias'.
12. McLennan's example here is the work of Manuel Castells, despite the latter's language leaning towards complexity analysis.
13. Tormey and Townshend referring, here, to Spivak's (1988) critique of Foucault and Deleuze's discussion of intellectuals.
14. In Laclau's last book, this Marxian complexity is acknowledged in passing (2014: 124), a mention uncomfortably embedded within a text that rehearses, again and again, arguments against an ineradicably flawed Marxism (for instance, 70–71).
15. This is a much stronger take than Sim's (2000: 2) later assessment of the 'hardly showbiz' role of a 'limited Marxism' that 'remains in dialogue with

other theoretical developments in an open-minded, non-doctrinal fashion'; and a post-*Marxism* that has the function of 'remaining in dialogue with that narrative [Marxism, thus keeping] ... some of its principles alive ... while also acting as a check on the more anarchic versions of the postmodern narrative' (171). It is much closer to Tormey and Townshend's (2006: 227) more strongly Marxian pluralism: 'just as "Post-marxism" represents a challenge to the reductive Marxism of "actually existing socialism", so Marxism can surely be regarded as a kind of corrective to the wilder flights of wishful thinking displayed by many post-Marxists. The world is still capitalist; the lives of the many are hostage to the wishes of the few. Inequality, powerlessness and oppression are, notwithstanding the heralds of the "End of History", still with us. ... we will probably need both Marxism and its sceptical "outside", Post-Marxism.'

2 'No, We Have Not Finished Reflecting on Communism': Castoriadis, Lefort and Psychoanalytic Leninism

1. Lefort (2007: 30).
2. See the extensive anonymous translator's Forewords to the first two Castoriadis volumes, *The Rising Tide of Insignificancy* and *Figures of the Thinkable*, Scott McLemee's (2004) 'The Strange Afterlife of Cornelius Castoriadis', and David Ames Curtis's (2005) 'Statement of David Ames Curtis Concerning the Announcement of the PDF Electronic Publication of Cornelius Castoriadis/Paul Cardan's *Figures of the Thinkable*'.
3. See, for instance, Bowman and Stamp (2007), Kay (2003), Parker (2004) and Sharpe and Boucher (2010).
4. See also Losurdo's (2004) devastating criticism of the category of totalitarianism.
5. See, for instance, Gregory Elliott (1994; 2006). It is interesting to note the peculiarly French turn to anti-totalitarianism, at a time when the concept was losing traction elsewhere, under pressure from changes taking place post-Stalin and challenges to 'really existing democracy' from the Left (Elliott, 1994; 2006). Castoriadis and Lefort are frequently, here, carelessly lumped together with the new philosophers and with a post-modern line that was to equate totalizing thought with totalitarianism and the erasure of difference, as well as a revisionist line of emboldened liberal thinking that came to lay the blame for the disasters of modernity with the French Revolution (Elliott, 1994; 2006). One sign of the vital differences, here, is given by Castoriadis's (2010a) insistence on the major discontinuities between communism and fascism.
6. See Castoriadis (1988a: 107–58), 'The Relations of Production in Russia', in *Political and Social Writings, Volume 1*.
7. Here, Lefort is fundamentally restating earlier (Lefort, 1986; 1988) arguments.
8. And Castoriadis (2003: 299) explicitly connects totalitarianism to capitalism – totalitarianism as 'immanent in the capitalist imaginary'.
9. The anonymous translator of *The Rising Tide of Insignificancy* notes that, in his last interview, Castoriadis insisted he would always remain a revolutionary.

10. Interestingly, returning again to a contention from his Socialism or Barbarism days, Castoriadis emphasizes the importance in the development of capitalism of internal contestation, of autonomy. Because individuals are creations of society, and because more and more our age is characterized by only 'unlimited expansion of the economy, of production, and of consumption' (2005: 226), where in the future, Castoriadis (2005: 237) asks, will we find the characters that have been central to the functioning and evolution of the social system – the dedicated teacher, the bureaucrat who is a stickler for rules, the honest judge?: 'we are also witnessing the destruction of the anthropological types that have conditioned the system's very existence' (2003: 89).
11. See Gauchet (2000) for a development of this analysis.
12. What Douzinas and Žižek (2010: ix) describe as the contemporary need to return 'to a popular voluntarism'.
13. And yet, this problem of spontaneity-organization remains a tension across Left communism – for instance, within the Socialism or Barbarism group. Lefort's exit in 1958 was occasioned by disagreements over this issue, with Lefort and Henri Simon taking a more anti-vanguardist, spontaneist and worker-centred socialist position, while Castoriadis emphasized the importance of organization. Castoriadis's (2010a) own view that he broke with the Leninist conception of the party in 1950 seems a little difficult to sustain, in the light of the Castoriadis–Pannekoek correspondence of 1953–4, where Pannekoek suggested Socialism or Barbarism was still infected by 'the Bolshevik virus' (Challard, 2012: 221). Challand (2012: 222) suggests Castoriadis can only be seen as a 'control freak' in the group and the new anti-vanguardist Castoriadis emerges much later, although, clearly, Castoriadis attempts some balance between the problematic of pure spontaneity and that of the leading role for revolutionary organizations, a more Gramscian-type of position. For further discussion, see Haider and Mohandesi (2013) and Simon (2013).
14. Perhaps we might include, under this designation, more recent work by first-phase post-Marxists such as Habermas (1999; 2001a; 2001b; 2006a; 2006b; 2006c), Bauman (1999), Laclau (2005a; 2005b) and Mouffe (2001–2; 2002; 2005), as well as thinkers sharing the basic orientation to post-Marxism phase I on those six problems, but striking a more positive, reconstructive note – Held (2003a; 2003b; 2004), Rorty (1997; 1999), Unger (2002; 2005a; 2005b), Vattimo (2004), Wallerstein (1995; 1998a; 2002b; 2004a), Wright (2006), for instance.

3 Forget Debord?

1. See Marcus's (1989) entertaining, more popular account of the Lettrists and the LI.
2. The drift – sometimes translated as '*derive*' – is defined by the SI (1989: 45) as a 'mode of experimental behaviour linked to the conditions of urban society: a technique of transient passage through varied ambiances'. In more deflated terms, this is wandering around city spaces, linked to the notion of 'psychogeography' – 'The study of the specific effects of the geographical

environment, consciously organized or not, on the emotions and behaviour of individuals' (SI, 1989: 45). Diversion – sometimes translated as '*detournement*' – is defined as the 'integration of present or past artistic production into a superior construction of a milieu ... [diversion] within the old cultural spheres is a method of propaganda, a method which testifies to the wearing out and loss of importance of those spheres' (SI, 1989: 45–6). Debord's films or the use of existing cartoon strips with alterations of the text would be examples here. Finally, constructed situations are defined as 'A moment of life concretely and deliberately constructed by the collective organization of a unitary ambiance and a game of events' (SI, 1989: 45). The construction of situations sits opposite the passivity, conformity and repetition attributed to the effects of spectacular society.

3. Of course, there are exceptions, such as Richard Gombin's *The Origins of Modern Leftism*, but, here, the SI are but one important moment in a much more wide-ranging discussion. Meanwhile, the SI's influence in academic circles can be seen early on, for instance, in Jean Baudrillard's (1996) 1968 work, *The System of Objects*.

4. One finds this sentiment in Jappe (1999: 161) who contends that an initial conspiracy of silence on Debord and the SI has given way to a 'conspiracy of chatter that is liable to distort their meaning beyond all recognition', an attempt 'to render them innocuous, to normalize them by one means or another'. Altogether more depressingly characteristic of situationist polemics is the mean-spirited and time-wasting attack mounted against Peter Wollen by former SI members T. J. Clark and Donald Nicolson-Smith (in McDonagh, 2004), including hysterical 'accusations' that Wollen had allowed himself to be published in *New Left Review* (a journal to which Clark himself would soon be contributing).

5. 'No one is indifferent to Debord today' (Kaufmann, 2006: 30), or 'It is not easy to live like Debord. It is not easy to think like him or even with him. Which is why it is not easy to forget him' (2006: 275).

6. Kaufmann (2006: 281, n.) comments on Hussey's book: 'It doesn't add more to what we know, but less: a thick layer of vulgarity, another of spite, and a third of incoherence. We can only hope that Hussey's book remains unparalleled.' This, without any attempt to refute some of the more damaging claims that Hussey makes. In addition, it is perhaps revealing to see Kaufmann (2006: 290, n.) deploying the situationist/Debordian pejorative slang 'Socio-Barbarian' to refer to a former member of Socialism or Barbarism. It should be said, though, that Kaufmann's situphilia is rather minor (with respect to the vituperation, if not in the attempt to defend Debord) in comparison to the chronic case of Jappe's book (1999). See, for instance, the latter's second bibliography on work on Debord and the SI.

7. Dauve, in this instance, is responding to Vaneigem's *The Revolution of Everyday Life*.

8. See, for instance, the *SI Anthology* or, more clearly still, *The Veritable Split in the International*.

9. Wark (2011) comes close to a similar justification, in suggesting that we see the exclusions in terms of tactical mobility and ruthless criticism of all that exists. In most other respects, though, Wark's book is excellent – covering a remarkably expansive terrain, giving attention to less well-known

situationists (such as De Jong, Jorn, Trocchi and Bernstein) and spanning the ideas, milieu and mood of the SI with great economy and elegance.

10. Aside from a very brief mention of the Jorn–Debord friendship in a footnote (Kaufmann, 2006: 299). It is interesting to compare Debord's tolerance here with the exclusions, where, in *The Veritable Split in the International*, we are told that Beaulieu was forced to resign 'because he was reproached for his silliness and lack of dignity' (Situationist International, 1990: 87). And Christian Sebastiani is criticized for 'casualness sometimes carried to the point of thoughtlessness' (1990: 93). Sebastiani was reproached by one of Debord's tendency (consisting of Debord, Rene Riesel and Rene Vienet) for 'a certain lifestyle', i.e., for being caught on a street corner in the company of a former SI member, Mustapha Khayati (see Sebastiani's [2004] response to the members of the tendency).

A couple of further instances serve to demonstrate Kaufmann's protective silence on such matters. First, Kaufmann (2006: 306, n.) notes the 1976 polemics over the republication of *On the Poverty of Student Life*. Here, Kaufmann appears to take the Debord position that this text could not be attributed solely to Mustapha Khayati (we might detect behind this Kaufmann's insistence that Debord *was* the SI). However, he does not mention what, for Khayati (2005), was a crucial issue: that the text wasn't 'made for the official commercial form' Champ Libre would give it.

Second, Kaufmann (2006: 318) refers simply and without elaboration to a 'break' between Debord and Lebovici's heirs. In fact, this apparently rather shocking and noteworthy 'break' led to the courts and to a sense among some observers that Debord had acted in a 'manipulative, underhand and greedy' manner (see Hussey, 2001: 361–2).

11. For instance, 'Cardan [Castoriadis] ... blathers on about "the imagination" in an attempt to justify the gelatinous flabbiness of his thought' (in SI, 1989: 374).

12. This account, by a former SoB member, Pierre Guillaume (1997), must be treated with some caution, because, as Hastings-King (1999) points out, and as Guillaume's text makes abundantly clear, the primary functions of the piece are to underscore Guillaume's personal connection with Debord and to suggest that the latter did not explicitly disapprove of Guillaume's subsequent journey into *negationisme*.

13. On this score, see, in particular, Debord's (2005) 1961 letters to Daniel Blanchard, *Pouvoir Ouvrier*, Attila Kotanyi, and J. L. Jollivet. Here, we find some lucid remarks by Debord on organizational questions. It is clear, though, both that such criticisms and Debord's withdrawal from a formal relationship with SoB (then PO) do not preclude political sympathies, and that similar criticisms regarding those dilemmas around organization, leadership, and representation can be made of virtually the entire span of the Marxian tradition (including the SI). It is also interesting, in line with Hastings-King's argument, to note the difference in tone between the aforementioned letters and, for instance, a letter to Edouard Taube dated 17 October 1964 (Debord, 2005).

14. On this score, the pessimism of Debord's (1990) *Comments on the Society of the Spectacle* – where a new integrated spectacle (characterized by generalized secrecy, the bovine compliance of the population, the loss of authentic

speech, and the crushing ubiquity of media discourse) has triumphed completely – can clearly be read as one logical trajectory out of the earlier characterization of the spectacle.

15. A very contestable position, given, most importantly, the contribution and influence of Raoul Vaneigem. See Hussey's (2001) very different reading.

16. As Boltanski (2002: 6) summarizes these, the social critique 'emphasises inequalities, poverty, exploitation and the egoism of a world that encourages individualism as opposed to solidarity'; the artistic critique, on the other hand, 'criticises oppression in the capitalist world (the domination of the market, the discipline of the factory), the uniformity of mass society and the commodification of everything, and it valorises an ideal of liberation and individual autonomy, of uniqueness and authenticity'.

17. Boltanski and Chiapello (2005: 203) suggest that Vaneigem's *The Revolution of Everyday Life* 'unquestionably contains the most concentrated version of the themes of the artistic critique'.

4 'Many Flowers, Little Fruit'?: The Dilemmas of Workerism

1. The volume *Futuro Anteriore* (Borio et al., 2002), based on nearly 60 interviews with workerists is another exception, but is not yet available in English. For a number of important texts on workerism, autonomy and the related categories of autonomist Marxism and open Marxism – including pieces by central Italian workerist figures such as Mario Tronti, Raniero Panzieri, Mariarosa Dalla Costa, Sergio Bologna, Franco 'Bifo' Berardi, Antonio Negri, secondary texts and interpretation from important commentators like Harry Cleaver and Nick Dyer-Witheford, even the full text of an autonomist novel, Nanni Balestrini's *The Unseen* – see the online Libertarian Communist library (https://libcom.org/library). For examples of more recent groups with a strong workerist slant, see the German Wildcat and British Aufheben websites (Wright, 2008). Of interest, too, is the rather notorious French group Tiqqun, which combines elements of situationism and autonomism. See, for instance, Invisible Committee (2008) *The Coming Insurrection*.

2. In this respect, Virno describes workerism as 'like Frankenstein', questioning whether it constitutes a 'true family of thought' (in Brophy, 2004: 286), and Bologna (2003) asks 'Is it possible to apply the category of continuity to this movement?', when continuity is a trope more fit for a history of dynasties and parties. In like fashion, elsewhere, Wright (2007) suggests the existence of three distinct generations within workerism as partly accounting for differences over theory, organization, and questions of struggle – three clusters of militants born in eight-year periods 1929–36, 1937–44, and 1945–52.

3. For an account of autonomist ideas in Germany, see Katsiaficas (2006).

4. See Negri (1991). The *Grundrisse* was translated into Italian 1968–70 and became, say Bellofiore and Tomba (2008), something of a bible of workerism, as emphasizing subjectivity against *Capital's* objectified analysis. Particularly important was the section 'Fragment on Machines', which was read in a way that gave great emphasis to the resistant reality of living labour (Wright, 2007).

5. See, for instance, Guattari and Negri (1990) and Lotringer and Marazzi (1980).
6. See, for instance, Tronti (2012) on this, which he reads as provoking a shift from the idea of 'party truth' to that of 'class truth'.
7. For more on anarchistic elements and influences in Gramsci's thought, see Levy (2012). For more on the reception of Gramsci, see Frosini (2008).
8. For such an analysis, see Haider and Mohandesi (2013) who trace the genealogy of the workers' inquiry from Marx's 1880 questionnaire to the Johnson-Forest Tendency to Socialism or Barbarism to workerism. The Italian link with Socialism or Barbarism is particularly important, transmitted, first and foremost, and directly by Danilo Montaldi from 1954 onwards. Montaldi and Alquati were, in this period, members of Gruppo di Unita Proletaria. Haider and Mohandesi's article is particularly probing on the tensions across all instances of such inquiries between the roles given to intellectuals and their analyses of capitalism and the direct experiences of, and knowledge produced by, workers. This is the issue at stake in the 1958 split in Socialism or Barbarism, a bone of contention among the workerists, and in play in fascinating ways in the creation of those documents associated with James, Boggs and Dunayevskaya in America, *The American Worker, Indignant Heart, Artie Cuts Out,* and *A Woman's Place.*
9. For more detail on these connections, see Hogsbjerg (2012).
10. While Wright does not explore the precise differences of emphasis and interest; clearly, cultural analyses of this type were, to some extent, present – for instance, prominent *Quaderni Rossi* author Alberto Asor Rosa produced an alternative to Gramsci's literary theory (Hardt, n.d.).
11. Katsiaficas (2006) provides an account that emphasizes and explores both the counter-cultural and women's movements and, more generally, develops a wide-ranging overview of the Italian context and contestations.
12. See, for instance, Castoriadis (1997a: 11).
13. Here, Bologna (2002) charges that Wright pays insufficient attention to the reasons for the departure of Tronti, Negri and Alquati from *Quaderni Rossi,* which he suggests was primarily centred on organizational questions – these three desiring a new movement, against Panzieri's hope for a shift within the existing workers' movement; and Bologna points to important gaps in the treatment of *Class Operaia* – especially around the already mentioned internationalism of Italian workerism, and, in particular, its relationship with the American Left. See also Turchetto (2008).
14. Murphy (2012) suggests that Negri only settled his account with Lenin after 1992.
15. In this respect, Bologna's journal *Primo Maggio* is interesting, seeking to develop a new type of militant history, and searching for a non-Leninist intellectual role as 'service provider', rather than political elite to the movements (Bellofiore and Tomba, 2008; Bologna, 1995; 2003).
16. On this, see, for instance, Magri (2011).
17. Here, Wright (2007) notes a certain vanguardism implicit in the idea of class composition, because this concept was, in large part, about identifying the strong points of capital, leading or hegemonic sectors.
18. In a particularly remorseless critique, Turchetto (2008) comments that workerism has tried to 'conjure up by the power of words the new redemptive subjects who never have the good grace to exist' (2008: 297), becoming a

'bad theory [...] which neither produces any critique, nor casts any light on the facts' (2008: 298).

19. Here, within the literature that has developed around Hardt and Negri's work, critics tend to raise, again and again, a number of important points: around the messianic, religious quality of the work – as Balakrishnan (2000: 147) says, Hardt and Negri's work involves 'an optimism of the will that can only be sustained by a millenarian erasure of the distinction between the armed and the unarmed, the powerful and the abjectly powerless'; around the super-extrapolation of certain trends, such as immaterial labour; around the lack of proper class analysis in the idea of multitude; around the neglect of the continuing central-ity of American and, more generally, Western power in the world-system – for example, when Hardt and Negri speak of imperial control operating through the bomb, money and ether, we could easily read this in the following way ... bomb=Washington, money=New York, ether=LA. For such criticisms, see, for instance, Balakrishnan (ed., 2003); Balibar (2013); Bates (2012); Boron (2005); Brennan (2003; 2006); Bull (2001); Callinicos (2001; 2002; 2007b); Camfield (2007); Dean and Passavant (eds, 2003); Dyer-Witheford (2001); Murphy (2012); Murphy and Mustapha (eds, 2007); Poster (2005); Resnick and Wolff (2001); Thompson (2005); Turchetto (2008); Žižek (2001b).

5 'Communism ... Is the Affirmation of a New Community': Notes on Jacques Camatte

1. Another more minor variety of acknowledgment of Bordiga and Bordigism is a scandal-mongering one. For instance, Bordigist 'fundamentalism' has been viewed as illustrative of a supposed meeting between ultra-Left and ultra-Right, in the small ruckus around the text 'Auschwitz, the Big Alibi', published by a French Bordigist group in 1960. Its later republication by French ultra-Leftists, some of whom subsequently became connected to *negationisme* (denial/down-playing of Nazi crimes against Jews during World War II), has been, for some, evidence enough of the direction in which Bordiga's ideas lead us.

2. For a good account of Bordiga and Gramsci, see Hoare and Smith (1998). For writings by Bordiga, see the following websites: International Library of the Communist Left (www.sinistra.net/lib); Amadeo Bordiga Archive (www.marxists.org/archive/bordiga); N + 1 Historical Archives of the 'Italian' Communist Left (www.quinterna.org/archivio/archivio_storico.htm).

3. For a detailed account of the young socialists in this period, see Craver (1996).

4. Which was to publish writings by Lukács, Pannekoek, Gorter and Pankhurst (Camatte, 1972).

5. As Bordiga expressed this in 1920, 'In our view, nothing does so much good as a split ... A good split clears the air. Communists to one side, reformists of all persuasions and gradations to the other' (in Davidson, 1977: 134).

6. To his credit, Gramsci refused to participate in such manoeuvring, stating that 'for general capability, and for work, he [Bordiga] is worth at least three' (in Cammett, 1967: 156).

7. Zinoviev had unsuccessfully attempted to buy Bordiga off by offering him the vice-presidency of the International (Fiori, 1970).

8. 'Lately, within the parties, a sport is practiced which consists in hitting, intervening, break, attack: and in these cases those who are hit are often excellent revolutionaries. I find this sport of terror within the party as having nothing in common with our work ... Unity is judged by facts and not by a regime of threats and terror ... We absolutely need a more healthy regime in the party; it is absolutely necessary to give the party the possibility to construct its opinion ... Factions do not represent the illness; they are nothing but a symptom of the illness, and if you want to cure the illness, you must first discover and understand it' (Bordiga in Piccone, 1983: 158).

9. See also the exchange of letters between Bordiga (1926d) and Trotsky in March that year.

10. The pair were imprisoned together for a period on the island of Ustica and, despite everything that had happened, were evidently close to one another, sharing meals, co-organizing classes, playing cards (Fiori, 1970; Gramsci, 1994). Bordiga and Gramsci also met a number of times between 1934–5, near the end of Gramsci's life (Bourrinet, 1998).

11. In a letter to his brother-in-law, Bordiga speaks of his political isolation during this period: 'It's necessary to distance oneself and wait ... wait not for this generation but for future generations ... I maintain my faith I am happy in my isolation' (in ICC, 1992: 29). For a detailed account of the activities of the Bordigists from 1926 to 1945, see ICC (1992).

12. The Bordigist groups were quite variegated at this point, with significant differences over a range of questions – relations with the PCI, ties with Trotskyist groups, and stances towards the Soviet Union, the unions and the notion of a transitional state. Bordiga's late membership can be attributed to hesitations over these variations (Bourrinet, 1998).

13. Evolving after the revolution into a simple organization for social research and study (Bordiga, 1946–8).

14. For Bordiga (1946–8), the stomach must be emancipated before the brain can be. The workers are subject, under the weight of their living conditions, to the 'whole traditional consensual ideology of the capitalist world', and communist consciousness is only to be found initially in organizations among restricted sectors of the population.

15. In these texts, Bordiga makes critical remarks on the obsessions with science, technology and production, considers the disasters and chain reactions (for instance, deforestation) provoked by the 'convulsive dynamic' of 'supercapitalism' (1951b), laments the consequences of urbanization, 'agglomerated monsters' (1952), and the impact of machines on human beings, and rejects the general capitalist neglect of thought for future generations.

16. Personal communication with Jacques Camatte, July 2013.

17. See, for instance, Camatte's 1965 letter to Bordiga.

18. Camatte (1977; 1995) continuing to extensively cite Marx and Bordiga, both in a critical vein and in support of his later primitivist positions. See, in particular, the four texts by Bordiga, as yet not translated into English, collected by Camatte in his 1972 book, *Bordiga et la passion du communism* – that is, a selection and prefatory reading of Bordiga made after Camatte's break from the International Communist Party.

19. The Rome Theses were drawn up by Bordiga and Umberto Terracini and contended that, with the disintegration of capitalism, communists needed

to prepare for revolutionary struggle, most importantly by developing a unitary, disciplined party equipped with a tight programme, involved in all aspects of working-class life and clearly differentiating itself from all other parties. The Draft Theses of the Left presented at Lyon rejected social democratic reformism and all forms of class collaboration (including electoral participation and the ideas of the United Front and a workers' government), insisting on the equal critique of fascism and liberal democracy, arguing for organic centralism and opposing bolshevization, and critical of the orientation of those who had been involved in *L'Ordine Nuovo*. See Bordiga (1926a).

20. In works such as the *Critique of Hegel's 'Philosophy of Right'*, *On the Jewish Question*, the *Economic and Philosophical Manuscripts*, 'On James Mill', and the *Grundrisse*.

21. This notion has its origins in the Lyons Theses presented by the Left, emphasizing the organic and unified development of the communist party and opposed, therefore, to bolshevization, as well as to what the Bordigists considered the misleading and potentially damaging emphasis on *democratic* centralism.

22. Camatte similarly rejects the direct democracy arguments of the council communists.

23. Althusser and his associates being, of course, the best known, but also including, a little later, Antonio Negri. On the latter, see, for instance, the use Negri (1996) makes of 'subsumption'. See also Negri (2010) for the continuing importance of this notion in his thought. In contrast to Camatte, though, Negri couples this with the Italian workerist emphasis on the priority of class contestation in the transformations in capitalism. Arguably, this protects Negri against the pessimistic direction in which the focus on subsumption might lead.

24. There is also some interesting discussion of the transition to socialism within *Capital and Community* – for instance, a 1972 note engaging with the Dutch council communist text of 1930, *Fundamental Principles of Communist Production and Distribution*.

25. Details on Camatte are scant, even in French, but it seems clear that the events of 1968 in France were important in his break from Marxism. See, for example, Camatte (1977).

26. Even though, as noted, Camatte continues to draw extensively from Marx. For instance, in his text on Russia from 1974, Camatte is still deploying work from the early Marx in favour of his enthusiasms for communism as Gemeinwesen.

27. Clearly, in his break from Marxism, here and in other emphases – for example, proletarian failure and integration, the new workings of ideology and wider consideration of cultural questions, scepticism about progress – Camatte is drawing close to ideas found within Western Marxism and the New Left – say Horkheimer and Adorno (1972) or Marcuse (1966; 1973). We can see this, for instance, in Camatte's (1977; 1995) explicit references to the ideas of Castoriadis, the Situationist International, Italian workerism, Norman O. Brown and the influence of Wilhelm Reich.

28. In Camatte's (1974) work on community and communism in Russia, he dates the real domination of capital to around 1945, with the impact of two World Wars, fascism, the New Deal and Peronism.

29. Camatte (1995: 236–7) suggests that we return animals to a state of nature, and he also argues for more natural behaviour on a number of fronts – abandoning meat-eating, even a fruitarian diet, natural childbirth, greater amounts of touching between people as 'psychogenetically important'.

30. Camatte (1995: 205) credits the feminist movement with drawing attention to the shortcomings of the revolutionary movement – the way it had become 'infested with notions of power and domination'.

31. Here Camatte (1995: 176) insists on the need to break with Bordigist revolutionary anonymity, which apparently now coincides too much with the suppression of genuine individuality under the domination of capital.

32. Which, again, appears very close to Marcuse (1965).

33. And, here, Camatte absolutely rejects any violence against people, say, the police: 'The revolutionary struggle is a human struggle, and it must recognize in every person the possibility of humanity' (1995: 118); 'the communist revolution is the triumph of life, it cannot in any way glorify death, or seek to exploit it, since this would be putting itself on the terrain of class society' (1995: 122).

34. Again, we see Camatte drawing on his Bordigist inheritance, using but diverting Bordiga's emphasis on the 'invariance' of the communist doctrine.

35. Fredy Perlman (1983), for instance, dismisses the term, suggesting that it is those in the wealthy capitalist nations who are living out primitive lives.

36. See, for instance, Perlman (1983) and Lorraine Perlman (1989).

37. See, for instance, Zerzan (1994) and Zerzan (ed.) (2005).

38. See Watson (1981–85/1997).

39. The key carrier of this influence is likely to have been Fredy Perlman who encountered Camatte's work in the early 1970s and translated the latter's 'The Wandering of Humanity' in 1975 (Perlman, 1989). The importance of Camatte's work is underscored in the early part of Perlman's (1983) primitivist masterpiece *Against HisStory, Against Leviathan!*, and Perlman's connection with *Fifth Estate* and other radical groups in Detroit and beyond was likely pivotal in the spread of Camatte's influence outwards. We see Camatte mentioned early on by a number of key primitivist thinkers: for instance, by Peter Werbe in 1977; in an exchange of letters between John and Paula Zerzan and *Fifth Estate* in 1978; by George Bradford (David Watson) in an essay of 1981 (see Various Authors, 2012). And, more recently, his work has featured in journals such as *Green Anarchy* and has been cited by Bob Black (1997) as an important influence in primitivist/green anarchist thinking about organization. See also the discussion of *Fifth Estate* by Millett (2004).

40. A 'community of freedoms', in Perlman's (1983: 7) estimation. Sometimes, too, contemporary indigenous cultures provide stark positive contrasts to elements of life in advanced societies.

41. For the above account, I am freely drawing from the following: Davidson (2009); Gordon (2008); Kinna (2005); Millett (2004); Moore (n.d.); Perlman (1983); Smith (2010); Watson (1981–5/1997); Williams (2007); Zerzan (1995).

42. Made not only by Marxists but also by anarchists such as Bookchin (1995a and b) and Booth (2001), and by other Left communists.

43. Because one finds these emphases and impulses in some late-nineteenth-century and earlier twentieth-century anarchist strands – anti-progressivism,

the critique of science, the desire for simplicity, the gestures to nature and the past – strands that were lambasted by anarchism's Marxist critics, who often unfairly generalized these emphases to the entirety of anarchism. Gustav Landauer (1978) is, for instance, a thinker in whose work we can find some elements congruent with contemporary primitivism.

44. Bookchin (1995b) feared a 'regression of rationality into intuitionism, of naturalism into supernaturalism, of realism into mysticism, of humanism into parochialism, and of social theory into psychology'. See also David Watson's – as George Bradford (1989) – critique of elements of primitivism.

45. For instance, Perlman had been associated with Glaberman's *Facing Reality* and Dunayevskaya's *News and Letters* (Perlman, 1989) and Zerzan was involved in union then ultra-Left politics in the 1960s and 1970s.

6 Anarchism as the Contemporary Spirit of Anti-Capitalism?: A Critical Survey of Recent Debates

1. On this conflict, see, for instance, the accounts of Thomas (1980) and Leier (2009).

2. Including, for instance, notable works such as Graeber's (2004) *Fragments of an Anarchist Anthropology*, Purkis and Bowen's (eds) (2004) *Changing Anarchism*, Anderson's (2005) *Under Three Flags*, Day's (2005) *Gramsci Is Dead*, Kinna's (2005) *Anarchism*, Critchley's (2007) *Infinitely Demanding*, Shukaitis et al.'s (eds) (2007) *Constituent Imagination*, Gordon's (2008) *Anarchy Alive*, Randall et. al.'s (eds) (2009) *Contemporary Anarchist Studies*, Newman's (2010) *The Politics of Postanarchism*, Sonn's (2010) *Sex, Violence, and the Avant-Garde*, Jun and Wahl's (eds) (2010) *New Perspectives on Anarchism*, Klausen and Martel's (eds) (2011) *How Not to Be Governed*, Rouselle and Evren's (eds) (2011) *Post-Anarchism: A Reader*, Jun's (2012) *Anarchism and Political Modernity*, Kinna's (ed.) (2012) *Continuum Companion to Anarchism*, Howarth's (ed.) (2012) *Anarchist Pedagogies*, and Clark's (2013) *The Impossible Community*. For a very good guide to various anarchist groups, networks, archives, projects and readings, see the 'Resources' and 'Bibliography' sections in Kinna (ed.) (2012).

3. See, for instance, Grubacic and Graeber (2004).

4. See, here, Kinna's (2005: 10–15) discussion in her concise but still expansive and subtle introduction, *Anarchism*.

5. By a resolution on the endorsement of the necessity of political action (Braunthal, 1966; Foster, 1955).

6. In a relatively early contribution, May (1994) pointed to the anarchist affinities of post-structuralist thought. See also Kuhn (2009) on the various connections between anarchism and post-structuralism.

7. For a contemporary defence of dialectical thinking for anarchism, see Clark (2013).

8. And, of course, when we consider that there are over 50 volumes of, say, Proudhon's work to consider (Prichard, 2012), there will always be major questions around simple characterizations.

9. For two intelligent attempts to mediate in this disagreement, see Kinna (2012) and Clark (2013), the latter seeking to steer a communitarian

anarchist path between Bookchinite abstract universalism and a particularist post-anarchism that caricatures the historic anarchist tradition.

10. A connected inclination in this literature and, more widely, I think, in anarchist discussions, is to combine the proclivity to confessional modes of self-placement with calculations (at times, justificatory, at times, self-deprecating) of various rankings within hierarchies of oppression and suffering.

11. Which both Critchley (2007) and de Rota (2011), for instance, champion as pivotal to anarchist politics today.

12. Interestingly, Laclau provides the foreword to Newman's 2001 work, *From Bakunin to Lacan*.

13. As Adams (2011: 131) formulates this, 'Today, informal affinity groups, multiply-linked individuals and spontaneous street formations form the primary basis of resistance, while increasingly anachronistic formal organizations act as a mere shell structure'.

14. However, Day (2005) remarks that there are dangers and limits to the notion of pure nomadism, implying an ethos of fleeting, individualistic encounters over more sustained and collective forms of contestation. In a similar vein, Franks (2007) charges that this Deleuzian–Guattarian variety of post-anarchism prioritizes elitist forms of resistance and agents of change, threatening to reinstall the idea of an egoistic vanguard elite. The worry here is that anarchism might end up with a narrowly artistic-bohemian appeal.

15. See also Jun (2012) and Grubacic and Graber (2004) for similar formulations.

16. See also, in this respect, the collection edited by Shukaitis et al.(2007), *Constituent Imagination*. For further reflections on the possibilities of anarchist sociology, anarchist social studies, anarchist education, anarchist geography and anarchist cultural studies, see Williams (2010), DeLeon (2010), Ince (2010) and Cohn (2010), respectively.

17. The Amster et al. (2009) collection contains much relevant material, especially in the 'methodology' section, with reflections on anarchism and ethnographic field research, activist geography and disability studies. Kinna's anthology (2012) also contains a range of valuable contributions and materials for further research on anarchism and the academy.

18. See also Klausen and Martel (2011) for this emphasis – for instance, in their championing of the concept of 'constellations', as a way of breaking from top-down, totalizing and deterministic theorizing. Here, recourse to an intellectual tool of Marxian provenance (Walter Benjamin) raises again the problem of the anarchism–Marxism dialogue.

19. In this vein of reconsideration of the Marxian–anarchist divide, see also a series of articles in the journal *Theory in Action* – Memos (2010), Armaline and Shannon (2010) and Garland (2010). See also the excellent Prichard et al. (2012) edited collection, *Libertarian Socialism*.

20. For recent reflections on this, see the 'Pedagogy' section of Amster et al.'s *Contemporary Anarchist Studies*, and Howarth (2012).

21. Along with the substance, if not the sometimes virulent form, of the critique of primitivism articulated by Murray Bookchin and others. For a contemporary defence of Bookchin in this debate and more widely, see Price (2012).

7 Reflections on Wallerstein: The Modern World-System, Four Decades On

1. See Chase-Dunn and Grimes (1995) for a good survey.
2. For further detail on the influence of the ECLA, Annales and dependency theory, see Wallerstein (2005a: 11–22).
3. For further information on A/B, expansion/stagnation phases and other long-term trends, see Chase-Dunn (1998), Kleinknecht et al. (1992) and Wallerstein (2005a).
4. The crucial lesson, for Wallerstein (1990a), from the defeat of the 1848 world-revolution was the need for long-term political organization to achieve movement objectives. Eventually, this issued in a triumph across the movements of a two-step strategy of capturing state power and then transforming life.
5. Or, as Wallerstein (2000a: 7) summarizes this elsewhere, the collapse of the myths of the free market, the sovereign state, the equal rights of citizens and the value-neutral scholar.
6. The ' serious assessment of historical alternatives, the exercise of our judgement as to the substantive rationality of alternative possible historical systems' (Wallerstein, 1998a: 1). See the further development of this in Tamdgidi (2007).
7. The so-called Industrial Revolution should be seen, says Wallerstein (1989: 78), 'as the reurbanization and reconcentration of the leading industries alongside an effort to increase scale'.
8. Skocpol (1977: 1078), too, focuses in on the explanatory problem in Wallerstein's account of the origins of capitalism, with respect to its unprecedented dynamism, arguing that, in Wallerstein, market processes are the only visible dynamics and once established 'everything reinforces everything else', the analysis flawed by teleology and functionalism.
9. For more detail on this issue, see Chase-Dunn and Anderson (2005), Frank (1998), Friedman and Chase-Dunn (2005) and Wallerstein's (1999d) critique of Frank. The same issue of *Review* in which Wallenstein's critique appears also contains responses to Frank by Amin and Arrighi.
10. On this score, Brenner (1977) criticizes the Third Worldist/socialism-in-one-country politics that displaces socialism among the neo-Smithian Marxists.
11. See, for instance, Arrighi (1990) for a broad analysis on the shifts of proletarian organization, in conversation with Marxian expectations; or Silver and Arrighi (2001) on the ambiguities of the labour movement with respect to issues of national protection and imperialism; or Silver (2005) on the question, over the long-term, of labour and globalization. See also Arrighi and Silver (1999).
12. For instance, that control of the state in the context of the international division of labour and the interstate system affords less power than was expected (Arrighi et al., 1989: 57).
13. And, on this issue, Wallerstein clearly refuses an obdurate Marxism that denies transformations in class structures. For instance, Wallerstein (1990b) rejects the leading role of the industrial proletariat, and acknowledges the growing occupational complexity of labour in core countries after the 1960s. See also Arrighi et al. (1989).

14. As 'a term of political exhortation' (Wallerstein, 2000b: 28).
15. Wallerstein (1998a, 2003a), for instance, drawing from Arrighi, notes the fluctuations across the life and times of the capitalist world-economy of periods of accumulation centred on production and phases centred on financial speculation. For Arrighi (2009) this financial phase is a sign of the 'Autumn' of a particular hegemonic cycle, though he insists that this is compatible with acknowledging the peculiarities of each cycle of accumulation and is not a narrative of merely the 'return of the same' across capitalism's life-span.
16. This he mostly attributes to changes in the geoculture (Wallerstein, 1999a), thus reading it in a very different way to many globalization thinkers, as another signal of the crisis of the system as a whole rather than attributable to merely the thickening of world interconnectedness.
17. A fairly common argument in historical and political sociology (for example, Mann, 2013), evidenced, say, in the American consequences of the recent recession, military quagmires, growing criticism of and rebellion against transnational institutions, or the rise of Tea Party Republicanism, 'the gangrene of imperial decline' (Davis, 2013: 52).
18. For instance, Wallerstein (1997a) will at times draw a very negative balance-sheet of modernity while at others seemingly committing himself to at least science and scientific progress (2004b). See McLennan (1998). This ties in with Wallerstein's (2006b) critique of Eurocentrism, which turns out to be a quest for a more universal universalism, rather than a rejection of universalism as such.
19. This very difficult debate cannot be adequately treated here, but again there is plenty to back a world-systems, state-capitalism interpretation of the countries of 'really existing socialism'. For more on this see, for instance, Fernandez (1997) or van der Linden (2007).
20. For multiple examples of this, see the *Journal of World-Systems Research*.

8 Narrating Socialism – Four Voices

1. Leon Trotsky (1907) and Rosa Luxemburg (1972[1910]) are early users of the phrase in this way.
2. In Badiou's (2013b: 7) version of reconsidering the meaning of 'failure' in the light of the communist hypothesis, he suggests a mathematics analogy – 'Fermat's theorem' in the case of which 'It was ... vital not to abandon the hypothesis for the three hundred years during which it was impossible to prove it'.
3. For Badiou (2011: 8, 12), the subjective type democracy moulds is 'egoism and desire for petty enjoyments', which explains 'the profound stupidity of contemporary democratic societies'. However, towards the close of this same piece, Badiou withdraws somewhat, denoting 'true' democracy as communist, 'the power of peoples over their own existence' (2011: 15).
4. Despite the apparent unrepentant Leninism, here Badiou (2013a: 8–9) has sought to distance communism from terror, seeing the latter as circumstantial, where inter-imperialist war, foreign intervention, attempted counter-revolution, amidst continuing 'contradictions among the people',

manifested in permanent 'insurrectional urgency or relentless violence', a brutal 'forcing of the situation', and an abandonment of the Idea of communism for competition with capitalism. That is, he gives an almost identical treatment to the Russian Revolution as Magri.

5. In this vein, the peculiarity of Antipodean capitalism and socialism are underscored by Beilharz (2001; 2005a; 2009) – statism, arbitration, the pragmatic ethos, fairness and reasonability as key ideas, practical egalitarianism, for instance.

6. For Badiou, fascist politics are the politics of the state, and communist politics are, despite the deformations of 'really existing socialism', antithetical to the state. As he puts this elsewhere, the event and truth are precisely and absolutely outside of the state; the idea of a 'communist state' is oxymoronic (Badiou, 2010a: 5–7).

7. Elsewhere, Badiou speaks of four 1968s – a youth revolt, a workers' rebellion, a 'libertarian May' (2010b: 49), and a political mediation seeking to move beyond classical revolutionism – this last being the most important way in which we remain contemporaries of 1968.

8. See, in particular, Beilharz (2009), Chapters Nine and Ten.

9. At the time, the journal had a circulation of around 50,000 (Anderson: 2011).

10. In other respects, though, Hellman (2012) is correct in noting how 'lenient' Magri is on Berlinguer.

11. Here Magri (2011: 5–6) notes that we have, now, 'a victorious capitalism'; 'Inequalities ... have asserted themselves in new and often sharper forms'; the decline of social gains such as universal welfare, and of national independence for poor countries; 'New and urgent problems ... from environmental degradation to a moral decay'; the crisis of the political system and the demise of the nation state; a crisis of hegemony and 'the multiplication of conflicts'.

12. To cite just one piece of evidence of this – the quality of the reflections in the journal *Historical Materialism*, especially those numerous contributions from a cohort of talented younger Marxian scholars.

13. '"Postmarxisms" regularly emerge at those moments in which capitalism itself undergoes a structural metamorphosis. Marxism is the science of capitalism ... it is incoherent to celebrate the "death of Marxism" in the same breath with which one announces the definitive triumph of capitalism and the market ... the various "post-Marxisms" ... along with their posited "crisis" or "death" of Marxism, have been simultaneous with precisely those moments in which capitalism is restructured and prodigiously enlarged. And these in turn have been followed by various theoretical projects of a more modern [type]... Marxism attempting to theorize the new and unexpected dimensions taken on by its traditional object of study, capitalism as such' (Jameson, 1996: 1, 3).

14. Interestingly, while declaring Marxism as, in some sense, of a previous sequence and, desperately separating himself from any sociology (Marxian or otherwise), Badiou (2012b) declares, more recently, that our present fully confirms all of Marx's diagnoses. This draws our attention to the really significant absence in Badiou of a replacement for the 'historical social science' point of the old Marxist triangle, which might incline us to classify him as

nearer to Rousseau (Critchley, 2012) and Plato than to Marx. This absence will be, for many, troublingly bound up with the decisionism (his emphasis on will, decision, choice) and irrationalism (say, the religiosity of truth procedures as a 'glorious body' [Badiou, 2010a: 7]) that might be detected in Badiou – for instance, in his lament for the contemporary 'lack of a great fiction' (Badiou, 2012a: 78) to replace masses, classes and parties; or, elsewhere, Badiou's (2010a: 12) insistence that 'every event is a surprise' and that the real of that event 'must be exposed in a fictional structure'. The mythic quality of the event/truth, as Balibar (2013; see also Laclau, 2014: 181–206) points out, is lent a religious intensity, an intensity reaching beyond that of religiosity proper or the imagined community of nation. See also Callinicos (2012) for a trenchant, more orthodox Marxist critique of Badiou, charging that the latter's work is hamstrung by an abstract ontology devoid of theoretical content, an inadequate treatment of the state and an underdeveloped account of politics, and a prioritization of subjective affects over location of communism in extant processes and struggles. On this, see also Keucheyan (2013: 178–9).

15. A very interesting question, given Badiou's focus on the importance of the quasi-mythical, relates to the problem of the eventual replacement term for the 'proletariat/working class'. This is a crucial issue for him, as we need a new 'creative affirmation' identifying 'the inexistents of the world' (2012b: 68), a new name of the 'power of the generic' (2012b: 79). Given this importance, one wonders at his absolute hostility to what is precisely Hardt and Negri's attempt to think this – 'multitude'.

16. Here, Badiou (2013b) contends that the fundamentally negative classical dialectic needs to be replaced by a new 'affirmative' logic, which is equivalent to his notion of the possibility represented by an event, and a 'heroic' anthropology animated by an idea of humankind's singularity as deeply connected with the Idea and truth procedures.

Bibliography

Adams, J. (2003) 'Postanarchism in a Nutshell'. Available (accessed 17 January 2012) at: http://info.interactivist.net/node/2475

Adams, J. (2011) 'The Constellation of Opposition'. In D. Rousselle and S. Evren (eds), *Post-Anarchism: A Reader*. London: Pluto.

Adamson, W. L. (1980) *Hegemony and Revolution: A Study of Antonio Gramsci's Political and Cultural Theory*. Berkeley: University of California Press.

Agger, B. (2004) *Speeding up Fast Capitalism: Cultures, Jobs, Families, Schools, Bodies*. Boulder: Paradigm.

Albert, M. (2004) *Parecon: Life after Capitalism*. London: Verso.

Alexander, J. C. (1995) 'Modern, Anti, Post and Neo'. *New Left Review*, I/210, 63–101.

Alexander, J. C. (2001) 'Robust Utopias and Civil Repairs'. *International Sociology*, 16 (4): 579–591.

Althusser, L. (1978) 'The Crisis of Marxism.' *Marxism Today*, July, 227, 215–220.

Amadeo Bordiga Archive. Available (accessed 8 August 2012) at: http://www.marxists.org/archive/bordiga/index.htm

Amin, S. (1994) *Re-reading the Postwar Period: An Intellectual Itinerary*. New York: Monthly Review Press.

Amin, S. (2003) *Obsolescent Capitalism: Contemporary Politics and Global Disorder*. London: Zed.

Amin, S. (2006) *A Life Looking Forward: Memoirs of an Independent Marxist*. London: Zed Books.

Amin, S., Arrighi, G., Frank, A. G. and Wallerstein, I. (1990) *Transforming the Revolution: Social Movements and the World-System*. New York: Monthly Review Press.

Amster, R., DeLeon, A., Fernandez, L, A., Nocella II, A, J. and Shannon, D. (2009) 'Introduction'. In R. Amster, A. DeLeon, L. A. Fernandez, A. J. Nocella II, and D. Shannon (eds), *Contemporary Anarchist Studies: An Introductory Anthology of Anarchy in the Academy*. London: Routledge.

Andersen, N. A. (2003) *Discursive Analytical Strategies: Understanding Foucault, Koselleck, Laclau, Luhmann*. Bristol: The Policy Press.

Anderson, B. (2005) *Under Three Flags: Anarchism and the Anticolonial Imagination*. London: Verso.

Anderson, P. (1976) *Considerations on Western Marxism*. London: New Left Books.

Anderson, P. (1983) *In the Tracks of Historical Materialism*. London: Verso.

Anderson, P. (2000) 'Renewals'. *New Left Review*, 1. Available (accessed 3 May 2003) at: www.newleftreview.net/NLR23501.shtml

Anderson, P. (2004) 'The River of Time'. *New Left Review*, 26, 67–77.

Anderson, P. (2007) 'Jottings on the Conjuncture'. *New Left Review*, 48, 5–37.

Anderson, P. (2011) 'Lucio Magri, 1932–2011'. *New Left Review*, 72, 111–121.

Anonymous (2003) 'Foreword'. In C. Castoriadis, *The Rising Tide of Insignificancy*. Available (accessed 1 October 2013) at: www.notbored.org/RTI.pdf

Anonymous (2005) 'Foreword'. In C. Castoriadis, *Figures of the Thinkable*. Available (accessed 1 October 2013) at: www.notbored.org/FTPK.pdf

Antliff, A. (2011) 'Anarchy, Power and Post-Structuralism'. In D. Rousselle and S. Evren (eds), *Post-Anarchism: A Reader*. London: Pluto.

Arjomand, S. A. (2004) 'Social Theory and the Changing World: Mass Democracy, Development, Modernization and Globalization'. *International Sociology*, 19, 321–53.

Armaline, W. T. and Shannon, D. (2010) 'Introduction: Toward a More Unified Libertarian Left'. *Theory and Action*, 3 (4), 1–7.

Aronowitz, S. (1981) *The Crisis of Historical Materialism: Class, Politics and Culture in Marxist Theory*. New York: Praeger.

Arrighi, G. and Silver, B. (eds) (1999) *Chaos and Governance in the Modern World System*. Minneapolis: University of Minnesota Press.

Arrighi, G. (1990) 'Marxist Century, American Century: The Making and Remaking of the World Labour Movement'. *New Left Review*, I/179, 29–63.

Arrighi, G. (1997) 'Capitalism and the Modern World-System: Rethinking the Non-Debates of the 1970s'. Available (accessed 13 December 2012) at: www2.binghamtom.edu/fbc/archive/gaasa96.htm

Arrighi, G. (2002) 'The African Crisis: World Systemic and Regional Aspects'. *New Left Review*, 15, 5–36.

Arrighi, G. (2005a) 'Hegemony Unravelling – I'. *New Left Review*, 32, 23–80.

Arrighi, G. (2005b) 'Hegemony Unravelling II'. *New Left Review*, 33, 83–116.

Arrighi, G. (2009) 'The Winding Paths of Capital: Interview with David Harvey'. *New Left Review*, 56, 61–94.

Arrighi, G. (2010) *The Long Twentieth Century: Money, Power, and the Origins of Our Times* (new updated edition). London: Verso.

Arrighi, G., Hopkins, T. and Wallerstein, I. (1989) *Anti-systemic Movements*. London: Verso.

Badiou, A. (2001) *Ethics*. London: Verso.

Badiou, A. (2003a) *Infinite Thought: Truth and the Return to Philosophy*. London: Continuum.

Badiou, A. (2003b) *Saint Paul: The Foundation of Universalism*. California: Stanford University Press.

Badiou, A. (2005a) 'The Adventure of French Philosophy'. *New Left Review*, 35, 67–77.

Badiou, A. (2005b) *Metapolitics*. London: Verso.

Badiou, A. (2006) 'Interview With Alain Badiou'. *Carceraglio*. Available (accessed 4 October 2011) at: http://scentedgardensfortheblind.blogspot.com/2006_10_15_scentedgardensfortheblin

Badiou, A. (2007a) *The Century*. Cambridge: Polity.

Badiou, A. (2007b) 'One Divides Itself Into Two'. In S. Budgen, S. Kouvelakis and S. Žižek (eds), *Lenin Reloaded: Toward a Politics of Truth*. Durham: Duke University Press.

Badiou, A. (2008a) *The Meaning of Sarkozy*. London: Verso.

Badiou, A. (2008b) '"We Need a Popular Discipline": Contemporary Politics and the Crisis of the Negative'. *Critical Inquiry*, 34 (Summer), 645–659.

Badiou, A. (2008c) 'The Communist Hypothesis'. *New Left Review*, 49, 29–42.

Badiou, A. (2010a) 'The Idea of Communism'. In C. Douzinas and S. Žižek (eds), *The Idea of Communism*. London: Verso.

Badiou, A. (2010b) *The Communist Hypothesis*. London: Verso.

Badiou, A. (2011) 'The Democratic Emblem'. In G. Agamben, A. Badiou, D. Bensaid, W. Brown, J. L. Nancy, J. Rancière and K. Ross, *Democracy in What State?* New York: Columbia University Press.

Badiou, A. (2012a) *Philosophy for Militants*. London: Verso.

Badiou A (2012b) *The Rebirth of History: Times of Riots and Uprisings*. London: Verso.

Badiou, A. (2013a) 'The Communist Idea and the Question of Terror'. In S. Žižek (ed.), *The Idea of Communism 2: The New York Conference*. London: Verso.

Badiou, A. (2013b) 'Affirmative Dialectics: From Logic to Anthropology'. *International Journal of Badiou Studies*, 2 (2), 1–13.

Bakunin, M. (1973) *Selected Writings*. New York: Grove Press.

Bakunin, M. (1990) *Statism and Anarchy*. New York: Knopf.

Balakrishnan, G. (2000) 'Hardt and Negri's Empire'. *New Left Review*, 5, 142–148.

Balakrishnan, G. (ed.) (2003) *Debating Empire*. London: Verso.

Balakrishnan, G. (2009) 'Speculations of the Stationary State'. *New Left Review*, 59, 5–26.

Balakrishnan, G. (2011) 'The Twilight of Capital?' In D. Palumbo-Lio, B. Robbins and N. Tanoukhi (eds), *Immanuel Wallerstein and the Problem of the World: System, Scale, Culture*. Durham: Duke University Press.

Balibar, E. (2007) 'The Philosophical Moment in Politics Determined by War: Lenin 1914–16'. In S. Budgen, S. Kouvelakis and S. Žižek (eds), *Lenin Reloaded: Toward a Politics of Truth*. Durham: Duke University Press.

Balibar, E. (2013) 'Communism as Commitment, Imagination, and Politics'. In S. Žižek (ed.), *The Idea of Communism 2: The New York Conference*. London: Verso.

Balibar, E. and Wallerstein, I. (1991) *Race, Nation, Class: Ambiguous Identities*. London: Routledge.

Bates, D. (2012) 'Situating Hardt and Negri'. In A. Prichard, R. Kinna, S. Saku and D. Berry (eds), *Libertarian Socialism: Politics in Black and Red*. London: Palgrave.

Baudrillard, J. (1983) *Simulations*. New York: Semiotext(e).

Baudrillard, J. (1996) *The System of Objects*. London: Verso.

Bauman, Z. (1976) *Socialism: The Active Utopia*. London: George Allen and Unwin.

Bauman, Z. (1987) *Legislators and Interpreters: On Modernity, Post-Modernity and Intellectuals*. Oxford: Polity.

Bauman, Z. (1999) *In Search of Politics*. California: Stanford University Press.

Bauman, Z. (2002) *The Bauman Reader* (Edited by Peter Beilharz). Oxford: Blackwell.

Beck, U. (1997) *The Reinvention of Politics: Rethinking Modernity in the Global Social Order*. Cambridge: Polity.

Beck, U. (1999) *World Risk Society*. Polity: Cambridge.

Beilharz, P. (1994) *Postmodern Socialism: Romanticism, City and State*. Melbourne: Melbourne University Press.

Beilharz, P. (1999) *Zygmunt Bauman: Dialectic of Modernity*. London: Sage.

Beilharz, P. (2001) 'Australian Civilization and Its Discontents'. *Thesis Eleven*, 64, February, 65–76.

Beilharz, P. (2002) 'Reading Zygmunt Bauman: Looking for Clues'. In P. Beilharz (ed.), *Zygmunt Bauman, Volume I*. London: Sage.

Beilharz, P. (2003) 'Socialism: Modern Hopes, Postmodern Shadows'. In G. Ritzer and B. Smart (eds), *Handbook of Social Theory*. London: Sage.

Beilharz, P. (2005a) 'Australia: the Unhappy Country, or, a Tale of Two Nations'. *Thesis Eleven*, 82, August, 73–87.

Beilharz, P. (2005b) 'Postmodern Socialism Revisited'. In P. Hayden and C. el-Ojeili (eds), *Confronting Globalization: Humanity, Justice and the Renewal of Politics*. London: Palgrave.

Beilharz, P. (2007) 'Post-Marxism'. In G. Ritzer (ed.), *The Blackwell Encyclopaedia of Sociology*. Cambridge: Blackwell.

Beilharz, P. (2009) *Socialism and Modernity*. Minnesota: University of Minneapolis Press.

Bell, D. (1999) *The Coming of Post-Industrial Society: A Venture in Social Forecasting* (Special Anniversary Edition). New York: Basic Books.

Bell, D. (2006) 'Ends an Rebirths: An Interview with Daniel Bell'. *Thesis Eleven*, 85, May, 93–103.

Bellofiore, R. (2006) 'Between Panziere and Negri: Mario Tronti and the Workerism of the 1960s and 1970s'. Available (accessed 26 July 2013) at: http://libcom.org/library/between-panzieri-negri-mario-tronti-workerism-1960s-1970s

Bellofiore, R. and Tomba, M. (2008) 'On Italian Workerism'. Available (accessed 26 July 2013) at: http://libcom.org/library/italian-workerism

Bensaid, D. (2007) 'Leaps! Leaps! Leaps!'. In S. Budgen, S. Kouvelakis and S. Žižek (eds), *Lenin Reloaded: Toward a Politics of Truth*. Durham: Duke University Press.

Bergesen, A. J. (2000) 'The Columbia Social Essayist'. *Journal of World-Systems Research*, VI (2), 198–213.

Berkman, A. (1972) *What Is Communist Anarchism?* New York: Dover.

Berman, M. (1984) 'The Signs in the Street: A Response to Perry Anderson'. *New Left Review*, I/144, 114–123.

Bertalan, H. (2011) 'When Theories Meet: Emma Goldman and "Post-Anarchism"'. In D. Rousselle and S. Evren (eds), *Post-Anarchism: A Reader*. London: Pluto.

Betz, H. G. (2003) 'The Growing Threat of the Radical Right'. In P. H. Merkl and L. Weinberg (eds), *Right-Wing Extremism in the Twenty-First Century*. London: Frank Cass.

Bey, H. (1995) 'Primitives and Extropians'. Available (accessed 7 August 2012) at: http://hermetic.com/bey/primitives.html

Bidet J. and Kouvelakis, S. (eds) (2008) *Critical Companion to Contemporary Marxism*. Leiden: Brill.

Black, B. (1997) *Anarchy after Leftism*. Columbia: A. A. L. Press.

Boggs, C. (1984) *The Two Revolutions: Gramsci and the Dilemmas of Western Marxism*. Boston: South End Press.

Boggs, C. (1993) *Intellectuals and the Crisis of Modernity*. New York: State University of New York Press.

Bohme, G. (2003) 'Contribution to the Critique of the Aesthetic Economy'. *Thesis Eleven*, 73, 71–82.

Boli, J. and Lechner, F. J. (2009) 'Globalization Theory'. In B. S. Turner (ed.), *The New Blackwell Companion to Social Theory*. Cambridge: Wiley-Blackwell.

Bologna, S. (1995) 'For an Analysis of Autonomia – An Interview with Sergio Bologna'. Available (accessed 26 July 2013) at: http://libcom.org/library/analysis-of-autonomia-interview-sergio-bologna-patrick-cunninghame

Bologna, S. (2003) 'Steve Wright's *Storming Heaven. Class Composition and Struggle in Italian Autonomist Marxism*'. Available (accessed 27 July 2013) at: http://libcom.org/library/review-storming-heaven-sergio-bologna

Boltanski, L. (2002) 'The Left after May 1968 and the Longing for Total Revolution'. *Thesis Eleven*, 69, 1–20.

Boltanski, L. and Chiapello, E. (2005) *The New Spirit of Capitalism*. London: Verso.

Bookchin, M. (1995a) *Social Anarchism or Lifestyle Anarchism: An Unbridgeable Chasm*. Edinburgh: AK Press.

Bookchin, M. (1995b) 'A Philosophical Naturalism'. Available (accessed 20 August 2012) at: http://dwardmac.pitzer.edu/anarchist_archives/bookchin/philosonatural.html

Booth, S. (2001) 'Primitivism: An Illusion with No Future. The Anarchist Library 2012'. Available (accessed 1 July 2013) at: http://theanarchistlibrary.org/library/stephen-booth-primitivism-an-illusion-with-no-future

Bordiga, A. (1922) 'The Democratic Principle'. Available (accessed 7 August 2012) at: www.marxists.org/archive/bordiga/works/1922/democratic-principle.htm

Bordiga, A. (1926a) 'Draft Theses for the Third Congress of the Communist Party of Italy Presented by the Left'. Available (accessed 20 August 2001) at: www.sinistra.net/lib/pre/lunita/dufeadixye.html

Bordiga, A. (1926b) 'The Communist Left in the Third International'. Available (accessed 14 February 2012) at: www.marxists.org/archive/bordiga/works/1926/comintern.htm

Bordiga, A. (1926c) 'Letter to Korsch'. Available (accessed 14 February 2012) at: www.marxists.org/archive/bordiga/works/1926/letter-korsch.html

Bordiga, A. (1926d) 'Correspondence Between Bordiga and Trotsky'. Available (accessed 14 August 2012) at: www.en.internationalism.org/ir/101_bordiga.htm

Bordiga, A. (1946) 'The Fundamentals For a Marxist Orientation'. Available (accessed 14 August 2012) at: www.marxists.org/archive/bordiga/works/1946/orientation.htm

Bordiga, A. (1946–8) 'Force, Violence and Dictatorship in the Class Struggle'. Available (accessed 20 August 2012) at: www.sinistra.net/lib/apt/compro/lipa/lipanbeboe.html

Bordiga, A. (1950) 'Why Dialectical Materialism?'. Available (accessed 7 August 2012) at: http://libcom.org/library/dialectical-method-amadeo-bordiga

Bordiga, A. (1951a) 'The Filling and Bursting of Bourgeois Civilization'. Available (accessed 7 August 2012) at: www.marxists.org/archive/bordiga/works/1951/civilisation.htm

Bordiga, A. (1951b) 'Murder of the Dead'. Available (accessed 1 July 2013) at: www.quinterna.org/lingue/english/historical_en/murder_of_dead.htm

Bordiga, A. (1952) 'The Human Species and the Earth's Crust'. Available (accessed 1 July 2013) at: www.quinterna.org/lingue/english/historical_en/human_species_and_earthcrust.htm

Bordiga, A. (1953) 'The Soul of Horse Power'. Available (accessed 1 July 2013) at: www.quinterna.org/lingue/english/historical_en/soul_of_horse power.htm

Bordiga, A. (1963) 'The Legend of Piave'. Available (accessed 7 August 2012) at: www.marxists.org/archive/bordiga/works/1963/legend.htm

Bordiga, A. (1965) 'Considerations on the Party's Organic Activity when the General Situation Is Historically Unfavourable'. Available (accessed 7 February 2012) at: www.marxists.org/archive/bordiga/1965/consider.htm

Bordiga, A. (1977) 'Bordiga's Polemic'. In A. Gramsci, *Selections From Political Writings (1910–20)*. London: Lawrence and Wishart.

Borio, G. et al. (2002) *Futuro Anteriore*. Rome: Derive Approdi.

Boron, A. A. (2005) *Empire and Imperialism: A Critical Reading of Michael Hardt and Antonio Negri*. London: Zed.

Bourdieu, P. (1998) 'A Reasoned Utopia and Economic Fatalism'. *New Left Review*, I/227. Available (accessed 13 July 2004) at: www.newleftreview.net/IssueI223.asp?Article=08

Bourg, J. (2007) 'Translator's Introduction'. In C. Lefort, *Complications: Communism and the Dilemmas of Democracy*. New York: Columbia University Press.

Bourrinet, P. (n.d.) 'An Important Book on Bordiga Unknown (1926–1946)'. Available (accessed 14 February 2012) at: www.left-dis.nl/uk/bordigaunknown.htm

Bourrinet, P. (1998) '"The Bordigist Current" (1912–1952)'. Available (accessed 27 June 2013) at: www.left-dis.nl/uk/bordigist.pdf

Bowen, J. (2004) 'Moving Targets: Rethinking Anarchist Strategies'. In J. Purkis and J. Bowen (eds), *Changing Anarchism: Anarchist Theory and Practice in a Global Age*. Manchester: Manchester University Press.

Bowman, P. and Stamp, R. (eds) (2007) *The Truth of Žižek*. London: Continuum.

Bracken, L. (1997) *Guy Debord – Revolutionary*. California: Feral House.

Bradford, G. (1989) *How Deep Is Deep Ecology?* California: Times Change.

Braunthal, J. (1966) *A History of the International 1864–1914*. London: Nelson.

Brennan, T. (2003) 'The Empire's New Clothes'. *Critical Inquiry*, 29 (2), 337–367.

Brennan, T. (2006) *War of Position: The Cultural Politics of Left and Right*. New York: Columbia University Press.

Brenner N. (2011) 'The Space of the World: Beyond State-Centrism?'. In D. Palumbo-Lio, B. Robbins and N. Tanoukhi (eds), *Immanuel Wallerstein and the Problem of the World: System, Scale, Culture*. Durham: Duke University Press.

Brenner, R. (1977) 'The Origins of Capitalist Development: A Critique of Neo-Smithian Marxism'. *New Left Review*, I/104, 25–92.

Brophy, E. (2004) '"Italian Operaismo Face to Face" A report on the "Operaismo a Convegno" Conference, 1–2 June 2002 – Rialto Occupato, Rome, Italy'. *Historical Materialism*, 12 (1), 277–298.

Budgen, S, Kouvelakis S. and Žižek S. (eds) (2007) *Lenin Reloaded: Toward a Politics of Truth*. Durham: Duke University Press.

Buick, A. (1987) 'Bordigism'. In A. Buick and J. Crump (eds), *Non-Market Socialism in the Nineteenth and Twentieth Centuries*. Basingstoke: Macmillan.

Bull, M. (2001) 'You Can't Build a New Society with a Stanley Knife'. *London Review of Books*, 23 (19), 3–7.

Butler, J. (1998) 'Merely Cultural'. *New Left Review*, 227/I, 33–44.

Butler, J. (2000) 'Ethical Ambivalence'. In M. Garber, B. Hanssen and R. L. Walkowitz (eds), *The Turn to Ethics*. New York: Routledge.

Butler, J, Laclau, E. and Žižek, S. (2000) *Contingency, Universality, Hegemony: Contemporary Dialogues on the Left*. London: Verso.

Callinicos, A. (2001) 'Tony Negri in Perspective'. *International Socialism*, 2, 92. Available (accessed 27 June 2013) at: www.marxists.org/history/etol/writers/callinicos/2001/xx/toninegri.htm

Callinicos, A. (2002) 'The Actuality of Imperialism'. *Millennium*, 31 (2), 319–326.

Callinicos, A. (2003) *An Anti-Capitalist Manifesto*. Cambridge: Polity.

Callinicos, A. (2007a) 'Leninism in the Twenty-First Century?: Lenin, Weber, and the Politics of Responsibility'. In S. Budgen, S. Kouvelakis and S. Žižek (eds), *Lenin Reloaded: Toward a Politics of Truth*. Durham: Duke University Press.

Callinicos, A. (2007b) 'Antonio Negri and the Temptation of Ontology'. In T. S. Murphy and A. K. Mustapha (eds), *The Philosophy of Antonio Negri: Revolution in Theory Volume Two*. London: Pluto.

Callinicos, A. (2012) 'Alain Badiou and the Idea of Communism'. In L. Panitch, G. Albo and V. Chibber (eds), *Socialist Register 2013: The Question of Strategy*. London: The Merlin Press.

Camatte, J. (1961) 'Origin and Function of the Party Form'. Available (accessed 7 August 2012) at: www.marxists.org/archive/camatte/origin.htm.

Camatte, J. (1969) 'The Democratic Mystification'. Available (accessed 1 October, 2003) at: www.Geocities.com/~johngray/demyst.htm

Camatte, J. (1964–72) *Capital and Community: The Results of the Immediate Process of Production and the Economic Works of Marx* (Translated by Unpopular Books, 1988). Available (accessed 7 August 2012) at: www.marxists.org/archive/camatte/capcom/index.htm

Camatte, J. (ed.) (1972) *Bordiga et la passion du communisme*. Paris: Spartacus.

Camatte, J. (1974) *Community and Communism in Russia*. Available (accessed 20 April 2001) at: www.geocities.com/~johngray/comrus01–3.htm

Camatte, J. (1977) 'May-June 1968: The Exposure'. Available (accessed 29 June 2013) at. http://theanarchistlibrary.org/library/jacques-camatte-may-june-1968-the-exposure

Camatte, J. (1995) *This World We Must Leave and Other Essays*. New York: Semiotext(e)/Autonomedia.

Camfield, D. (2007) 'The Multitude and the Kangaroo: A Critique of Hardt and Negri's Theory of Immaterial Labour'. *Historical Materialism*, 15 (2), 21–52.

Cammett, J. M. (1967) *Antonio Gramsci and the Origins of Italian Communism*. Stanford: Stanford University Press.

Castells, M. (1997) *The Information Age: Economy, Society and Culture: The Power of Identity*. Oxford: Blackwell.

Castells, M. (1998) *The Information Age: Economy, Society and Culture: End of Millennium*. Oxford: Blackwell.

Castells, M. (2000) *The Information Age: Economy, Society and Culture: The Rise of the Network Society*. Oxford: Blackwell.

Castoriadis, C. (1987) *The Imaginary Institution of Society*. Cambridge: Polity.

Castoriadis, C. (1988a) *Political and Social Writings Volume I, 1946–1955*. Minneapolis: University of Minnesota Press.

Castoriadis, C. (1988b) *Political and Social Writings Volume 2, 1955–1960*. Minneapolis: University of Minnesota Press.

Castoriadis, C. (1991) *Philosophy, Politics, Autonomy*. Oxford: Oxford University Press.

Castoriadis, C. (1993) *Political and Social Writings Volume 3, 1961–1979*. Minneapolis: University of Minnesota Press.

Castoriadis, C. (1997a) *The Castoriadis Reader*. Cambridge: Blackwell.

Castoriadis, C. (1997b) *World in Fragments: Writings on Politics, Society, Psychoanalysis, and the Imagination*. Stanford: Stanford Press.

Castoriadis, C. (2003) *The Rising Tide of Insignificancy*. Available (accessed 1 October 2013) at: www.notbored.org/RTI.pdf

Castoriadis, C. (2005) *Figures of the Thinkable.* Available (accessed 1 October 2013) at: www.notbored.org/FTPK.pdf

Castoriadis, C. (2010a) *A Society Adrift: More Interviews and Discussions on* The Rising Tide of Insignificancy, *Including* Revolutionary Perspectives Today. Available (accessed 1 October 2013) at: www.notbored.org/ASA.pdf

Castoriadis, C. (2010b) *A Society Adrift, Interviews and Debates 1974–1997.* New York: Fordham University Press.

Castoriadis, C. (2011) *Postscript on Insignificancy, Including More Interviews and Discussions on* The Rising Tide of Insignificancy. *Followed by Five Dialogues, Four Portraits, and Two Book Reviews.* Available (accessed 1 October 2013) at: www.notbored.org/PSRTI.pdf

Challard, B. (2012) 'Socialism or Barbarism or the Partial Encounters between Critical Marxism and Libertarianism'. In A. Prichard, R. Kinna, S. Saku and D. Berry (eds), *Libertarian Socialism: Politics in Black and Red.* Basingstoke: Palgrave.

Chase-Dunn, C. (1998) *Global Formation: Structures of the World-Economy* (updated edition). Lanham: Rowman and Littlefield.

Chase-Dunn, C. and Anderson, E. N. (eds) (2005) *The Historical Evolution of World-Systems.* Basingstoke: Palgrave.

Chase-Dunn, C. and Grimes, P. (1995) 'World-Systems Analysis'. *Annual Review of Sociology,* 21, 387–417.

Chase-Dunn, C. and Inoue, H. (2011) 'Immanuel Wallerstein'. In G. Ritzer and J. Stepmisky (eds), *The Wiley-Blackwell Companion to Major Social Theorists: Volume II, Contemporary Social Theorists.* Cambridge: Wiley-Blackwell.

Chibber, V. (2013) *Postcolonial Theory and the Specter of Capital.* London: Verso.

Clark, J. P. (2013) *The Impossible Community: Realizing Communitarian Anarchism.* New York: Bloomsbury.

Clark, T. J. (2012) 'For a Left With No Future'. *New Left Review,* 74, 53–75.

Clark, T. J. and Nicolson-Smith, D. (2004) 'Why Art Can't Kill the SI'. In T. McDonagh (ed.), *Guy Debord and the SI: Texts and Documents.* Cambridge: MIT Press.

Cleaver, H. (n.d.) 'Autonomist Marxism'. Available (accessed 13 July 2001) at: www.eco.utexas.edu/Homepage-/Faculty/Cleaver

Cleaver, H. (1993) 'An Interview with Harry Cleaver'. Available (accessed 27 June 2013) at: https://webspace.utexas.edu/hcleaver/www/Interviewwith HarryCleaver.html

Cloud, D. L. (1994) '"Socialism of the Mind": The New Age of Post-Marxism'. In T. W. Simons and M. Billig (eds), *After Postmodernism: Reconstructing Ideology Critique.* London: Sage.

Cohn, J. (2010) 'What is Anarchist Cultural Studies? Precursors, Problems, and Prospects'. In: N. J. Jun and S. Wahl (eds), *New Perspectives on Anarchism.* Lanham: Lexington Books.

Cole, G. D. H. (1954) *Socialist Thought: Marxism and Anarchism 1850–1890.* London: Macmillan.

Coleman, S. (1987) 'Impossibilism'. In M. Rubel and J. Crump (eds), *Non-Market Socialism in the Nineteenth and Twentieth Centuries.* London: Macmillan.

Cornell, A. (2011) 'A New Anarchism Emerges, 1940–1954'. *Journal for the Study of Radicalism,* 5 (1), 105–132.

Craig, J. (2004) 'Spectacle, Attention, Counter-Memory'. In T. McDonagh (ed.), *Guy Debord and the SI: Texts and Documents.* Cambridge: MIT Press.

Craver, E. (1996) 'The Third Generation: The Young Socialists in Italy, 1907–1915'. *Canadian Journal of History/Annales canadiennes d'histoire* XXXI, August/août,

199–226. Available (accessed 7 August 2012) at: www.usask.ca/history/cjh/f/iss/text/96/craver_896.shtml

Critchley, S. (2007) *Infinitely Demanding: Ethics of Commitment, Politics of Resistance*. London: Verso.

Critchley, S. (2009) 'Infinitely Demanding Anarchism: An Interview with Simon Critchley'. Available (accessed 23 October 2011) at: www.ucd.ie/philosophy/perspectives/resources/Simon_critcheley_interview.pdf

Critchley, S. (2012). 'Why Badiou is a Rousseauist'. *International Journal of Badiou Studies*, 1 (1), 1–8.

Crouch, C. (2004) *Post-Democracy*. Cambridge: Polity.

Cuninghame, P. (1995) 'For an Analysis of Autonomia – An Interview with Sergio Bologna'. Available (accessed 26 July 2013) at: http://libcom.org/library/analysis-of-autonomia-interview-sergio-bologna-patrick-cunninghame

Curtis, D, A. (1988) 'Foreword'. In C. Castoriadis. *Political and Social Writings Vol I 1946–55*. Minneapolis: University of Minnesota Press.

Curtis, D. A. (1997) 'Foreword'. In C. Castoriadis, *The Castoriadis Reader*. Cambridge: Blackwell.

Curtis, D, A. (2005) 'Statement of David Ames Curtis Concerning the Announcement of the PDF Electronic Publication of Cornelius Castoriadis/Paul Cardan's *Figures of the Thinkable* (Including *Passion and Knowledge*). Available (accessed 1 October 2013) at: http://perso.orange.fr/www.kaloskaisophos.org/rt/rtdac/rtdactf/rtdacftp&kblogstatement1.html

Dauve, G. [aka Jean Barrot] (1979) *Critique of the Situationist International*. Available (accessed 1 October 2013) at: www.geocities.com/~johngray/barsit.htm

Davidson, A. (1977) *Antonio Gramsci: Towards an Intellectual Biography*. London: Merlin Press.

Davidson, S. (2009) 'Ecoanarchism: A Critical Defence'. *Journal of Political Ideologies*, 14 (1), 47–67.

Davis, M. (2013) 'The Last White Election?' *New Left Review*, 79, 5–52.

Dawson, M. (2013) *Late Modernity, Individualization and Socialism: An Associational Critique of Neoliberalism*. Basingstoke: Palgrave Macmillan.

Day, R. J. F. (2005) *Gramsci Is Dead: Anarchist Currents in the Newest Social Movements*. London: Pluto.

Day, R. J. F. (2011) 'Hegemony, Affinity and the Newest Social Movements: At the End of the 00s'. In D. Rousselle and S. Evren (eds), *Post-Anarchism: A Reader*. London: Pluto.

Dean, J. and Passavant, P (eds) (2003) *Empire's New Clothes: Reading Hardt and Negri*. London: Routledge.

Debord, G. (1990) *Comments on the Society of the Spectacle*. London: Verso.

Debord, G. (1991) *Panegyric* (Volume 1). London: Verso.

Debord, G. (1995) *The Society of the Spectacle*. New York: Zone.

Debord, G. (2005) Letters (in English translation and available online). Available (accessed 1 October 2013) at: www.notbored.org/debord.html

Debray, R. (2007) 'Socialism: A Life-Cycle'. *New Left Review*, 5–28.

de Goede, M. (2005) 'Carnival of Money: Politics of Dissent in the Era of Globalizing Finance'. In L. Amoore (ed.), *The Global Resistance Reader*. London: Routledge.

De Landa, M. (2006) *A New Philosophy of Society: Assemblage Theory and Social Complexity*. New York: Continuum.

DeLeon, A. P. (2010) 'Sabotaging the System! Bringing Anarchist Theory into Social Studies Education'. In N. J. Jun and S. Wahl (eds), *New Perspectives on Anarchism*. Lanham: Lexington Books.

de Rota, A. F. (2011) 'Acracy_Reloaded @ Post-1968/1989: Reflections on Postmodern Revolutions'. In D. Rousselle and S. Evren (eds), *Post-Anarchism: A Reader*. London: Pluto.

Docherty, T. (1996) *After Theory: Postmodernism/Postmarxism*. London: Routledge.

Dolgoff, S. (1972) *Bakunin on Anarchy*. New York: Knopf.

Douzinas, C. and Žižek, S. (2010) 'Introduction: The Idea of Communism'. In C. Douzinas and S. Žižek (eds), *The Idea of Communism*. London: Verso.

Dyer-Witheford, N. (2001) 'Empire, Immaterial Labour, the New Combinations, and the Global Worker'. *Rethinking Marxism*, 13 (3–40), 70–80

Eagleton, T. (2007) 'Lenin in the Postmodern Age'. In S. Budgen, S. Kouvelakis and S. Žižek (eds), *Lenin Reloaded: Toward a Politics of Truth*. Durham: Duke University Press.

Ebert, T. (2002 [1995]) 'Untimely Critiques for a Red Feminism'. Available (accessed 21 August 2001) at: www.angelfire.com/on/pisd/TeresaEbert.htm

Elliott, G. (1994) 'Contentious Commitments: French Intellectuals and Politics'. *New Left Review*, I/206. Available (accessed 1 October 2013) at: http://newleftreview.org/I/206/gregory-elliott-contentious-commitments-french-intellectuals-and-politics

Elliott, G. (2006) 'Parisian Impostures'. *New Left Review*, 41. Available (accessed 1 October 2013) at: http://newleftreview.org/II/41/gregory-elliott-parisian-impostures

el-Ojeili, C. (2003) *From Left Communism to Post-Modernism: Reconsidering Emancipatory Discourse*. Lanham: University Press of America.

Epstein, B. (2001) 'Anarchism and the Anti-Globalization Movement'. *Monthly Review*, 53, 1–14.

Evren, S. (2011) 'Introduction'. In D. Rousselle and S. Evren (eds), *Post-Anarchism: A Reader*. London: Pluto.

Feher, F., Heller, A. and Markus, G. (1986) *Dictatorship over Needs: An Analysis of Soviet Societies*. Oxford: Blackwell.

Feher, F. and Heller, A. (1987) *Eastern Left, Western Left: Totalitarianism, Freedom and Democracy*. Cambridge: Polity.

Femia, J. V. (1993) *Marxism and Democracy*. Oxford: Clarendon.

Fernandez, N. C. (1997) *Capitalism and Class Struggle in the USSR: A Marxist Theory*. London: Ashgate.

Fiori, G. (1970) *Antonio Gramsci: Life of a Revolutionary*. New York: Schocken Books.

Fleming, M. (1979) *The Anarchist Way to Socialism: Elisee Reclus and Nineteenth-Century European Anarchism*. London: Croom Helm.

Foster, W. Z. (1955) *History of the Three Internationals*. Westpoint: Greenwood Press.

Fotopoulos, T. (1997) *Towards an Inclusive Democracy: The Crisis of the Growth Economy and the Need for a New Liberatory Project*. London: Cassell.

Foucault, M. (1980) *Power/Knowledge: Selected Interviews and Other Writings, 1972–1977*. Brighton: Harvester.

Frank, A. G. (1998) *Re-ORIENT: The Global Economy in the Asian Age*. Berkeley: University of California Press.

Frank, A. G. (2000) 'Immanuel and Me With-Out Hyphen'. *Journal of World-Systems Research*, VI (2), 216–231.

Franks, B. (2007) 'Postanarchism: A Critical Assessment'. *Journal of Political Ideologies*, 12 (2), 127–145.

Franks, B. (2010) 'Vanguards and Paternalism'. In N. J. Jun and S. Wahl (eds), *New Perspectives on Anarchism*. Lanham: Lexington Books.

Franks, B. (2012) 'Between Anarchism and Marxism: The Beginnings and Ends of the Schism'. *Journal of Political Ideologies*, 17 (2), 207–227.

Fraser, N. (2003) 'Introduction: The Radical Imagination – Between Redistribution and Recognition'. Available (accessed 24 September 2006) at: www.newschool.edu/gf/polsci/faculty/fraser/NancyFraser_Intro-TheRadical Imagination.pdf

Friedman, J. (1995) *Cultural Identity and Global Process*. London: Sage.

Friedman, J. (2000) 'Globalization, Class and Culture in Global Systems'. *Journal of World-Systems Research*, VI (3), 636–656.

Friedman, J. and Chase-Dunn, C. (eds) (2005) *Hegemonic Decline: Present and Past*. Boulder: Paradigm.

Frosini, F. (2008) 'Beyond the Crisis of Marxism: Gramsci's Contested Legacy'. In J. Bidet and S. Kouvelakis (eds), *Critical Companion to Contemporary Marxism*. Leiden: Brill.

Fuller, S. (2006) *The Intellectual*. London: Totem Books.

Furet, F. (2000) *The Passing of an Illusion*. Chicago: University of Chicago Press.

Gaarder, E. (2009) 'Addressing Violence against Women: Alternatives to State-Based Law and Punishment'. In R. Amster A. DeLeon, L. A. Fernandez, A. J. Nocella II and D. Shannon (eds), *Contemporary Anarchist Studies: An Introductory Anthology of Anarchy in the Academy*. London: Routledge.

Gabay, C. (2010) 'What Did the Anarchists Ever Do For Us? Anarchism, Decentralization, and Autonomy at the Seattle anti-WTO Protests'. In N. J. Jun and S. Wahl (eds), *New Perspectives on Anarchism*. Lanham: Lexington Books.

Galtung, J. (1971) 'A Structural Theory of Imperialism'. *Journal of Peace Research*, 8 (2), 81–117.

Garber M, Hanssen, B. and Walkowitz, R. L. (eds) (2000) *The Turn to Ethics*. New York: Routledge.

Garland, C. (2010) 'The (Anti-) Politics of Autonomy: Between Marxism and Anarchism'. *Theory in Action*, 3 (4), 8–16.

Gauchet, M. (2000) 'A New Age of Personality: An Essay on the Psychology of Our Times'. *Thesis Eleven*, 60, 23–41.

Geras, N. (1987) 'Post Marxism?' *New Left Review*, 163(I), 40–82.

Geras, N. (1988) 'Ex-Marxism Without Substance: Being a Real Reply to Laclau and Mouffe'. *New Left Review*, 169(I), 34–61.

Giddens, A. (1991) *Modernity and Self-Identity*. Stanford: Stanford University Press.

Goldfrank, W. L. (2000) 'Paradigm Regained? The Rules of Wallerstein's World-Systems Method'. *Journal of World-Systems Research*, VI (2), 150–195.

Goldner, L. (1991) 'Communism Is the Material Human Community: Amadeo Bordiga Today'. Available (accessed 7 August 2012) at: http://home.earthlink. net/~lrgoldner/bordiga.html.

Gombin, R. (1975) *The Origins of Modern Leftism*. Middlesex: Penguin.

Gordon, U. (2008) *Anarchy Alive: Anti-Authoritarian Politics from Practice to Theory*. London: Pluto.

Graeber, D. (2004) *Fragments of an Anarchist Anthropology*. Chicago: Prickly Paradigm Press.

Graeber, D. (2011) 'Occupy Wall Street's Anarchist Roots'. *Al-Jazeera*, 30 November. Available (accessed 5 February 2012) at: www.aljazeera.com/indepth/opinion/2011/11/2011112872835904508.html

Gramsci, A. (1977) *Selections from Political Writings (1910–20)*. London: Lawrence and Wishart.

Gramsci, A. (1978) *Selections from Political Writings (1921–26)*. London: Lawrence and Wishart.

Gramsci, A. (1994) *Letters from Prison, Volume I*. New York: Columbia University Press.

Gramsci, A. (1998) *Selections from the Prison Notebooks*. London: Lawrence and Wishart.

Grubacic, A. and Graeber, D. (2004) 'Anarchism, or the Revolutionary Movement of the Twenty-First Century'. Available (accessed 2 April 2012) at: www.theanarchistlibrary.org

Guattari, F. and Negri, A. (1990) *Communists Like Us*. New York: Semiotext(e).

Guerin, D. (1970) *Anarchism*. New York: Monthly Review Press.

Guillaume, P. (1997) 'Debord'. Available (accessed 29 September 2013) at: www.notbored.org/guillaume.html

Gupta. S. (2000) *Marxism, History, and Intellectuals: Towards a Reconceptualized Transformative Socialism*. Cranbury: Associated University Presses.

Habermas, J. (1999) 'The European Nation-State and the Pressures of Globalization'. *New Left Review*, 235(I), 46–59.

Habermas, J. (2001a) *The Postnational Constellation: Political Essays*. Cambridge: Polity.

Habermas, J. (2001b) 'Why Europe Needs a Constitution'. *New Left Review*, 11, 5–26.

Habermas, J. (2006a) *Time of Transitions*. Cambridge: Polity.

Habermas, J. (2006b) *The Divided West*. Cambridge: Polity.

Habermas, J. (2006c) 'Towards a United States of Europe', *Der Standard*, 10–11 March. Available (accessed 27 September 2013) at: www.signandsight.com/features/676.html

Habiby. E. (2003) *The Secret Life of Saeed: The Pessoptimist*. Northampton: Interlink Books.

Haider, A. and Mohandesi, S. (2013) 'Workers' Inquiry: A Genealogy', *Viewpoint Magazine*, 27 September 2013. Available (accessed 31 October 2013) at: http://viewpointmag.com/2013/09/27/workers-inquiry-a-genealogy/

Hall, S. (1988) *The Hard Road to Renewal: Thatcherism and the Crisis of the Left*. London: Verso.

Hardt, M. (n.d.) *Dissertation*. Available (accessed 12 September 2003) at: www.duke.edu/~hardt/Dissertation.htm

Hardt, M. (1996) 'Introduction: Laboratory Italy'. In P. Virno and M. Hardt (eds), *Radical Thought in Italy: A Potential Politics*. Minneapolis: University of Minnesota Press.

Hardt, M. (n.d.) 'On Negri's Return to Prison'. Available (accessed 1 October 2013) at: http://multitudes.samizdat.net/On-Toni-Negri-and-his-intention-to

Hardt, M. (2010) 'The Common in Communism'. In C. Douzinas and S. Žižek, (eds), *The Idea of Communism*. London: Verso.

Hardt, M and Negri, A. (2000) *Empire*. Cambridge, MA: Harvard University Press.

Hardt, M. and Negri, A. (2003) 'The Rod of the Forest Warden: A Response to Timothy Brennan'. *Critical Inquiry*, 29 (2), 368–372.

Hardt, M. and Negri, A. (2004) *Multitude: War and Democracy in the Age of Empire*. New York: Penguin.

Hardt, M. and Negri, A. (2009) *Commonwealth*. Cambridge, MA: The Belknap Press.

Harvey, D, (1989) *The Condition of Postmodernity: An Enquiry into the Origins of Cultural Change*. Blackwell: Oxford.

Harvey, D. (2000a) *Spaces of Hope*. Berkeley: University of California Press.

Harvey, D. (2005) *The New Imperialism*. New York: Oxford University Press.

Harvey, D. (2007). *A Brief History of Neoliberalism*. Oxford: Oxford University Press.

Hastings-King, S. (1999) 'L'Internationale Situationniste, Socialisme ou Barbarie, and the Crisis of the Marxist Imaginary'. *Substance*, 28 (3), 26–54.

Heckert, J. (2011) 'Sexuality as State Form'. In D. Rousselle and S. Evren (eds), *Post-Anarchism: A Reader*. London: Pluto.

Held, D. (2003a) 'Global Social Democracy'. In A. Giddens (ed.), *The Progressive Manifesto*. Cambridge: Polity.

Held, D. (2003b) 'From Executive to Cosmopolitan Multilateralism'. In D. Held and M. Koenig-Archibugi (eds), *Taming Globalization: Frontiers of Governance*. Cambridge: Polity.

Held, D. (2004) *Global Covenant: The Social Democratic Alternative to the Washington Consensus*. Cambridge: Polity.

Held, D. and Kaya, A. (eds) (2007) *Global Inequality: Patterns and Explanations*. Cambridge: Polity.

Heller, A. and Feher, F. (1988) *The Postmodern Political Condition*. Cambridge: Polity.

Heller, A and Feher, F. (1991) *The Grandeur and Twilight of Radical Universalism*. London: Transaction.

Hellman, S. (2012) 'Whatever Happened to Italian Communism? Lucio Magri's *The Tailor of Ulm*'. In L. Panitch, G. Albo and V. Chibber (eds), *Socialist Register 2013: The Question of Strategy*. London: The Merlin Press.

Hoare, Q. and Smith, G. N. (1998) 'General Introduction'. In *Antonio Gramsci: Selections from the Prison Notebooks*. London: Lawrence and Wishart.

Hobsbawm, E. J. (1963) *Primitive Rebels: Studies in Archaic Forms of Social Movement in the 19th and 20th Centuries*. New York: Frederick and Praeger.

Hobsbawm, E. J. (1973) *Revolutionaries: Contemporary Essays*. New York: Pantheon Books.

Hobsbawm, E. (2003) *Interesting Times: A Twentieth Century Life*. New York: Pantheon.

Hogsbjerg, C. (2012) 'A "Bohemian Freelancer"? C. L. R. James, His Early Relationship to Anarchism and the Intellectual Origins of Autonomism'. In A. Prichard, R. Kinna, S. Saku and D. Berry (eds), *Libertarian Socialism: Politics in Black and Red*. Basingstoke: Palgrave Macmillan.

Homer, S. (1998) *Fredric Jameson: Marxism, Hermeneutics, Postmodernity*. New York: Routledge.

Horkheimer, M. and Adorno, T. (1972) *Dialectic of Enlightenment*. New York: Herder and Herder.

Howard, D. (2007) 'Foreword'. In C. Lefort, *Complications: Communism and the Dilemmas of Democracy*. New York: Columbia University Press.

Howard, D. and Pacom, D. (1998) 'Autonomy – The Legacy of the Enlightenment: A Dialogue with Castoriadis'. *Thesis Eleven*, 52, 83–101.

Howarth, D. (1998) 'Post-Marxism.' In A. Lent (ed.), *New Political Thought: An Introduction*. London: Lawrence and Wishart.

Howarth, R. H. (ed.) (2012) *Anarchist Pedagogies: Collective Actions, Theories, and Critical Reflections on Education*. Oakland: PM Press.

Hudson, W. (2003) *The Reform of Utopia*. Ashgate: Aldershot.

Hussey, A. (2001) *The Game of War: The Life and Death of Guy Debord*. London: Jonathan Cape.

ICC (International Communist Current) (1992) *The Italian Communist Left, 1926–45*. London: ICC.

Ince, A. (2010) 'Whither Anarchist Geography?' In N. J. Jun and S. Wahl (eds), *New Perspectives on Anarchism*. Lanham: Lexington Books.

Ingram, J. D. (2006) 'The Politics of Claude Lefort's Political: Between Liberalism and Radical Democracy'. *Thesis Eleven*, 87 (1), 33–50.

International Library of the Communist Left. Available (accessed 7 August 2012) at: www.sinistra.net/lib/app/alen/alphaen.html

Invisible Committee (2009) *The Coming Insurrection*. Available (accessed 29 July 2013) at: http://archive.org/details/TheComingInsurrectionByTheInvisible Committee

Jacoby, R. (1981) *Dialectic of Defeat: Contours of Western Marxism*. Cambridge: Cambridge University Press.

Jacoby, R. (2005) *Picture Imperfect: Utopian Thought for an Anti-Utopian Age*. New York: Columbia University Press.

Jameson, F. (1984a) 'Postmodernism, Or, The Cultural Logic of Late Capitalism'. *New Left Review*, 146(I), 52–92.

Jameson, F. (1984b) 'Periodizing the '60s'. *Social Text*, No. 9/10, Spring-Summer, 178–209.

Jameson, F. (1989) 'Marxism and Postmodernism'. *New Left Review*, 176(I), 31–45.

Jameson, F. (1996) 'Five Theses on Actually Existing Marxism'. *Monthly Review*, 47 (11), 1–10.

Jameson, F. (2002) *A Singular Modernity: Essay on the Ontology of the Present*. London: Verso.

Jameson, F. (2005) *Archaeologies of the Future: The Desire Called Utopia and Other Science Fictions*. London: Verso.

Jameson, F. (2007) 'Lenin and Revisionism'. In S. Budgen, S. Kouvelakis and S. Žižek (eds), *Lenin Reloaded: Toward a Politics of Truth*. Durham: Duke University Press.

Jameson, F. (2009) *Valences of the Dialectic*. London: Verso.

Jappe, A. (1999) *Guy Debord*. Berkeley: University of California Press.

Jeppesen, S. (2011) 'Things to Do With Post-Structuralism in a Life of Anarchy: Relocating the Outpost of Post-Anarchism'. In D. Rousselle and S. Evren (eds), *Post-Anarchism: A Reader*. London: Pluto.

Joll, J. (1966) *The Second International: 1889–1914*. New York: Harper Row.

Joll, J. (1979) *The Anarchists* (Second Edition). London: Methuen.

Jun , N. J. (2011) 'Reconsidering Post-Structuralism and Anarchism'. In D. Rousselle and S. Evren (eds), *Post-Anarchism: A Reader*. London: Pluto.

Jun, N. (2012) *Anarchism and Political Modernity*. London: Continuum.

Jun, N. J. and Wahl, S. (eds) (2010) *New Perspectives on Anarchism*. Lanham: Lexington Books.

Karagiannis, N. and Wagner, P. (eds) (2007) *Varieties of World-Making: Beyond Globalization*. Liverpool: Liverpool University Press.

Katsiaficas, G. (2006) *The Subversion of Politics: European Autonomous Social Movements and the Decolonization of Everyday Life*. Oakland: AK Press.

Kaufmann, V. (2006) *Guy Debord: Revolution in the Service of Poetry*. Minneapolis: University of Minnesota Press.

Kay, S. (2003) *Žižek: A Critical Introduction*. Cambridge: Polity.

Keucheyan, R. (2013) *The Left Hemisphere: Mapping Critical Theory Today*. London: Verso.

Khayati, M. (2005) Letter to Champ Libre, 12 October 1976. Available (accessed 27 September 2013) at: www.notbored.org/khayati-12October1976.html

Kinna, R. (2005) *Anarchism: A Beginner's Guide*. London: Oneworld.

Kinna, R. (2012) 'Introduction'. In R. Kinna (ed.), *The Continuum Companion to Anarchism*. New York: Continuum.

Kinna, R. (ed.) (2012) *The Continuum Companion to Anarchism*. New York: Continuum.

Kinna, R. and Prichard, A. (2012) 'Introduction'. In A. Prichard, R. Kinna, S. Saku and D. Berry (eds), *Libertarian Socialism: Politics in Black and Red*. Basingstoke: Palgrave Macmillan.

Klausen, J. C. and Martel, J. (2011) 'Introduction: How Not to be Governed'. In J. C. Klausen and J. Martel (eds), *How Not to Be Governed: Readings and Interpretations from a Critical Anarchist Left*. New York: Lexington Books.

Kleinknecht, A., Mandel E. and Wallerstein, I. (eds) (1992) *New Findings in Long-Wave Research*. London: Macmillan.

Klooger, J. (2009) *Castoriadis: Psyche, Society, Autonomy*. Leiden: Brill.

Koch, A. M. (2011) 'Post-Structuralism and the Epistemological Basis of Anarchism'. In D. Rousselle and S. Evren (eds), *Post-Anarchism: A Reader*. London: Pluto.

Kolakowski, L. (1990) *Modernity of Endless Trial*. Chicago: University of Chicago Press.

Kouvelakis, S. (2008) 'The Crises of Marxism and the Transformation of Capitalism'. In J. Bidet and S. Kouvelakis (eds), *Critical Companion to Contemporary Marxism*. Leiden: Brill.

Kovacevic, F. (2007) *Liberating Oedipus? Psychoanalysis as Critical Theory*. Lanham: Lexington Books.

Kuhn, G. (2009) 'Anarchism, Postmodernity, Poststructuralism'. In R. Amster, A. DeLeon, L. A. Fernandez, A. J. Nocella II and D. Shannon (eds), *Contemporary Anarchist Studies: An Introductory Anthology of Anarchy in the Academy*. London: Routledge.

Kumar, K. (1993) 'The End of Socialism? The End of Utopia? The End of History?' In K. Kumar and S. Bann (eds), *Utopias and the Millennium*. London: Reaktion Books.

Labica, G. (2007) 'From Imperialism to Globalization'. In S. Budgen, S. Kouvelakis, and S. Žižek (eds), *Lenin Reloaded: Toward a Politics of Truth*. Durham: Duke University Press.

Laclau, E. (1990) *New Reflections on the Revolution of Our Times*. London: Verso.

Laclau, E. (1996) *Emancipations*. London: Verso.

Laclau, E. (2005a) *On Populist Reason*. London: Verso.

Laclau, E. (2005b) 'The Future of Radical Democracy'. In L. Tonder and L. Thomassen (eds), *Radical Democracy: Politics between Abundance and Lack*. Manchester: Manchester University Press.

Laclau, E. (2014) *The Rhetorical Foundations of Society*. London: Verso.

Laclau, E and Mouffe, C. (1985) *Hegemony and Socialist Strategy*. London: Verso.

Landauer, G. (1978) *For Socialism*. St Louis: Telos.

Lash, S. and Urry, J. (1987) *The End of Organized Capitalism*. Cambridge: Polity.

Latour, B. (2004) 'Why Has Critique Run Out of Steam? From Matters of Fact to Matters of Concern'. *Critical Inquiry*, 30, Winter, 225–248.

Latour, B. (2005) *Reassembling the Social: An Introduction to Actor-Network Theory*. Oxford: Clarendon.

Lazarus, S. (2007) 'Lenin and the Party, 1902-November 1917'. In S. Budgen, S. Kouvelakis and S. Žižek (eds), *Lenin Reloaded: Toward a Politics of Truth*. Durham: Duke University Press.

Lecercle, J. J. (2007) 'Lenin the Just, or Marxism Unrecycled'. In S. Budgen, S. Kouvelakis and S. Žižek (eds), *Lenin Reloaded: Toward a Politics of Truth*. Durham: Duke University Press.

Lee, R. E. (2011) 'The Modern World-System: Its Structures, Its Geoculture, Its Crisis and Transformation'. In D. Palumbo-Lio, B. Robbins, and N. Tanoukhi (eds), *Immanuel Wallerstein and the Problem of the World: System, Scale, Culture*. Durham: Duke University Press.

Lefort, C. (1986) *The Political Forms of Modern Society: Bureaucracy, Democracy, Totalitarianism*. Cambridge: Polity.

Lefort, C. (1988) *Democracy and Political Theory*. Cambridge: Polity.

Lefort, C. (2000) *Writing: The Political Test*. Durham: Duke University Press.

Lefort, C. (2007) *Complications: Communism and the Dilemmas of Democracy*. New York: Columbia University Press.

Leier, M. (2009) *Bakunin: The Creative Passion*. London: Seven Stories Press.

Lenin, V. I. (1966) *Collected Works, Volume 31*. Moscow: Progress Publishers.

Levin, Thomas, Y. (1989) 'Dismantling the Spectacle: The Cinema of Guy Debord'. In E. Sussman (ed.), *On the Passage of a Few People through a Rather Brief Moment of Time: The Situationist International 1957–1972*. Cambridge, MA: MIT.

Levitas, R. (1990) *The Concept of Utopia*. Syracuse: Syracuse University Press.

Levitas, R. (2003) 'The Elusive Idea of Utopia'. *History of the Human Sciences*, 16 (1), 1–10.

Levitas, R. (2005) 'The Imaginary Reconstitution of Society or Why Sociologists and Others Should Take Utopia More Seriously'. Inaugural Lecture, University of Bristol, 4 October. Available (accessed 1 October 2013) at: www.bris.ac.uk/spais/files/inaugural.pdf

Levitas, R. (2007) 'Looking for the Blue: The Necessity of Utopia'. *Journal of Political Ideologies*, 12 (3), 289–306.

Levitas, R. (2013) *Utopia as Method: The Imaginary Reconstitution of Society*. Basingstoke: Palgrave Macmillan.

Levy, C. (2012) 'Antonio Gramsci, Anarchism, Syndicalism and Sovversivismo'. In A. Prichard, R. Kinna, S. Saku and D. Berry (eds), *Libertarian Socialism: Politics in Black and Red*. Basingstoke: Palgrave Macmillan.

Libertarian Communist Library (n.d.) Available (accessed 26 July 2013) at: http://libcom.org/

Losurdo, D. (2004) 'Towards a Critique of the Category of Totalitarianism'. *Historical Materialism*, 12 (2), 25–55.

Lotringer, S. and Marazzi, C. (1980) (eds) *Autonomy: Post-political Politics*. New York: Semiotext(e).

Lovell, D. W. (1986) *From Marx to Lenin: An Evaluation of Marx's Responsibility for Soviet Authoritarianism*. Cambridge: Cambridge University Press.

Luxemburg, R. (1972 [1910]) 'The Next Step'. Available (accessed 30 September 2013) at: www.marxists.org/archive/luxemburg/1910/03/15.htm

Lynd, S. and Grubacic, A. (2008) *Wobblies and Zapatistas: Conversations on Anarchism, Marxism and Radical History*. Oakland: PM Press.

Magnus, B. and Cullenberg, S. (1995) *Wither Marxism? Global Crises in International Perspective*. New York: Routledge.

Magri, L. (2005) 'Parting Words'. *New Left Review*, 31, 93–105.

Magri, L. (2008) 'The Tailor of Ulm'. *New Left Review*, 51, 47–62.

Magri, L. (2011) *The Tailor of Ulm: Communism in the Twentieth Century*. London: Verso.

Mair, P. (2006) 'Ruling the Void? The Hollowing of Western Democracy'. *New Left Review*, 42, 25–51.

Malia, M. (1995) *The Soviet Tragedy*. New York: Free Press

Mann, M. (1988) *States, War and Capitalism: Studies in Political Sociology*. Oxford: Basil Blackwell.

Mann, M. (1993) *The Sources of Social Power, Volume Two: The Rise of Classes and Nation States, 1760–1914*. Cambridge: Cambridge University Press.

Mann, M. (1995) 'As the Twentieth Century Ages'. *New Left Review*, I/214, 104–124.

Mann, M. (2001) 'Globalization and September 11'. *New Left Review*, 12, 51–72.

Mann, M. (2013) *The Sources of Social Power, Volume Four: Globalizations, 1945–2011*. Cambridge: Cambridge University Press.

Marcos, Subcommandante (2001) 'The Punch Card and the Hour Glass'. *New Left Review*, 9, 69–79.

Marcus, G. (1989) *Lipstick Traces: A Secret History of the Twentieth Century*. Cambridge, MA: Harvard University Press.

Marcuse, H. (1966) *One-Dimensional Man: Studies in the Ideology of Advanced Industrial Society*. Boston: Beacon Press.

Marcuse, H. (1973) *Eros and Civilization*. London: Abacus.

Marshall, P. (1992) *Demanding the Impossible: A History of Anarchism*. London: HarperCollins.

Martin, H. P. and Schumann, H. (1998) *The Global Trap: Globalization and the Assault on Democracy and Prosperity*. New York: Zed.

Martin, W. G. (2000) 'Still Partners and Still Dissident After All These Years? Wallerstein, World Revolutions and the World-Systems Perspective'. *Journal of World-Systems Research*, VI (2), 234–63.

Marx, K. (1978) *The Marx-Engels Reader* (Second Edition), Edited by R. C. Tucker. New York: W. W. Norton and Company.

Marx, K. (1993) *Grundrisse*. London: Penguin.

Marx, K and Engels, F. (1994) *Collected Works, Volume 34, Marx: 1861–64*. London: Lawrence and Wishart.

Masters, A. (1974) *Bakunin: The Father of Anarchism*. London: Sidgwick and Jackson.

May, T. (1994) *The Political Philosophy of Poststructuralist Anarchism.* University Park: Penn State University Press.

May, T. (2009) 'An Interview With Todd May: Rancière, Deleuze and Anarchism'. Available (accessed 7 August 2013) at: http://notes-taken.blogspot.co.nz/2009/11/interview-with-toddy-may-ranciere.html

Maximoff, G. P. (ed.) (1953) *The Political Philosophy of Bakunin.* London: Free Press of Glencoe.

McDonagh, T. (ed.) (2004) *Guy Debord and the Situationist International: Texts and Documents.* Cambridge, MA: MIT Press.

McLemee, S. (2004) 'The Strange Afterlife of Cornelius Castoriadis'. *The Chronicle of Higher Education,* March 26. Available (accessed 30 September 2013) at: www.notbored.org/strange-afterlife.html

McLemee, S. and Le Blanc, P. (1994) *C. L. R. James and Revolutionary Marxism: Selected Writings of C. L. R. James.* New Jersey: Humanities Press.

McLennan, G. (1996) 'Post-Marxism and the 'Four Sins' of Modernist Theorizing'. *New Left Review,* 218(I), 53–74.

McLennan, G. (1998) 'The Question of Eurocentrism: A Comment on Immanuel Wallerstein'. *New Left Review,* 231(I), 153–158.

McLennan, G. (1999) 'Recanonizing Marx'. *Cultural Studies,* 13 (4), 555–576.

Mclennan, G. (2000) 'The New Positivity'. In J. Eldridge (ed.), *For Sociology: Legacies and Prospects.* Durham: Sociology Press.

McLennan, G. (2002) 'Sustaining Sociology: An Interview With Gregor McLennan'. *New Zealand Sociology,* 17 (2), 322–337.

McLennan, G. (2003) 'Maintaining Marx.' In G. Ritzer and B. Smart (eds), *Handbook of Social Theory.* London: Sage.

McLennan, G. (2006) *Sociological Cultural Studies: Reflexivity and Positivity in the Human Sciences.* Basingstoke: Palgrave Macmillan.

McLennan, G. (2010) 'The Postsecular Turn'. *Theory, Culture and Society,* 27 (4), 3–20.

McMichael, P. (2000) 'World-Systems Analysis, Globalization, and Incorporated Comparison'. *Journal of World-Systems Research,* VI (3), 68–99.

Meade, R. C. (1990) *Red Brigades: The Story of Italian Terrorism.* London: Macmillan.

Memos, C. (2010) 'Reconsidering the Marxist-Anarchist Controversy in and Through Radical Praxis: Lessons Taken From the Greek Uprising, December 2008'. *Theory in Action,* 3 (4), 17–37.

Merrifield, A. (2005) *Guy Debord.* London: Reaktion Books.

Michael-Matsas, S. (2007) 'Lenin and the Path of Dialectics'. In S. Budgen, S. Kouvelakis and S. Žižek (eds), *Lenin Reloaded: Toward a Politics of Truth.* Durham: Duke University Press.

Millett, S. (2004) 'Technology is Capital: Fifth Estate's Critique of the Megamachine'. In J. Purkis and J. Bowen (eds), *Changing Anarchism: Anarchist Theory and Practice in a Global Age.* Manchester: Manchester University Press.

Milner, A., Ryan, M. and Savage, R. (2006) 'Introduction'. In A. Milner, M. Ryan and R. Savage (eds), *Imagining the Future: Utopia and Dystopia.* North Carlton: Arena.

Moore, J. (n.d.) 'A Primitivist Primer'. Available (accessed 13 March 2012) at: www.Primitivism.com/primer.htm

Moretti, F. (2011) 'World-Systems Analysis, Avolutionary Theory, *weltliteratur*'. In D. Palumbo-Lio, B. Robbins and N. Tanoukhi (eds), *Immanuel Wallerstein and the Problem of the World: System, Scale, Culture*. Durham: Duke University Press.

Morton, A. (2007) *Unravelling Gramsci: Hegemony and Passive Revolution in the Global Economy*. London: Pluto.

Mouffe, C. (2000) 'What Ethics for Democracy?' In M. Garber, B. Hanssen and R. L. Walkowitz (eds), *The Turn to Ethics*. New York: Routledge.

Mouffe, C. (2001–2) 'Democracy: Radical and Plural'. *CSD Bulletin*, 9 (1), Winter.

Mouffe, C. (2002) *Politics and Passions: The Stakes of Democracy*. London: Centre for the Study of Democracy.

Mouffe, C. (2005) 'For an Agonistic Public Sphere'. In L. Tonder and L. Thomassen (eds), *Radical Democracy: Politics Between Abundance and Lack*. Manchester: Manchester University Press.

Mouzelis, N. (1988) 'Marxism or Postmarxism?'. *New Left Review*, 167(I), 107–123.

Mouzelis, N, P. (1990) *Post-Marxist Alternatives: The Construction of Social Orders*. London: Macmillan.

Mueller, T. (2011) 'Empowering Anarchy: Power, Hegemony and Anarchist Strategy'. In D. Rousselle and S. Evren (eds), *Post-Anarchism: A Reader*. London: Pluto.

Murden, S, W. (2002) *Islam, the Middle East, and the New Global Hegemony*. Boulder: Lynne Rienner.

Murphy, T. S. (2012) *Antonio Negri*. London: Routledge.

Murphy, T. S. and Mustapha, A. K. (eds) (2007) *The Philosophy of Antonio Negri: Revolution in Theory, Volume Two*. London: Pluto.

Negri, A. (1988) *Revolution Retrieved: Writings on Marx, Keynes, Capitalist Crisis and New Social Subjects*. London: Red Notes.

Negri, A. (1989) *The Politics of Subversion: A Manifesto for the 21st Century*. Cambridge: Polity.

Negri, A. (1991) *Marx Beyond Marx: Lessons on the* Grundrisse. New York: Autonomedia.

Negri, A. and Hardt, M. (1994) *Labour of Dionysis: A Critique of the State-Form*. Minneapolis: University of Minnesota Press.

Negri, A. (1996) 'Twenty Theses on Marx: Interpretation of the Class Situation Today'. In S. Makdisi, C. Casarino and R. E. Karl (eds), *Marxism Beyond Marxism*. New York: Routledge.

Negri, A. (2004) *Negri on Negri: Antonio Negri with Anne Dufourmantelle*. London: Routledge.

Negri, A. (2007) 'What to Do Today with *What is to be Done?*, or Rather: The Body of the General Intellect'. In S. Budgen, S. Kouvelakis and S. Žižek (eds), *Lenin Reloaded: Toward a Politics of Truth*. Durham: Duke University Press.

Negri, A. (2010) 'Communism: Some Thoughts on the Concept and Practice'. In C. Douzinas and S. Žižek (eds), *The Idea of Communism*. London: Verso.

N + 1 'Historical Archives of the "Italian" Communist Left'. Available (accessed 15 August 2012) at: www.quinterna.org/lingue/english/historical_en/0_historical_archives.htm

Newman, S. (2001) *From Bakunin to Lacan: Anti-Authoritarianism and the Dislocation of Power*. New York: Lexington Books.

Newman, S. (2010) *The Politics of Postanarchism*. Edinburgh: Edinburgh University Press.

Newman, S. (2011a) 'Post-Anarchism and Radical Politics Today'. In D. Rousselle and S. Evren (eds), *Post-Anarchism: A Reader*. London: Pluto.

Newman, S. (2011b) 'Postanarchism: A Politics of Anti-Politics'. *Journal of Political Ideologies*, 16 (3), 313–327.

Nicolaus, M. (1993) 'Foreword'. In K. Marx *Grundrisse*. London: Penguin.

Nolan, P. and Zhang, J. (2010) 'Global Competition after the Financial Crisis'. *New Left Review*, 64, 97–108.

Offe, C. (1985) *Disorganized Capitalism: Contemporary Transformations of Work and Politics*. Cambridge: Polity.

Ollman, B. (1976) *Alienation: Marx's Conception of Man in Capitalist Society*. New York: Cambridge University Press.

O'Malley, J. (1970) 'Editor's Introduction'. In K. Marx, *Critique of Hegel's 'Philosophy of Right'*. Cambridge: Cambridge University Press.

Outhwaite, W. and Ray, L. (2005) *Social Theory and Postcommunism*. Oxford: Blackwell.

Palumbo-Lio D., Robbins B. and Tanoukhi N. (2011) 'Introduction: The Most Important Thing Happening'. In D. Palumbo-Lio,B. Robbins and N. Tanoukhi (eds), *Immanuel Wallerstein and the Problem of the World: System, Scale, Culture*. Durham: Duke University Press.

Parker, I. (2004) *Slavoj Žižek: A Critical Introduction*. London: Pluto.

Pengam, A. (1987) 'Anarcho-Communism'. In M. Rubel and J. Crump (eds), *Non-Market Socialism in the 19th and 20th Centuries*. London: Macmillan.

Perlman, F. (1983) *Against His-Story, Against Leviathan! An Essay*. Detroit: Black and Red.

Perlman, L. (1989) *Having Little Being Much: A Chronicle of Fredy Perlman's 50 Years*. Detroit: Black and Red.

Petras, J. and Veltmeyer, H. (2001) *Globalization Unmasked: Imperialism in the Twenty-First Century*. New York: Zed Books.

Piccone, P. (1983) *Italian Marxism*. Berkeley: University of California Press.

Pieterse, J. N. (2005) 'Global Inequality: Bringing Politics Back In'. In C. Calhoun, C. Rojek and B. Turner (eds), *Handbook of Sociology*. London: Sage.

Pitts, J. (2012) 'A Liberal Geoculture?' *New Left Review*, 78, 136–144

Plant, S. (1992) *The Most Radical Gesture*. London: Routledge.

Poster, M. (2005) 'Hardt and Negri's Information Empire: A Critical Response'. *Cultural Politics*, 1 (1), 101–118.

Price, A. (2012) *Recovering Bookchin: Social Ecology and the Crises of Our Times*. Porsgrunn: New Compass.

Prichard, A. (2012) 'Anarchy, Anarchism and International Relations'. In R. Kinna (ed.), *The Continuum Companion to Anarchism*. New York: Continuum.

Prichard, A., Kinna, R., Saku, S. and Berry, D. (eds) (2012) *Libertarian Socialism: Politics in Black and Red*. Basingstoke: Palgrave Macmillan.

Purkis, J. (2004) 'Towards an Anarchist Sociology'. In J. Purkis and J. Bowen (eds), *Changing Anarchism: Anarchist Theory and Practice in a Global Age*. Manchester: Manchester University Press.

Purkis, J. and Bowen, J. (2004a) 'Introduction: Why Anarchism Still Matters'. In J. Purkis and J. Bowen (eds), *Changing Anarchism: Anarchist Theory and Practice in a Global Age*. Manchester: Manchester University Press.

Purkis, J. and Bowen, J. (2004b) 'Conclusion: How Anarchism Still Matters'. In J. Purkis and J. Bowen (eds), *Changing Anarchism: Anarchist Theory and Practice in a Global Age*. Manchester: Manchester University Press.

Rancière, J. (2008) 'Democracy, Anarchism and Radical Politics Today: An Interview With Jacques Rancière'. *Anarchist Studies*, 16 (2), 173–185.

Randall A., DeLeon A., Fernandez L. A., Nocella II A.J. and Shannon D. (eds) (2009) *Contemporary Anarchist Studies: An Introductory Anthology of Anarchy in the Academy*. New York: Routledge.

Rawls, J. (1999) *A Theory of Justice*. Cambridge, MA: Belknap.

Resnick, S. and Wolff, S. (2001) '*Empire* and Class Analysis'. *Rethinking Marxism*, 13 (3–4), 61–69.

Ritzer, G. and Stepnisky, J. (eds) (2011) *Blackwell Companion to Major Social Theorists, Volume Two*. Malden: Wiley-Blackwell.

Robbins, B. (2011) 'Blaming the System'. In D. Palumbo-Lio, B. Robbins and N. Tanoukhi (eds), *Immanuel Wallerstein and the Problem of the World: System, Scale, Culture*. Durham: Duke University Press.

Roberts, D. (2003a) 'Illusion Only Is Sacred: From the Culture Industry to the Aesthetic Economy'. *Thesis Eleven*, 73, 83–95.

Roberts, D. (2003b) 'Towards a Genealogy and Typology of Spectacle: Comments on Debord'. *Thesis Eleven*, 75, November, 54–68.

Robertson, G. (1988) 'The Situationist International'. *Block*, 14, 39–53.

Robinson, W. I. (2011a) 'Globalization and the Sociology of Immanuel Wallerstein: A Critical Appraisal'. *International Sociology*, 26 (6), 723–745.

Robinson, W. I. (2011b) 'Global Capitalist Theory and the Emergence of Transnational Elites'. *Critical Sociology*, 38 (3), 349–363.

Rorty, R. (1997) *Achieving Our Country: Leftist Thought in Twentieth-Century America*. Cambridge, MA: Harvard University Press.

Rorty, R. (1999) *Philosophy and Social Hope*. London: Penguin.

Rose, N. (1996) 'The Death of the Social? Re-Figuring the Territory of Government'. *Economy and Society*, 25 (3), 327–356.

Ross, K. (2002) *May '68 and Its Afterlives*. Chicago: University of Chicago Press.

Rousselle, D. and Evren, S. (eds) (2011) *Post-Anarchism: A Reader*. London: Pluto.

Rubel, M. and Crump, J. (eds) (1987) *Non-Market Socialism in the Nineteenth and Twentieth Centuries*. London: Macmillan.

Sadler, S. (1999) *The Situationist City*. Cambridge, MA: MIT Press.

Said, E. W. (1994) *Culture and Imperialism*. London: Vintage.

Said, E. W. (2001) *Power, Politics, and Culture: Interviews with Edward W. Said*. New York: Pantheon.

Salvadori, M. (ed.) (1968) *Modern Socialism*. London: Macmillan.

Sanderson, S. K. (2005) 'World-Systems Analysis after Thirty Years: Should It Rest in Peace'. *International Journal of Comparative Sociology*, 46 (3), 179–213.

Santos, B. (2005a) 'Preface'. In B. Santos (ed.), *Democratizing Democracy: Beyond the Liberal Democratic Canon*. London: Verso.

Santos, B. (2005b) 'General Introduction'. In B. Santos (ed.), *Democratizing Democracy: Beyond the Liberal Democratic Canon*. London: Verso.

Santos, B. (2006) *The Rise of the Global Left: The World Social Forum and Beyond*. London: Zed Books.

Santos, B. and Rodriguez-Garavito, C. A. (2006) 'Introduction: Expanding the Economic Canon and Searching for Alternatives to Neoliberal Globalization'. In B. Santos (ed.), *Another Production Is Possible: Beyond the Capitalist Canon*. London: Verso.

Santos, B. (2008) 'The World Social Forum and the Global Left'. *Politics and Society*, 36 (2), 247–270.

Santucci, A. A. (2010) *Antonio Gramsci*. New York: Monthly Review Press.

Schecter, D. (1994) *Radical Theories: Paths beyond Marxism and Social Democracy*. Manchester: Manchester University Press.

Schecter, D. (2007) *The History of the Left From Marx to the Present: Theoretical Perspectives*. London: Continuum.

Sebastiani, C. (2004) 'To the Tendency Constituted 11 November 1970' (Letter 19 November 1970). Available (accessed 30 September 2013) at: www.notbored.org/orientation31.html

Sennett, R. (1998) *The Corrosion of Character: The Personal Consequences of Work in the New Capitalism*. New York: W. W. Norton and Company.

Sennett, R. (2006) *The Culture of the New Capitalism*. Yale: New Haven Press.

Shandro, A. (2007) 'Lenin and Hegemony: The Soviets, the Working Class, and the Party in the Revolution of 1905'. In S. Budgen, S. Kouvelakis and S. Žižek (eds), *Lenin Reloaded: Toward a Politics of Truth*. Durham: Duke University Press.

Sharpe, M. and Boucher, G. (2010 *Žižek and Politics: A Critical Introduction*. Edinburgh: Edinburgh University Press.

Shatz, M. S. (1990) 'Introduction'. In M. Bakunin, *Statism and Anarchy*. Cambridge: Cambridge University Press.

Showstack-Sassoon, A. (1980) *Gramsci's Politics*. London: Croom Helm.

Showstack-Sassoon, A. (2000) *Gramsci and Contemporary Politics: Beyond Pessimism of the Intellect*. London: Routledge.

Shukaitis S., Graeber D. and Biddle, E. (eds) (2007) *Constituent Imagination: Militant Investigations/Collective Theorizations*. Oakland: AK Press.

Silver, B. (2005) *Forces of Labour: Workers' Movements and Globalization Since 1870*. Cambridge: Cambridge University Press.

Silver, B. and Arrighi, G. (2001) 'Workers North and South'. *Socialist Register*, 37, 53–76.

Sim, S. (1998*) Post-Marxism: A Reader*. Edinburgh: Edinburgh University Press.

Sim, S. (2000) *Post-Marxism: An Intellectual History*. London: Routledge.

Simon, H. (2013) 'Workers' Inquiry in Socialisme ou barbarie'. *Viewpoint Magazine*, 5 September 2013. Available (accessed 31 October 2013) at: http://viewpointmag.com/2013/09/26/workers-inquiry-in-socialisme-ou-barbarie/

SI (Situationist International) (1989) *Situationist International Anthology* (edited by Ken Knabb). Berkeley: Bureau of Public Secrets.

Situationist International (1990) *The Veritable Split in the International: Public Circular of the Situationist International*. London: Chronos Publications.

Sivanandan, A. (1990) *Communities of Resistance: Writings on Black Struggles for Socialism*. London: Verso.

Skocpol, T. (1997) 'Wallerstein's World Capitalist System: A Theoretical and Historical Critique'. *American Journal of Sociology*, 82 (5), 1075–1090.

Smith, M. (2010) 'The State of Nature'. In N. J. Jun and S. Wahl (eds), *New Perspectives on Anarchism*. Lanham: Lexington Books.

Snyder, D. and Kick, E. L. (1979) 'Structural Position in the World System and Economic Growth, 1955–1970: A Multiple Network Analysis of Transnational Interaction'. *American Journal of Sociology*, 84 (5), 1096–1126.

So, A. Y. (1990) 'How to Conduct Class Analysis in the World Economy?: Reply to Dawson'. *Sociological Perspectives*, 33 (3), 423–427.

So, A. Y. and Hikam, M. (1989) '"Class" in the Writings of Wallerstein and Thompson: Toward a Class Struggle Analysis'. *Sociological Perspectives*, 32 (4), 453–467.

Sonn, R. D. (1992) *Anarchism*. New York: Twayne Publishers.

Sonn, R. D. (2010) *Sex, Violence, and the Avant-Garde: Anarchism in Interwar France*. University Park: Pennsylvania State University Press.

Spivak, G. C. (1988) 'Can the Subaltern Speak?' In C. Nelson and L. Grossberg (eds), *Marxism and the Interpretation of Culture*. Urbana: University of Illinois Press.

Spivak, G. C. (1990) *The Post-Colonial Critic: Interviews, Strategies, Dialogues*. New York: Routledge.

Spivak, G. C. (1995) 'Supplementing Marxism'. In B. Magnus and S. Cullenberg (eds), *Wither Marxism? Global Crises in International Perspective*. New York: Routledge.

Stavrakakis, Y. (1997) 'Green Ideology: A Discursive Reading'. *Journal of Political Ideologies*, 2 (3), 259–281.

Sussman, E. (ed.) (1989) *On the Passage of a Few People Through a Rather Brief Moment of Time: The Situationist International 1957–1972*. Cambridge, MA: MIT Press.

Tamdgidi, M. H. (2007) *Advancing Utopistics: The Three Component Parts and Errors of Marxism*. Boulder: Paradigm.

Therborn, G. (1976) *Science, Class and Society: On the Formation of Sociology and Historical Materialism*. London: New Left Books.

Therborn, G. (1980) *The Ideology of Power and the Power of Ideology*. London: Verso.

Therborn, G. (1995) 'The Autobiography of the Twentieth Century'. *New Left Review*, 214(I), 81–90.

Therborn, G. (2000a) 'Time, Space, and Their Knowledge: The Times and Place of the World and Other Systems'. *Journal of World-Systems Research*, VI (2), 266–84.

Therborn, G. (2000b) 'At the Birth of Second Century Sociology: Times of Reflexivity, Spaces of Identity, and Nodes of Knowledge'. *British Journal of Sociology*, 51 (1), 37–57.

Therborn, G. (2000c) 'Reconsidering Revolutions'. *New Left Review*, 2, 148–53.

Therborn, G. (2001) 'Into the 21st Century'. *New Left Review*, 10, 87–110.

Therborn, G. (2003) 'Entangled Modernities'. *European Journal of Social Theory*, 6 (3), 293–305.

Therborn, G. (2007) 'After Dialectics: Radical Social Theory in a Post-Communist World'. *New Left Review*, 43, 63–114.

Therborn, G. (2008) *From Marxism to Post-Marxism?* London: Verso.

Therborn G. (2011) *The World: A Beginner's Guide*. Cambridge: Polity.

Therborn G. (2012) 'Class in the Twenty-First Century'. *New Left Review*, 78, 5–29.

Theses of Lyons (1926) Draft for the 3rd Congress of the Communist Party of Italy Presented by the Left. Available (accessed 20 October 2001) at: www.sinistra.net/lib/pre/lunita/dufeadixye.html

Thomas, P. (1980) *Karl Marx and the Anarchists*. London: Routledge and Kegan Paul.

Thomas, P. (2009) 'The Moor's Italian Journeys'. *New Left Review*, 58, 119–132.

Thomas, P. (2011) *The Gramscian Moment: Philosophy, Hegemony, and Marxism*. London: Haymarket Books.

Thompson, P. (2005) 'Foundation and Empire: A Critique of Hardt and Negri'. *Capital and Class*, 29, 73–98.

Tonder, L. and Thomassen, L. (eds) (2005) *Radical Democracy: Politics Between Abundance and Lack*. Manchester: Manchester University Press.

Tormey, S. (2001a) *Agnes Heller: Socialism, Autonomy and the Postmodern*. Manchester: Manchester University Press.

Tormey, S. (2001b) 'Agnes Heller: "Radical Universalism" after the "Grand Narrative"'. In L. Wilde (ed.), *Marxism's Ethical Thinkers*. New York: Palgrave.

Tormey, S. (2004) *Anti-Capitalism: A Beginner's Guide*. London: Oneworld Publications.

Tormey, S. and Townshend, J. (2006) *Key Thinkers from Critical Theory to Post-Marxism*. London: Sage.

Tosel, A. (2008) 'The Development of Marxism: From the End of Marxism-Leninism to a Thousand Marxisms – France-Italy, 1975–2005'. In J. Bidet and S. Kouvelakis (eds), *Critical Companion to Contemporary Marxism*. Leiden: Brill.

Touraine, A. (2000) 'A Method for Studying Social Actors'. *Journal of World-Systems Research*, VI (3), 900–918.

Tronti, M. (2010) 'Workerism and Politics'. *Historical Materialism*, 18, 186–189.

Tronti, M. (2012) 'Our Operaismo'. *New Left Review*, 73, 119–139.

Trotsky, L. (1907) *1905*. Available (accessed 30 September 2012) at: www.marxists.org/archive/trotsky/1907/1905/index.htm

Turchetto, M. (2008) 'From "Mass Worker" to "Empire": The Disconcerting Trajectory of Italian *Operaismo*'. In J. Bidet and S. Kouvelakis (eds), *Critical Companion to Contemporary Marxism*. Leiden: Brill.

Unger, R. M. (2002) 'The Boutwood Lectures: The Second Way'. Available (accessed 30 September 2013) at: www.law.harvard.edu/faculty/unger/english/docs/corpus1.doc

Unger, R. M. (2005a) *What Should the Left Propose?* London: Verso.

Unger, R. M. (2005b) 'The Future of the Left'. *Renewal*, 13 (2), 172–184.

Urry, J. (2005) 'The Complexity Turn'. *Theory, Culture and Society*, 22 (5), 1–14.

Vaneigem, R. (1983) *The Revolution of Everyday Life*. London: Aldgate Press.

van der Linden, M. (2007) *Western Marxism and the Soviet Union: A Survey of Critical Theories and Debates since 1917*. London: Brill.

van Der Linden, M. and Thorpe, W. (eds) (1990) *Revolutionary Syndicalism: An International Perspective*. Aldershot: Scholar.

Various Authors (2012) *The Origins of Primitivism (1977–1988)*. Available (accessed 27 June 2013) at: http://theanarchistlibrary.org/library/various-authors-the-origins-of-primitivism-1977–1988

Vattimo, G. (2004) *Nihilism and Emancipation: Ethics, Politics, and Law*. New York: Columbia University Press.

Virno, P. et al. (1996) 'Do You Remember Revolution?'. In P. Virno and M. Hardt (eds), *Radical Thought in Italy: A Potential Politics*. Minneapolis: University of Minnesota Press.

Wade, R. (2007) 'Why Inequality Matters'. In D. Held and A. Kaya (eds), *Global Inequality: Patterns and Explanations*. Cambridge: Polity.

Wagner, P. (2001a) *A History and Theory of the Social Sciences*. London: Sage.

Wagner, P. (2001b) 'Modernity, Capitalism and Critique'. *Thesis Eleven*, 66, 1–31.

Wallerstein, I. (1974) *The Modern World-System: Capitalist Agriculture and the Origins of the European World-Economy in the Sixteenth Century*. New York: Academic Press.

Wallerstein, I. (1980a) *The Modern World-System II: Mercantilism and the Consolidation of the European World-Economy, 1600–1750.* New York: Academic Press.

Wallerstein, I. (1980b) *The Capitalist World-Economy.* Cambridge: Cambridge University Press.

Wallerstein, I. (1989) *The Modern World-System III: The Second Era of Great Expansion of the Capitalist World-Economy, 1730–1840s.* San Diego: Academic Press.

Wallerstein, I. (1990a), in S. Amin, G. Arrighi, A. G. Frank, and I. Wallerstein I (eds), *Transforming the Revolution: Social Movements and the World-System.* New York: Monthly Review Press.

Wallerstein, I. (1990b) 'Culture as the Ideological Battleground of the Modern World-System'. *Theory, Culture and Society,* 7, 31–55.

Wallerstein, I. (1991a), in E. Balibar and I. Wallerstein (eds), *Race, Nation, Class: Ambiguous Identities.* London: Routledge.

Wallerstein, I. (1991b) *Geopolitics and Geoculture: Essays on the Changing World-System.* Cambridge: Cambridge University Press.

Wallerstein, I. (1991c) *Unthinking Social Science: The Limits of Nineteenth Century Paradigms.* Cambridge: Polity.

Wallerstein, I. (1995) *After Liberalism.* New York: The New Press.

Wallerstein, I. (1997a) 'Eurocentrism and its Avatars: The Dilemmas of Social Sciences'. *New Left Review,* 226(I), 93–107.

Wallerstein, I. (1997b) 'Social Sciences and the Communist Interlude, or Interpretations of Contemporary History'. Available (accessed 10 October 2006) at: www.Binghamton.edu/fbc/iwpoland.htm

Wallerstein, I. (1997c) Intellectuals in an Age of Transition. Available (accessed 12 September 2006) at: www.binghamton.edu/fbc/iwguatpews.htm

Wallerstein, I. (1998a) *Utopistics, or Historical Choices of the Twenty First Century.* New York: New Press.

Wallerstein, I. (1998b) 'The So-Called Asian Crisis: Geopolitics in the Longue Durée'. Available (accessed 28 September 2006) at: www.Binghamton.edu/fbc/iwasncrs.htm

Wallerstein, I. (1998c)' Questioning Eurocentrism: A Reply to Gregor McLennan'. *New Left Review,* 231(I), 159–160.

Wallerstein, I. (1999a) *The End of the World as We Know It: Social Science for the Twenty First Century.* Minneapolis: University of Minnesota Press.

Wallerstein, I. (1999b) 'Interview with Professor Immanuel Wallerstein, Maison de Sciences de l'Home, June 25, 1999'. Available (accessed 12 September 2006) at: www.zmk.uni-freiburg.ed/Wallerstein/wallitext.htm

Wallerstein, I. (1999c) 'The Heritage of Sociology, the Promise of Social Science'. *Current Sociology,* 47 (1), 1–37.

Wallerstein, I. (1999d) 'Frank Proves the European Miracle'. *Review,* 22 (3), 355–371.

Wallerstein, I. (2000a) 'Intellectuals in an Age of Transition'. Available (accessed 12 September 2006) at: www.Binghamton.edu/fbc/iwguatpews.htm

Wallerstein, I. (2000b) 'From Sociology to Historical Social Science: Prospects and Obstacles'. *British Journal of Sociology,* 51 (1), 25–35.

Wallerstein, I. (2000c) 'A Left Politics for the Twenty First Century? Or, Theory and Praxis Once Again'. *New Political Science,* 22 (2), 143–159.

Wallerstein, I. (2002a) 'New Revolts against the System'. *New Left Review*, 18. Available (accessed 26 February 2003) at: www.newleftreview.net/NLR 25202.shtml

Wallerstein, I. (2002b) 'A Left Politics for an Age of Transition'. *Monthly Review*, 53 (8), 17–23.

Wallerstein, I. (2003a) 'Entering Global Anarchy'. *New Left Review*, 22, 27–35.

Wallerstein, I. (2003b) *The Decline of American Power: The US in a Chaotic World*. New York: New Press.

Wallerstein, I. (2004a) 'The Dilemmas of Open Space: The Future of the World Social Forum'. *International Social Science Journal*, 56, 629–637.

Wallerstein, I. (2004b) *The Uncertainties of Knowledge*. Philadelphia: Temple University Press.

Wallerstein, I. (2005a) *World-Systems Analysis: An Introduction*. Durham: Duke University Press.

Wallerstein, I. (2005b) 'After Developmentalism and Globalization, What? *Social Forces*, 83 (3), 321–336.

Wallerstein, I. (2006a) 'The Curve of American Power'. *New Left Review*, 40, 77–94.

Wallerstein, I. (2006b) *European Universalism: The Rhetoric of Power*. New York: The New Press.

Wallerstein, I. (2009) 'Reading Fanon in the Twenty First Century'. *New Left Review*, 57, 117–125.

Wallerstein, I. (2010a) 'Structural Crises'. *New Left Review*, 62, 133–142.

Wallerstein, I. (2010b [1976]) 'A World-Systems Perspective on the Social Sciences'. *British Journal of Sociology*, 61 (1), 167–176.

Wallerstein, I. (2011a) *The Modern World-System IV: Centrist Liberalism Triumphant, 1789–1914*. Berkeley: University of California Press.

Wallerstein, I. (2011b) 'Thinking about the Humanities'. In D. Palumbo-Lio, B. Robbins and N. Tanoukhi (eds), *Immanuel Wallerstein and the Problem of the World: System, Scale, Culture*. Durham: Duke University Press.

Ward, C. (1988) *Anarchy in Action*. London: Freedom Press.

Ward, C. (2004) *Anarchism: A Very Short Introduction*. Oxford: Oxford University Press.

Wark, M. (2011) *The Beach Beneath the Street: The Everyday Life and Glorious Times of the Situationist International*. London: Verso.

Wark, M. (2013) *The Spectacle of Disintegration: Situationist Passages out of the Twentieth Century*. London: Verso.

Warren, B. (1973) 'Imperialism and Capitalist Industrialization. *New Left Review*, I/81, 3–44.

Watson, D. (1981–5/1997) 'Against the Megamachine'. Available (accessed 13 March 2012) at: www.radical archives.org/2010/09/06/dw-against-the-megamachine

Wigen, K. (2011) 'Cartographies of Connection: Ocean Maps as Metaphors for Inter-area History'. In D. Palumbo-Lio, B. Robbins, and N. Tanoukhi (eds), *Immanuel Wallerstein and the Problem of the World: System, Scale, Culture*. Durham: Duke University Press.

Williams, D. M. (2010) An Anarchist-Sociologist Research Program: Fertile Areas for Theoretical and Empirical Research. In N.M. Jun and S. Wahl (eds), *New Perspectives on Anarchism*. Lanham: Lexington Books.

Williams, L. (2007) 'Anarchism Revived'. *New Political Science*, 29 (3), 297–312.

Webster, F. (2002) *Theories of the Information Society*. London: Routledge.

Wilde, L. (ed.) (2001) *Marxism's Ethical Thinkers*. New York: Palgrave.

Wollen, P. (1989) 'Bitter Victory'. In E. Sussman (ed.), *On the Passage of a Few People through a Rather Brief Moment of Time: The Situationist International 1957–1972*. Cambridge, MA: MIT Press.

Wood, E. M. (1986) *The Retreat from Class: A New 'True' Socialism*. London: Verso.

Woodcock, G. (1962) *Anarchism*. Middlesex: Pelican.

Worth, O. (2013) *Resistance in the Age of Austerity: Nationalism, the Failure of the Left and the Return of God*. London: Zed Books.

Wright, C. (2005) 'A Libertarian Marxist Tendency Map.' Available (accessed 29 July 2013) at: http://libcom.org/library/libertarian-marxist-tendency-map

Wright, E. O. (2006) 'Compass Points: Towards a Socialist Alternative'. *New Left Review*, 41. Available (accessed 21 March 2007) at: http://newleftreview.org/?view=2638

Wright, S. (1980) 'Left Communism in Australia: J. A. Dawson and the "Southern Advocate for Workers' Councils"'. *Thesis Eleven*, 1, 43–77.

Wright, S. (2002) *Storming Heaven: Class Composition and Struggle in Autonomist Marxism*. London: Pluto.

Wright, S. (2007) 'Back to the Future: Italian Workerists Reflect upon the Operaista Project'. *Ephemera: Theory and Politics in Organization*, 7 (1), 270–281.

Wright, S. (2008) 'Mapping Pathways within Italian Autonomist Marxism: A Preliminary Survey'. *Historical Materialism*, 16, 111–140.

Wyatt, C. (2011) *The Defetishized Society: New Economic Democracy as a Libertarian Alternative to Capitalism*. London: Continuum.

Zerzan, J. (1995) *Future Primitive and Other Essays*. New York: Autonomedia.

Zerzan, J. (ed.) (2005) *Against Civilization: Readings and Reflections*. London: Feral House.

Žižek, S. (2001a) *Did Somebody Say Totalitarianism? Five Interventions in the (Mis) Use of a Notion*. London: Verso.

Žižek, S. (2001b) 'Have Michael Hardt and Antonio Negri Rewritten the Communist Manifesto for the Twenty-First Century ?' *Rethinking Marxism*, 13 (3–4), 190–198.

Žižek, S. (2001c) 'Repeating Lenin'. Available (accessed 23 August 2013) at: www.lacan.com/replenin.htm

Žižek, S. (2003) *The Puppet and the Dwarf: The Perverse Core of Christianity*. Cambridge, MA: MIT Press.

Žižek, S. (2004) *Organs without Bodies: On Deleuze and Consequences*. New York: Routledge.

Žižek, S. (2005) 'Against Human Rights'. Available (accessed 3 November 2011) at: www.libcom.org/library/against-human-rights-Žižek

Žižek, S. (2009) 'How to Begin From the Beginning'. *New Left Review*, 57, 43–55.

Žižek, S. (ed.) (2013) *The Idea of Communism 2: The New York Conference*. London: Verso.

Zolo, D. (2001) '"The Singapore Model": Democracy, Communication, and Globalization'. In K. Nash and A. Scott (eds), *The Blackwell Companion to Political Sociology*. Oxford: Blackwell.

Index

Printed and bound by CPI Group (UK) Ltd, Croydon, CR0 4YY